D1557875

THE DESTROYING ANGEL

SEX, FITNESS & FOOD
IN THE LEGACY OF
DEGENERACY THEORY,
GRAHAM CRACKERS,
KELLOGG'S CORN FLAKES &
AMERICAN HEALTH HISTORY

THE DESTROYING ANGEL

SEX, FITNESS & FOOD IN THE LEGACY OF DEGENERACY THEORY, GRAHAM CRACKERS, KELLOGG'S CORN FLAKES & AMERICAN HEALTH HISTORY

John Money

PROMETHEUS BOOKS

Buffalo, New York

Library of Congress Catalog Card No. 84-43104
ISBN 0-87975-277-7

To my sister, Joyce Elizabeth Hopkins,
my brother, Donald Frank Light Money,
and their families

Contents

Acknowledgments

Brigitte Lhomond made selected translations from an early French edition of Tissot's *L'Onanisme*. Elizabeth Connor and Doris E. Thibodeau both were unusually helpful in library reference searches. Helen Cutler and Kate Jakobsen were patient and exceptionally accurate in typing.

John Money's research is supported by USPHS Grant HD00325 and Grant #83086900 from The William T. Grant, Jr. Foundation.

Introduction

This book was conceived in Auckland, New Zealand, on Tuesday, October 6, 1981, in the interval between breakfast and leaving my cousin's home to lecture at ten o'clock on "Pairbonding, Love, and Sex" in the Department of Psychiatry at the University of Auckland. The timing is so precisely recalled because it was during this interval that my cousin, Meredith Money, who is my own age, showed me an old "doctor's book" he had retrieved from his mother's estate. It was J. H. Kellogg's *The Ladies' Guide in Health and Disease.* Based on Kellogg's earlier writings from the 1880s, it had been published in 1908, by the Signs of the Times Publishing Association, in Australia, England, South Africa, and India. My cousin thought I would be interested in what the author had to say about vicious habits and solitary vice in the section on "The Little Girl." Indeed I was! Here in my own hands I held, and with my own eyes I read, the very words that had shaped the sex-phobic child-rearing policies of the generation that had reared the both of us.

Two days later, in the city of Wanganui to the south, I was busy in the public library photocopying pages from a similar old doctor's book, this one from the estate of the parents of my friend Dr. Janet Frame Clutha. Dated 1905, it had the same publisher, in the same four countries as had *The Ladies' Guide,* and was called *The Ladies' Handbook of Home Treatment,* by F. C. Richards and Eulalia S. Richards. Each was a medical graduate of Edinburgh.

A few days later still, I hit the jackpot when I was in Wellington, the city of my own university years. On one of the city's early-spring days of sunlight-blue water and sky, I was exploring familiar streets near the harbor and found, unchanged, Smith's secondhand-book store. Far to the rear of the store, at floor level, and stacked behind other books, I dug out my archaeological treasure: *Man the Masterpiece, or Plain Truths Plainly Told About Boyhood, Youth and Manhood,* 1906. It was the male companion volume to *The Ladies' Guide,* by the same author, John Harvey Kellogg, M.D., of Battle Creek, Michigan. The chapter on "Sexual Sins and Their Consequences" was itself a masterpiece of Victorian sexual folly.

Kellogg's folly has its counterpart in those masterpieces of Victorian architectural conceit that had bankrupted their builders. Never completed, they have names like Burton's Folly. The master plan had failed. Either some of its essential parts had been omitted, or the parts had failed to synthesize into a whole in proper sequence. Kellogg's folly was a challenge—a failed medical theory that needed to be analyzed.

I already knew that the analysis would need to be done in historical perspective. I was reasonably certain that the history would trace back at least to the first edition, 1758, in Latin of Simon André Tissot's treatise, *Onanism: Dissertation on Maladies Produced by Masturbation,* of which I owned a copy of the 1781 edition, in French.

Otherwise, I was historically at sea. My landfall was back in Baltimore: the Welch Medical Library at Johns Hopkins. Here were the books and bibliographies I would need, and which I used, in writing this book.

The destroying angel from which the book takes its title is *Amanita phalloides*, the pure white mushroom that has the look of an unblemished angel, but harbors within itself a deadly toxin of destruction. It is an apt symbol of sex, for it grows first within a *volva* or womb, from which its cap and stem burst out, phallus-like (Gr. *phalloides*). In Christendom, the destroying angel is also a symbol of the ambivalence, the ecstasy and the agony of sex, to which we are all heir.

CHAPTER

1

F Is for Food, Fitness, and F------

Fornication, you can say, can be used to replace F------. But of course you know that's not really correct. F------ was a quite respectable Anglo-Saxon four-letter word until it fell on evil days and became an unspeakable, unprintable outcast. Nowadays, there are signs that it may emigrate from the gutter and again inhabit the voices of respectability.

Outcasts become heroes, and forbidden words exercise a secret fascination. F------ certainly does that. It is one of the Three Great Fs that are the mainstay of the entertainment industry. They are rivaled only by Fighting and Fashion. Anyone who follows the soaps on television or keeps up with the media magazines knows full well about that.

The Food, Fitness, and F------ formula for healthful living fills today's popular magazines with articles on diet, exercise, and sex. As a formula with tried and true sales appeal, it has a long history that traces back to the 1700s and beyond. The diet and the exercise regimens have not changed too much, but the hands on the sexual clock have turned from midnight to midday. The diets and the exercises that formerly were touted for their value in controlling sex now are recommended to augment sexual expression and enjoyment.

The resetting of the sexual clock was a consequence of the commercial application of the vulcanization of rubber, a process initiated in 1839 by Charles Goodyear in the United States and extended in 1840 by Thomas Hancock in England. According to one probably apocryphal story (quoted in Himes, 1963) the date when the clock was reset was 1876, and the occasion was the display of the vulcanized rubber condom at the Centennial Exposition in Philadelphia.

Mass production of the rubber condom marked the beginning, it may be said, of the birth-control age. Slow at first, the momentum of the birth-control age accelerated in the 1920s, by which time the liquid-latex process had made possible a thinner, more acceptable condom. Mass-produced, it was cheap. Mass distributed in vending machines, it could be purchased anonymously, and under the fiction of being exclusively "for

15

protection against disease." Thus did the trade circumvent the law against the dissemination of contraception.

Contraception permitted the progressive growth of positive approval of sexuality instead of prohibiton, especially for women, because it made possible the desired timing and frequency of pregnancy. This positive change was further enhanced with the discovery of penicillin and, from the 1940s onward, the mass production of antibiotics that were effective in the rapid cure of syphilis and gonorrhea, two of the greatest scourges among sexually transmitted diseases.

The change from negative toward positive public acceptance of sexuality in the media, though still incomplete, illustrates a general rule of change, well understood by cultural anthropologists. According to this rule, a change in human affairs from old to new customs, values, and beliefs, and the practices that uphold them, typically is set in motion by the invention or borrowing of a new material, object, or artifact. The preaching, politicking, feuding, and educating for or against the change comes second, not first. In most instances, the change cannot be held back, except temporarily. It rolls on like a tide. Human beings are too curious and fascinated by novelty to forgo an opportunity to explore and experience something new.

The tide of change set in motion by the discovery of effective contraception is not likely to roll back, regardless of the guerrilla attacks and rear-guard actions of those who romanticize the past as a golden age. The romantic idealization of sexlessness, abstinence, continence, and chastity has had its day. So also has the idealization of health foods and exercise as effective formulas for sexual restraint. But the doctrine held sway for more than a hundred years.

CHAPTER
2

The Diet That Cured Sex

Sylvester Graham and His Crackers

The name of Sylvester Graham (1794-1851) is today remembered not for his ideas about sex or physical exercise, but for its use in commercially produced graham crackers.[1] Graham had a fanatic's zeal for whole-grain bread, fresh-air exercise, and sexual abstinence to conserve vital fluids. Ralph Waldo Emerson (1803-1882) nicknamed him the prophet of bran-bread and pumpkins, because his vegetarian doctrine excluded meat eating.

Meat was prohibited because carnivorous food, Graham taught, caused carnal desire. According to the same principle of word magic, salt caused salaciousness and spices excited the passions as well as the taste. Graham didn't invent his dietary prohibtions. He borrowed them from books he read. Some of them were hundreds of years old—for example, the prohibition against eating the flesh of three unclean animals, the hare, the hyena, and the weasel. Here are the ancient theories regarding the consequences of eating the meat of these unclean animals.[2]

If you eat the meat of the hare (or rabbit), you will become an adult lover of the underaged and you will be unclean, having anal intercourse with an adolescent boy, because these animals grow a new anal opening each year, one for every year they have lived.

If you eat the meat of the hyena, you will become unclean and will practice seduction and adultery with both men and women, because this animal changes its sex every year; one year it copulates with males and the next with females.

If you eat the meat of the weasel, you will commit unclean sexual acts with your mouth, or have unclean sexual acts performed on you by mouth, because this animal conceives through its mouth.

If Sylvester Graham had read the Epistle of Barnabas, once a part of the New Testament but now removed and part of the Apocrypha, he would have known these ancient teachings, which St. Barnabas had copied from even more ancient writings now lost. There is no evidence, however, that Graham actually did read the Epistle or any references to it. He didn't pick out any particular animals as being unclean. The meat of all animals was unclean in the vegetarianism of Graham's religion.

Vegetarianism was not a religion of Graham's own making. It was the official teaching of the New Church of the Reverend William Cowherd, in Manchester, England, and had been transplanted to Philadelphia in 1817 by the Reverend William Metcalfe.[3] There it took root, along with Metcalfe's homeopathic medical beliefs, and became part of the great American health-reform movement.

Whereas Metcalfe preached vegetarianism on moral grounds and for health, Graham did so for a third reason. He connected the arousal of carnal passion with being carnivorous. Meat, he preached, stimulates the baser propensities, the sexual longings of the flesh, which, besides being unclean, are debilitating. They rob the body of its strength to resist illness.

Graham's personal brand of vegetarianism was shaped above all else by his nostalgic mania for homemade brown bread. For him, it promised to unlock the gateway of return to the lost paradise of infancy, before he had been deprived of his mother. His paradise had been shattered when he was only two years old and his father, a clergyman, died at the age of seventy-four. Sylvester was his father's seventeenth child, and the youngest of his second wife, who, as a widow, could not take care of her seven underaged children. Off and on, Sylvester lived with neighbors until, when he was six, the county probate court appointed a local farmer as his legal guardian. Ruth Graham, his mother, was decreed to be in a deranged state of mind and unable to carry out the responsibilities of parenthood.

Mother's home-grown, homemade, stone-ground, whole-wheat bread was his idealized, symbolic memory of mother and home. "Who," he asked, "that can look back 30 or 40 years to those blessed days of New England's prosperity and happiness, when our good mothers used to make the family bread, but can well remember how long and patiently those excellent matrons stood over their bread troughs, kneading and molding their dough? And who with such recollections cannot also well remember the delicious bread that those mothers used invariably to set before them? There was a natural sweetness and richness in it which made it always desirable; and which we cannot now vividly recollect, without feeling a strong desire to partake again of such bread as our mothers used to make for us in the days of our childhood" (quoted by Nissenbaum, 1980).

Graham insisted not only on family bread, but also on family flour, grown on the family farm. Graham bread was made from whole-wheat grain, home grown and home baked.

For its first thirty years, Graham's life lacked focus and initiative. He was occupationally a drifter until, when at a tavern with friends one night, he dramatically refused a glass of rum. He walked out of the tavern and found direction to his life in the temperance movement, fighting the evils of alcohol. He trained as an evangelist. Ordained at the age of thirty-four, he left the farms of the Connecticut valley in New England for Philadelphia. where in 1830 he became a mouthpiece for the Pennsylvania State Society for the Suppression of the Use of Ardent Spirits—a temperance society.

For nine years, Graham rode the crest of the wave that had formerly kept him in its trough. He achieved a reputation as a charismatic speaker and was sought after in New England and along the Atlantic seaboard. His success lay not only in his rhetoric but also in his construction of a health theory that popularized the latest medical teachings of the day. The appeal of this theory to listeners in a nonmedical audience was that it gave them a personal method of keeping healthy. They could apply it to themselves, without having to go to a physician.

Graham's method required adherence to his fixed rules of temperance as they pertained to diet (including no alcohol, coffee, tea, or tobacco); to exercise and fresh air; and to sexual abstinence. Intemperance debilitated the body, whereas temperance kept all of the organs and the nervous system in harmonious balance and gave the body health, strength, and resistance against disease.

Graham filled the lecture halls when he guaranteed that his method would succeed in warding off cholera. In the early 1830s, an epidemic of that disease had spread from Asia into Europe and killed people by the thousands. It was only a matter of time, as everyone knew, before the plague would hit America. People were desperate. They would try anything.

Of course Graham's promises mounted to naught, but no one kept statistics to make him accountable. His opposition came instead, in Boston, from citizens enraged that he, a man, would lecture on chastity and the unspeakable secret vice (masturbation) to an all-female audience.

Butchers and bakers also mobbed him, because they saw in him a threat to their livelihood. He angered butchers with his recommended abstinence from meat and his claim that a carnivorous diet caused evil in the form of carnal desire. Commercial bakers brought their wrath on his head because he preached against their using white flour, imported in bulk from Ohio. It was grown, Graham decried, on debauched and exhausted soil, artificially stimulated with animal manure. He would tolerate only unbolted flour made from whole grain grown on the home farm.

By 1840, Graham's public career was finished. His magnum opus, *Lectures on the Science of Human Life,* embodying all of his teachings, had appeared in print in 1839. It was not anything new that challenged him. The depression and debility that had marred his younger years returned. His loss of health resisted the cure that his own health system had guaranteed to the thousands who had attended his lectures or read his books. Before he died at the age of fifty-seven, vainly searching for recovery, he violated his own doctrine by eating meat and drinking liquor. His wife did not agree with his dietary restrictions. What he did about sex is not recorded, but for fresh air and exercise he bathed in the Mill River every day in the year.

Graham's position as a charismatic leader would have been dramatized for posterity had he been assassinated or imprisoned by his enemies while at the height of his fame. Instead, he was attacked only in writing. The *Boston Medical and Surgical Journal* accused him of being a charlatan. (See Nissenbaum, 1980, p. 10.) That was not persecution enough to immortalize him in the eyes of his followers. Their god revealed his feet of clay by his retreat from public life. He alienated his worshippers with his intolerance and apparent contempt for them. He was indifferent toward the *Graham Journal of Health and Longevity,* with which they had honored his doctrines. He never stayed in one of the Graham boarding-houses, in Boston and New York, which offered to young adults an environment based on Graham's principles of health-food diet, healthy exercise, and health-conserving abstinence from sex. In the end, posterity would grant his name not to a system of health, not to graham flour or graham bread, but to graham crackers. Though they are made of whole-wheat flour, they are a product of the commercialization of food production that he abhorred, and they are contaminated with commercially refined sugar, which he abominated.

James Caleb Jackson and Granula

Graham's personal eclipse did not spell the eclipse also of his health system. The system continued its appeal to health reformers as well as to the public. Part of this appeal was mercenary: people would pay for a health cure based on Graham's principles of temperance applied to diet, exercise, and sex. Beyond profits, Graham's system had also a scholarly appeal, because it was to some extent a popularization of the new thinking of the day regarding the physiology of the body in health and disease.

Graham's system had also a populist appeal, because it broke away from blind faith in the established authority of official medicine. It was on the authority of official medicine that, in 1799, George Washington's physicians had bled him to death, at the age of sixty-seven, though they believed that they were draining away bad humors in the blood.

Graham's system had the additional appeal that, even though its roots came from Europe, it was home grown. Americans of the day, remembering the Revolution, and newly recovered from the War of 1812, had great confidence in what they could do for themselves. They also were in the mood to try out new ways. In religion, for example, new sects and churches were founded. The same spirit permeated medicine. In those times, physicians were free to try out new cures without having to offer proof of their effectiveness.

James Caleb Jackson (1814-1895) promoted a new health cure that adapted Graham's health reform ideas in conjunction with hydropathy.[4] Hydropathic therapy, also known as the water-cure, involved especially cold water: showers, spouts, tubs, soaks, irrigations, and wet-packs applied to different parts of the body, along with frictions and massage. The water-cure had been developed first in Austria, in the 1820s, by Vincent Priessnitz (1799-1851).

In 1859, Jackson opened a health resort and sanitarium in Dansville, in rural upstate New York, under the name of Our Home on the Hillside. It offered accommodations for guests who did not seek treatment, as well as for those who did. The program included outings, lectures, concerts, dances, and theater. The cures were hydropathic, nutritional, and athletic. Printed material included tracts against eating meat, drinking alcohol, and smoking tobacco; and, in book form, *Hints on the Reproductive Organs,* 1853, and *The Sexual Organism and Its Healthy Management,* 1861 (Nissenbaum, 1980).

As in a modern hospital's canteen or gift store, Our Home on the Hillside offered for sale a line of health-foods. Graham bread was perishable. Jackson in 1863 devised a wafer made of graham flour and water, baked or dried in a slow oven, broken into small pieces, and then baked again. After the second baking, the pieces were ground into coarse particles. This product was called Granula. It was not too palatable and not a great commercial success. Moreover, it was too dry to eat without first being soaked in water or milk, and it needed sweetening. Nonetheless, it was the first cold breakfast cereal and would shape American food history quite apart from of its Grahamite connections with sexual purity and abstinence. It was marketed, at ten times the price of raw flour, by Our Home Granula Company, along with a coffee substitute.

Granula Goes to Battle Creek

One visitor to Our Home on the Hillside with a favorable response to Granula was Ellen Harmon White (1827-1915), a founder and the prophetess of the Seventh-day Adventist church.[5] She was the wife of James White (1821-1881), who led a congregation of followers from New England in 1855 to establish the headquarters of their religious movement in Battle Creek, Michigan. Without Ellen White, there would be no story about Granula, Granola, and Corn Flakes.

The Adventist church grew out of a failed prophecy preached interdenominationally by William Miller (1782-1849). This was the prophecy of Christ's second coming, the Advent. It was based on the Book of Daniel 8:13, 14, from which the date of the Advent was calculated to be in 1843, and then revised to October 22, 1844. When the end of the world failed to materialize on either date, the Millerite movement was largely discredited, except by a small following of the faithful who reinterpreted the prophecy and continued to await the Advent. They also took up the belief that Saturday, the seventh day of the week, was the true Christian Sabbath. The official name of the church, Seventh-day Adventist, was adopted in 1860 at a conference in Battle Creek.

Ellen White's revelations were delivered to her in visions and often contained excerpts or paraphrases of the writings of others. She was influenced by the works of both Sylvester Graham and James Caleb Jackson. One of her revelations caused her to publish, in 1864, a book on the evils of masturbation, under the title of *An Appeal to Mothers: The Great Cause of the Physical, Mental, and Moral Ruin of Many of the Children of Our Time*. This book drew heavily on quotations from Graham, expounding his theories of health through nutrition, exercise, and sexual abstinence. It also quoted passages from Jackson.

Mrs. White's revelations pointed the way to Jackson's health reforms being included as tenets and practices of the new church. In 1864, she led a deputation to visit Jackson at Our Home on the Hillside. The following year, the visit was repeated, this time with a patient, Pastor White, Ellen's husband, who had been stricken with a mysterious paralysis. The hydropathic treatments were tried in vain. His wife blamed the social distractions of Jackson's establishment. They were too sinful and did not conform to her own ultraconservative fundamentalist religious doctrine. She retained her faith in Jackson's premises selectively. For her, health resided only in nutrition, bodily exercise, and sexual restraint.

It was in 1865, the year of the end of the Civil War and Lincoln's assassination, that Jackson's health doctrine and Mrs. White's Adventist religious doctrine found their inevitable conjunction. It was the evening of Christmas Day, to be exact, when Mrs. White received a divine instruction to call on Adventists for funds to establish their own health facility, the Western Health Reform Institute.

Opened in 1866, the Institute was undistinguished for its first ten years, and the victim of disputatious leadership. The turnabout was effected by John Harvey Kellogg (1852-1943), who became its church-appointed medical superintendent in 1876, at the age of twenty-four.[6]

Kellogg was born into a local family that had been converted to the Adventist faith in the year of his birth. Though his formal schooling in boyhood was scrappy, he was manifestly bright. At twelve, he became employed by the Seventh-day Adventist Publishing Association. There he learned printing and proof-reading, whereby he became acquainted with the church's health-reform literature. At the age of twenty, he began training as a schoolteacher at Ypsilanti. He was already set to be a missionary of health food. At college he maintained himself inexpensively, he recorded, on a vegetarian diet of vegetables, nuts, fruits, and graham bread.

During the fall semester, he was recalled to Battle Creek, where Ellen and James White and other Adventists had embarked on a plan to send his older half-brother, Merrit, back East for further training in health care. They proposed that John Harvey and three other young people get the same training. They would attend Dr. Russell Trall's Hygeio-Therapeutic College in Florence Heights, New Jersey, a noted hydropathic school, where a degree cost twenty-five dollars and a reference.

Russell Thacher Trall (1812-1877) had been a founder of the American Hydropathic Society. He helped organize the American Anti-Tobacco Society and the American Vegetarian Society. As a follower of Graham, he forbade meat, sugar, salt, pepper, vinegar, and of course coffee and tea in the college kitchen, and served graham mush once a day, with fruit only as dessert.

Trall's hydropathic water-cure system had been widely disseminated. It was known to the Adventists not only by way of James Caleb Jackson but through Trall in person, when he had been a guest lecturer at their Western Health Reform Institute.

The course at Trall's college required six months. Its level of scholarship failed to satisfy John Harvey Kellogg. He spent the ensuing year as a medical student in Ann Arbor, at the University of Michigan. From there he transferred to Bellevue Hospital Medical College in New York City, which had an outstanding reputation in clinical teaching. He graduated in February 1875, at the college's fourteenth annual graduation ceremony. He stayed in New York for a few more months to gain experience in the then new method of electrical-stimulation therapy.

The next year he went to Wilmington, Delaware, home of the Hygeian Home water-cure establishment, and from there to Philadelphia, to arrange a health and temperance exhibit at the great Centennial Exposition, celebrating the nation's hundredth birthday.

It was after he returned to Battle Creek that, on October 1, 1876, he became superintendent of the Institute. The next year he renamed it the Medical and Surgical Sanitarium and defined it as a place where people learn to stay well. It was familiarly known as the Battle Creek Sanitarium.

By the turn of the century, Kellogg undertook postdoctoral training in surgery and became celebrated for his skill as an abdominal surgeon. But, throughout his life, he never gave up the early health precepts that had been passed down to him from Graham, Trall, Jackson, and others. His doctrines on nutrition, exercise, and sexual abstinence are still official in Adventist college and medical education.

Kellogg himself did not remain an Adventist. By 1907, he had incurred the wrath of Mrs. Ellen White for becoming too independent of the church elders in the governance and financial management of the Sanitarium and the breakfast-food industry. She expelled him and his younger brother from the church.

Wherever sex is equated with Victorianism, Kellogg's antisexual influence continues to be felt, even though his name may not be mentioned. The name, as everyone knows, is attached to corn flakes. Before corn flakes came into being, however, there was Granula, which became Granola.

John Harvey Kellogg and Corn Flakes

As a medical student in New York City, Kellogg lived in a third-floor room on the corner of 28th Street and Third Avenue. Later he would give this as the address of the place where the breakfast-food idea had its birth, for it was while he lived there that he began thinking about cooked and ready to eat cereals. His actual breakfast menu, based on Grahamite principles, consisted of seven graham crackers and an apple, supplemented with a weekly coconut and, occasionally, a side dish of potatoes or oatmeal.

It was in 1878, two years after his return to Battle Creek as superintendent of the Sanitarium, that he devised an alternative to the graham crackers of his student days. It was a breakfast-cereal health-food made by grinding up slowly dried and toasted meal cakes made of ground wheat, oats, and corn. He called the product Granula, thus infringing on the rights of James Caleb Jackson to exclusive use of this name for his own cereal. Jackson sued Kellogg and, in 1881, won. Thereafter Kellogg called his product Granola.

Granola recipes were featured in the health-food cookbooks compiled by Ella E. Kellogg (1853-1920), the wife of John Harvey Kellogg. The palatability of health-food was one of her concerns. So also was the experimental kitchen, attached to the main kitchen of the Sanitarium in 1883.

Dozens of new health-food recipes and products were perfected in this kitchen, but none rivaled flaked cereals in the magnitude of their effect on the world's breakfast habits. The impetus to the discovery of the flaking process came from a rivalry between·John Harvey Kellogg and Henry D. Perky (1843-1906), inventor of the recipe and industrial process of shredded wheat. Kellogg visited Perky in Denver in 1894, At that time, shredded wheat was made from flour dough. It was cooked soft and moist, like bread, and was perishable. After the meeting, Perky baked his shredded wheatcakes until they were dry and crisp, like Kellogg's Granola. Conversely, Kellogg cooked his whole grains soft, like Perky did his unshredded dough, before he squashed them flat and baked them dry and crisp.

Kellogg's first experiments failed. The wet flakes stuck together to form a mush. The secret of keeping them separate was discovered serendipitously. The cooked, wet grains had to be put aside to soak for several hours before being put through the rollers.

The name for the first crisp-baked wheat flakes was Granose. They were officially introduced to the world at the General Conference of the Seventh-day Adventists at Battle Creek Sanitarium early in 1895. Wheat was softer than other grains and easier to flake. It took three more years before the first Sanitas Corn Flakes were on the market, but it was not until 1906 that today's product was perfected.

From the outset, Kellogg was more interested in experimenting with new processes and recipes for producing health-foods than in applying his discoveries commercially. Business administration he delegated to his subordinate younger brother, Will Keith Kellogg (1860-1951). This arrangement worked for the best part of a quarter-century. Then, in 1906, Will Keith at last broke away. He formed a new corporation, the Battle Creek Toasted Cornflake Company, which later became the Kellogg Company. Though John Harvey was the major stockholder, he lacked the executive power to dictate policy to his junior brother as he formerly had done.

As it turned out, Will Keith Kellogg needed his new power, for in 1906 his chief rival, Charles W. Post (1854-1914), introduced his own line of corn flakes, Elijah's Manna, later renamed Post Toasties. Will Keith needed the power to override his medical brother's sanction against using the family name commercially and against sweetening corn flakes with commercial sugar. Sugar was not a health-food according to John Harvey Kellogg's system of diet.

Will Keith Kellogg, like C. W. Post, his competitor, was an entrepreneurial genius of advertising and marketing. Corn flakes rapidly elevated him, along with Post, to the rank of multimillionaire. His success no doubt fueled the fire of sibling rivalry that had always existed between the two brothers. Their power struggle was now free to become one not of managerial dominance only but of wealth also, for in 1907 both brothers, having been expelled by the Seventh-day Adventists, owed them no further financial fealty.

Feuding between the brothers escalated. Twice they faced each other in corporate battles fought out in the courts of law. In the overall, W. K. Kellogg was the victor. John Harvey had, in effect, fallen victim to his own puritanical vanity and presumptions of always being right. By the time he accepted his brother's secular and commercial heresies, he could be only his enemy, not his partner.

Henceforth, to the doctrinally faithful of the health-food cults, corn flakes were so contaminated by containing commercially refined sugar that they would be held in contempt as junkfood. Just as surely as if their name had been changed from corn flakes to porn flakes, they had lost their virtue as the diet of chastity, abstinence, and sexual purity.

The cult of doctrinally pure health-food did not, however, die out. It was given a great new birth of popularity in the Hippie era of the 1960s. Granola was revived as a trade name. Today, it is widely known among those whose breakfast cereals or snack bars lack the sinful sweetness of commercially refined white sugar and contain the innocent sweetness of honey and raisins instead.

The Granola revival can be taken as a symbol of the whole health-food revival of our time. The wheels of change that powered this revival of health-food doctrine, and at the same time of fresh-air-and-exercise health theory, did not revive the sexual-abstinence theory of health. The new health-cure doctrine combined nutrition and fitness with positive sex. The old theory of sexual debility and degeneracy was upended. Positive sex to prevent sexual debility and degeneracy became the new revised version. The sin of Onan no longer held its terror.

Reference Notes

See Bibliography for complete citations.

1. The reference sources used for biographical information on Sylvester Graham are R. H. Shyrock (1931), G. Carson (1957), and S. Nissenbaum (1980).

2. Information about the meat of unclean animals is paraphrased from J. Boswell (1980).

3. G. Carson (1957) briefly outlines the origin of religious vegetarianism in America.

4. S. Nissenbaum (1980) shows the historical continuity of health theory from Graham through Jackson to Kellogg.

5. The history of Seventh-day Adventism, its origin in Millerism, and the role of Mrs. E. H. White is drawn from S. Nissenbaum (1980), R. W. Schwarz (1970), and the *Encyclopaedia Britannica*.

6. Biographical data on Kellogg and those who influenced his career are drawn from G. Carson (1957), R. W. Schwarz (1970), and S. Nissenbaum (1980).

CHAPTER
3

The Saving of the Seed

The Sin of Onan

It may have been as early as fifteen or twenty thousand years ago, in the era when human beings left their gigantic zoo of murals in the caves at Lascaux and Altamira, that they also first developed the proverbial wisdom that loss of semen causes loss of strength. They may have been impressed by the effects of castration on male animals.

Proverbs are in all likelihood the earliest attempt at scientific wisdom. The appeal of a good proverb is the conviction that it embodies a self-evident truth. This truth can be appropriately modified to suit different times and places.

The proverbial equation of loss of semen with loss of strength not only has great antiquity but also is widely diffused among the peoples of the world, from India through Africa and Europe. In Tantric Yoga, it has long been basic to an entire philosophy of serenity and slowness. The quietness of a slow stroll through the field is to be preferred to the vigorous effort of scaling the high mountain, so to speak. Erotically, it is better to prolong the rocking of the penis in the cradle of the vagina, and to retain the orgasm, than to discharge the climactic energy and waste it. It is also better to space intercourse at long intervals rather than short ones.

In the nineteenth century, Tantric erotic philosophy found its way into America, without acknowledgment of its origins. It was written about under the name of male continence in 1872 by John Humphrey Noyes (1811-1886), who founded and ran the Oneida Community in upstate New York. Alice B. Stockham in 1896 idealized it in marriage under the name *karezza,* which she defines as meaning "to express affection in both words and actions." Formerly she had called it Sedular Absorption (absorption of the seed), but then conceded that to be in error, as no seed is released in the "exquisite exaltation" of karezza.

Noyes was indifferent to the idea that loss of semen meant loss of strength. His main concern was with retention of the orgasm to prevent pregnancy without restricting sexual pleasure. Adolescents at Oneida learned from experienced partners how to prolong intercourse while withholding orgasm. Men and women of the community both were at liberty to extend an erotic invitation, and to change partners. The restriction was not on copulation, but on procreation. A couple had to request community consent before they could try for a pregnancy.

Noyes was serious about women's erotic emancipation so that they would be able to enjoy sex without the threat of pregnancy. Dr. Stockham extolled the virtues of karezza for the same reason, as well as because of its erotic superiority over sex with ejaculation. She accepted conventional marriage and did not associate karezza with changing partners, as was done at Oneida.

It goes without saying that sex-positive writings like those of Noyes and Stockham were not in the mainstream of sexual teachings of the day and were not acceptable to traditionalists like Kellogg and his followers. For these traditionalists, erotic pleasure was a sin, with or without the climax of ejaculation. For them the value of conserving semen instead of wasting it was based not on Tantra but on the Bible.

Biblical and Tantric teachings regarding the saving of semen probably descend from the same source in prerecorded history. There is, however, no place in the Bible for Tantric ideas of saving semen for purposes of sexual pleasure. The biblical point of view is negative—semen is unclean. In Leviticus 15:16-18, it says:

> And if any man's seed of copulation go out from him, then shall he wash all his flesh in water, and be unclean until the even. And every garment, and every skin, whereon is the seed of copulation, shall be washed with water, and be unclean until the even. The woman also with whom man shall lie with seed of copulation, they shall both bathe themselves in water, and be unclean until even.

It is easy enough to interpret these verses as applying to either wet dreams or masturbation, as well as, when with a partner, to premature ejaculation or premature withdrawal. In all four instances, the seed was wasted instead of being used for procreation. The sin for which Onan died was the sin of spilling his seed on the ground, in premature withdrawal, instead of inseminating his brother's widow, according to the law. In Genesis 38:7-10, it says:

> And Er, Judah's firstborn, was wicked in the sight of the Lord, and the Lord slew him. And Judah said unto Onan, Go in unto thy brother's wife, and marry her, and raise up seed to thy brother. And Onan knew

that the seed should not be his; and it came to pass when he went in unto his brother's wife, that he spilled it on the ground, lest that he should give seed to his brother. And the thing which he did displeased the Lord: wherefore he slew him also.

Hundreds of years after the Lord slew Onan for failing to make his brother's widow pregnant, the Old Testament accompanied the followers of Jesus Christ when they moved out of the synagogue and into the churches of their new religion, Christianity. The early scholars, or fathers of the church, agreed with the biblical teaching that the man's seed should be used only for begetting children.[1] But that was not all. They added a new restriction, making it a sin to obtain passionate pleasure from the sexual organs, even when having sexual intercourse as man and wife. As a further restriction, man and wife were enjoined to abstain from intercourse on Mondays, Wednesdays, and Fridays; and to abjure completely for forty days before and after both Christmas and Easter.[2] Intercourse was forbidden also when the woman was menstruating, not to mention when she was heavy with child or recovering from childbirth.

The Sin of Sexual Passion

Sexual passion is not a sin in the Old Testament, which is quite forthright in recognizing the right and obligation of husband and wife to provide each other with sexual pleasure. Sexual delight is quite explicit in the Song of Solomon 7:6-10, which, in contemporary translation, says:

> How fair, how pleasant you are!
> O Love, daughter of delights,
> Your stature resembles the palm,
> Your breasts the clusters.
> Me thinks I'll climb the palm,
> I'll grasp its branches.
> Let your breasts be like grape clusters,
> The scent of your vulva like apples,
> Your palate like the best wine
> Flowing (for my love) smoothly,
> Stirring sleepers' lips.
> I belong to my beloved,
> And for me is her desire.

Early Christian teachers, from St. Paul onward, added the idea of denial of the passions of the flesh to what they found in the sexual precepts of the Old Testament. This addition had its most ancient roots in the mists of unrecorded history, when human beings first discovered the idea of taboo. The discovery may have been made by the ruler-priests of the people who made the great cave paintings of Lascaux and Altamira, aforementioned. Some people in that remote era had very high IQs, just as do some people today. They almost certainly did more with their intelligence than simply decorate caves. The Einsteins among them applied themselves to thinking great systems of explanation, just as great thinkers do today. One of their great discoveries may well have been the invention of taboo.

A taboo is a policy of prohibiting something that members of the human species would normally do in the course of their development, and of chastising and punishing those who disobey. The great taboos of the world are prohibitions applied to sex, food, corpses, speech, and elimination. Children who disobey a taboo are victimized by adults and others who obey the taboo. They are forbidden even to speak the words that are prohibited by the taboo. If they are defiant, they are further victimized until the mental lever of shame and guilt gets set into place and they become subservient and obedient. Like untamed horses, they become broken in. Thereafter, those who have power over them need only threaten to pull the lever to command conformity. Eventually the threat can be dispensed with, and conformity becomes habitual, or even fanatical.

Preachers and politicians know full well the power of taboo, and they exercise it to control people's lives. That is why, today, the democracy in which we live is not a democracy but a dictatorship with respect to our sexual lives. The sexual taboo has long been the major taboo of our culture. It is deeply imbedded into our religion.

There is more of the sexual taboo in the New Testament than in the Old Testament. The addition, insofar as it can be traced, goes back to the Stoic School of Greek philosophical thought dating from the fourth century B.C. The Stoic ideal was a life undisturbed by passions like grief, hatred, joy, tragedy, hunger, and sexual desire. With the passage of centuries, the Stoic ideal became absorbed into the new Gnostic religion as renunciation of passion and acceptance of the ascetic life of self-denial. In Gnostic mysticism there were two worlds, the divine world of good and light and the material world of evil and darkness. Marriage, sexual propagation, and carnal passion belonged to the world of evil. Woman, the temptress, could not be saved without becoming masculinely transformed, so as not to be sexually arousing to man. Sexuality had to be renounced, according to the ascetic school of Gnostic thought, or, according to the opposing view, openly indulged because bodily existence was too far removed from true spiritual existence to harm it. The ascetics despised the sensualists and accused them of celebrating love feasts, or sexual orgies, as a means of mystical communion that brought them closer to the Kingdom of God.

There was much overlap and borrowing of the older Gnostic teaching by the newer Christian teaching, and vice versa. Eventually Gnosticism disappeared, much of its teaching permanently absorbed by the church. The renunciation and negation of sexual passion and erotic pleasure was one of the teachings that was absorbed. It became part of official church doctrine. Gnostic sensualism was abhorred as the work of the devil.

The extreme form of renunciation doctrine declares that spiritual purity can be achieved by denial of all the fleshly appetites and passions by means of self-imposed starvation, sexual abstinence, isolation, silence, restricted movement, mutilation of the body, and perpetual praying.

In today's language, this is the doctrine of self-imposed brain-washing and self-imposed abuse and deprivation. It is a little recognized law of human existence that a person can become so brain-washed as to become addicted to abuse and deprivation, including that which is self-imposed. Eventually it produces a mental state of being euphoric or "high," which at its highest becomes a peak of ecstasy. The changes in brain chemistries that produce this ecstasy are quite probably the same as those produced by psychedelic drugs, especially opiates, and psychedelic mushrooms.

The practice of achieving spiritual purity by denial of the appetites of the flesh became embodied in the teachings of some early monastic orders. In varying degrees, it persists in some monastic orders today. It has never been assumed, however, that all Christians could be obedient to the most extreme discipline of self-denial.

There are two strategies for a less extreme degree of self-denial. One is to use the sexual organs as infrequently as possible, and then only because it is unavoidably necessary to do so for the procreation of offspring. The other is to perform the procreative act as a test of spiritual purity by not enjoying it and by experiencing the least possible degree of erotic passion and pleasure.

Both of these practices were given a plausible Christian doctrinal justification by being linked to the story in Genesis of the fall of Adam and Eve in the Garden of Eden, when they yielded to the temptation of the serpent and lost their innocence by having sexual intercourse. It was from this story that the doctrine of original sin evolved. Jesus alone had escaped the taint of original sin by reason of his having been conceived without sexual intercourse and born to a virgin.

The early Christian writers struggled with how to reconcile the contradiction between the sanctity of virginity, celibacy, and perfect chastity, on the one hand, and the sanctity of marriage and childbearing on the other. Tertullian (160-230) combined with contradiction in the saying that woman is a temple built over a sewer. Origen (185-284) attempted to resolve the contradiction in favor of personal celibacy by castrating himself. St. Jerome (340-420) taught that uncleanness and corruption were attached to all acts of sexual intercourse. He held women in low esteem as sacks of filth, and wedlock as a perpetual bondage and impediment to prayer. Jerome's personal struggle to attain sexual purity was undermined by his having recurrent erotic dreams inhabited by bevies of young women.

Whereas St. Jerome left Christianity with a heritage of the denigration of women, St. Augustine (354-430) left Christianity with a fixation on the sexual organs as the seat of sin. The source of that sin is the concupiscence and lustful passion that arouses the organs.

St. Augustine was converted to Christianity and baptized at the age of thirty-three. His mother, St. Monica, was always a Christian and his father a convert. In his *Confessions,* he attributed the lateness of his own conversion to his own concupiscence. As a teenager, in what he called "a bargain struck for lust," he found a lover to live with him as his concubine. It was according to the custom of the day. When he was twenty, a son was born. For fifteen years the couple lived together. Then, at his mother's insistence on arranging a family-approved marriage, he sent his lover back home to North Africa. "This was a blow which crushed my heart to bleeding," he wrote, "because I loved her dearly." He stayed in Milan, teaching. His bride-to-be was not yet of marriageable age. "Give me chastity," he prayed, "and continence, but no, not yet." He took another concubine until, soon, his conflict was resolved by the ecstasy of religious conversion. He did not marry, but from then on gave up "lust and wantonness." He returned to his home in North Africa and at the age of forty-two became Bishop of Hippo.

The guilt of original sin, according to Augustine, is possessed by a baby at birth because of the depravity of nature manifested in the sexual passion (concupiscence) and genital union of the parents. Moreover, we all enter the world, he said, "between the feces and the urine." In his book *On Marriage and Concupiscence,* Augustine crystallized the negative doctrine of sex on which subsequent writers would expound until the present. Eight hundred years later, St. Thomas Aquinas (1225-1274) pronounced involuntary nocturnal emission of semen, the so-called wet dream, a sin; and rated masturbation a greater sin than fornication.

The *Speculum Doctrinale* of Vincent of Beauvais, a manual of moral doctrine very much adhered to in the Middle Ages, specified that "a man who loves his wife very much is an adulterer. Any love for someone else's wife, or too much love for one's own, is shameful. The upright man should love his wife with his judgment, not his affections" (quoted from

Boswell, 1980, p. 164).

Reference Notes

1. Material related to early Christian doctrine and teachers is drawn from articles by John Wright and John R. Gaden in a special issue, "Sexuality," of the *St. Mark's Review* (June 1981), published by the St. Mark's Institute of Theology in Canberra, Australia; from an address by Father Felix Donnelly delivered at the Annual Conference of the New Zealand Society of Sexology (1980); and from the *Encyclopaedia Britannica*. See also Bullough, 1976.

2. Felix Donnelly, ibid.

CHAPTER

4

The Troubadours Sing of Love

Husbands, Wives, and Lovers

There is no word in the Bible for falling in love or being love-smitten. This absence of a word for the very dramatic human experience of becoming erotically pairbonded perhaps reflects the fact that, in the ancient times of the Old Testament, the marriage of a daughter or a son was arranged by the families. Each marital union was arranged not only to produce children but also so that it would effect a proper union of the status, power, and wealth of the two families. In early biblical times, it was legal to arrange for a man to have more than one wife, as it still is in the Moslem religion. In later biblical times, however, polygamy changed to monogamy.

The tradition of the arranged marriage, especially among the upper classes, held sway in the days of Imperial Rome. It was adopted by the early Christian church. To some degree, it is still in existence today. Royal marriages are arranged or, at a minimum, require official family approval. In families of lesser rank, parental approval of the future bride or bridegroom may be a matter of supreme importance, especially with respect to religion or race, if not wealth, political power, nationality, or social class. Parental disapproval nowadays cannot prevent a legal marriage, but it does sometimes bring a halt to family participation in the ceremonial. If the lovers are defiantly determined to wed, they need only to elope and get married secretly.

The love affair belongs to the human species, and has done so throughout history. There have always been couples who fall in love, no matter what the rules of marriage. In the biblical age of arranged marriages, the experience of the love affair certainly was known at first hand by the author of the love songs of the Song of Solomon. It was known also to St. Augustine, and he suffered from lovesickness when, bowing to parental authority, he agreed to a marriage arranged by his mother, St. Monica, and sent his live-in lover, or concubine, of fifteen years back to

37

her home.[1]

St. Augustine wrote as his predecessors had written, making a separation between the bond of devotion that two lovers have for each other and the bond of passion that they have in bodily union. This two-way split between love and sex derives directly from the Gnostic duality of good and evil. Love is good and spiritual. It belongs to the kingdom of light. Passion is bad and of the flesh, carnal. It belongs to the kingdom of darkness.

The early Christian writers, struggling to think out a doctrine for their new religion, removed spiritual love from its association with carnal union of the flesh in sexual intercourse and used it as a symbol to illustrate man's relationship to God. The symbolism sometimes was quite specific (and for males somewhat embarrassing), as the church was said to be the bride of Christ—but without a nuptial bed, of course! The relationship between Christ and his bride was patterned after the relationship of his Father with the Virgin Mary. Christ was conceived by divine intervention, without the seed of Joseph, her husband.

The example of the Virgin Mary became more and more important in the era when Christianity attained its thousandth birthday. The church increasingly acknowledged a significant place to the Mother of God as a counterbalance to an all-male Godhead, the Father, the Son, and the Holy Ghost.

"The Virgin," wrote Peter of Blois, Archdeacon of Bath, "is the only mediatrix between man and Christ. We were sinners and we were afraid to appeal to the Father because he is Terrible; but we have the Virgin in whom there is no terror, for in her is the plenitude of grace and purity."[2] The Virgin, symbol of the grace and purity of love, was, of course, unspoiled by the sinful lust of sex.

The meaning of this symbolism was not lost on the dissidents of the age who yearned to be allowed to celebrate the triumph of the love affair over the dictatorship of the arranged marriage. They found their voice, as dissidents always do, in art and entertainment. Their heroes were the troubadours,[3] the wandering minstrels and performers of Provence, in the region stretching from the mountains of the eastern Pyrenees in Spain across Mediterranean France. They sang not in the Latin of hymns in church but in the vernacular language of the people. Their influence spread with great speed to the poets of other languages—to the Jewish love poets of Spain, southward through Italy to Sicily, and in the north to the German meistersingers. It was an influence that, adapting to the ages, would become a permanent feature of European culture.

The first troubadour poet whose name remains known was William of Poitiers, the Ninth Duke of Aquitaine (1071-1127). In Italy Dante (1265-

1321) inherited the tradition. He denatured and idealized it extravagantly in the poetical history of his mystical love for Beatrice. They were both nine years old when first they saw each other, and his love unattainable remained forever spiritualized. She died at the age of twenty-five.

Love and Sex

The troubadour tradition was infused permanently into the English language by Shakespeare (1564-1616) in Romeo and Juliet. Since then, the drama of young love thwarted and doomed to be never consummated with the sex organs has been a mainstay of drama, opera, cinema, and television shows. Indeed, the distinction between love and sex permeates Western civilization and affects all our lives.

The troubadours were to the ten and eleven hundreds what the rock-and-roll performers are to the nineteen hundreds. Each troubadour group roved from one castle town to another. Wherever they went, they could always count on bringing out a crowd. In the audience, young people no doubt predominated, as the songs of the troubadours celebrated the triumphs and the tragedies of love. They were addressed especially to young women.

Historians have no certainty as to where the troubadours discovered the new philosophy of romantic love. One likely guess points to the Arabic poets of the Islamic courts of the Moroccan rulers of southern Spain. Their poetic tradition may have reached back beyond Byzantium and the Hellenistic age to ancient Persia and the East.

Another likely guess is that the celebration of the love affair in troubadour song was a new flowering, home-grown, of a once nearly endangered species kept alive and revived in the hidden gardens of the common people. Before Imperial Rome, followed by the Roman Church, spread over Europe, union in marriage was not an arrangement decided by the two families. It required that two young people in love first become betrothed, then prove that they could have a pregnancy, and then be married. This system of pregnancy after betrothal and before marriage became progressively encroached upon by the Roman and Christian system of marriage before pregnancy. In northern Scandinavia and Iceland, the betrothal system has remained totally intact until this very day. Up until the ten hundreds, betrothal may well have been preserved among the common people of southern France (Wikman, 1937). There the troubadours may have found their inspiration.

Understandably, it was not the experience of being love-smitten, or limerent, that the troubadours discovered. Writers long before them had described it. Plato was one of them. Of the man who is love-smitten, he wrote: "He whose initiation is recent, and who has been the spectator of many glories in the other world, is amazed when he sees anyone having a godlike face or form which is the expression or imitation of divine beauty; and at first a shudder runs through him, and some misgiving of a former world steals over him; then looking upon the face of his beloved as a god, he reverences him, and if he were not afraid of being thought a downright madman, he would sacrifice to his beloved as to the image of a god; then as he gazes on him there is a sort of reaction, and the shudder naturally passes into an unusual heat and perspiration; he receives the effluence of beauty through the eyes, and he warms. And this state is by men called love." Plato, being Greek, knew that the state of being love-smitten is independent of the sex of the partner. The troubadours knew the same, though they sang chiefly of the knight and his lady love.

What differentiates the love songs of the troubadours from Plato and other Greek and Roman writers is that the troubadours went far beyond simply giving an accurate description or declaration of being in love. They became the leaders of a people's movement to rehabilitate the love affair in Christian society.

To rehabilitate the love affair meant also to recognize a new status for women, giving them a new strategy of power over their lovesick men. "Never was archer able to draw more straight than she who shot into my heart the sweet death of which I wish to die," lamented one poet who was without hope "unless she restore my joy with a glance of love."

Eleanor of Aquitaine (1122-1204) acted on the potential of woman's new power inherent in the new movement. In youth she had married Louis VII and was Queen of France until her husband had the marriage annulled. She then became Queen of England, wife of Henry II and mother of Richard the Lionhearted and King John. In her French castle at Poitiers, as an older woman, she and her daughter Marie presided over a Court of Love, a tribunal of some sixty women, the function of which was to educate noblemen in the art of love, according to the troubadour tradition.[4] The rules were set forth in a Treatise on Love and Remedies of Love, commissioned by Eleanor from the court chaplain, André le Chaplain, known also by his Latin name, Andreas Capellanus (twelfth century, dates unknown).

Regarding both the power of women and the power of love the troubadours were in defiance of the church's doctrine. They refuted the church's contemporary ruling that erotic passion, even in marriage, is equivalent to the sin of adultery because every Christian man and woman is already promised in marriage as the bride of Christ. Therefore, to love another with erotic passion is a betrayal of one's love of God.

Eleanor of Aquitaine, presiding over a disputation in her Court of Love, is on record as having expressed doubt that true love could exist between a husband and wife. But she deferred to her daughter's opposing view, saying that it would be admirable if a woman could find love in her marriage.

Andreas Capellanus, writing about 1175, also addressed the issue of true love in marriage: "Many evils come from love," he wrote, "but I do not see that anything that is good for men comes from it; that delight of the flesh which we embrace with such great eagerness is not in the nature of a good, but rather, as men agree, it is a damnable sin which even in married persons is scarcely to be classed among the venial faults which are not sins, according to the word of the psalmist, who said, 'For behold I was conceived in iniquities and in sins did my mother conceive me.'"[5]

In this statement from his closing chapter, Andreas Capellanus completely contradicts the main purpose of his entire book, which is to give instruction on the art of true love. There was wisdom in his having his cake and eating it too: he was protecting himself from the wrath of the church. He had given such detailed instruction on the sin of passion, he claimed, only in order to show that its repudiation was the test of true faith.

The troubadours had their own formula for compromise with the church. They did not attack the institution of marriage. They sang not of marriage but of love; and not of lechery (which derives from the same root as "licking") but of true love. The dividing line between true love and sensuous longing was pretty thin in the early troubadour songs. Later, true love became more mystical and spiritualized. Until then, the dividing line between sensuous love and lechery was ill defined. However, there was escape from lechery: the formula was that the man importuned the woman, and the woman made his heart leap by giving him a clandestine glance, though in the end she said no, and thus saved him from the adulterous embrace of passion.

Troubadour love was destined to be love unrequited. It was a wound inflicted by Cupid's arrow that entered through the eyes and went straight to the heart, the organ of the vital spirit. Love was an affair of the heart, and a heartbreak: "A thousand times a day I wish to die," run the lines of one song, "so much the dart pains me with which love has wounded my heart."

In their defiance of religious doctrine, the troubadours accomplished for love between the sexes a change of its status from sin to sickness—the same change as happened in the nineteenth century for love between members of the same sex. The next step was the change from sickness to being acceptable as an alternative social norm. This step, the change whereby the love affair would become fully integrated with the marital arrangement, was mercilessly suppressed by the Inquisition, which came by papal decree in 1233 to Provence, the troubadour homeland. The bishops there lost no time in gearing up for a reign of terror that laid waste to the region for more than a century.

Reference Notes

1. Biological data for St. Augustine are from J. R. Gaden (1981); and from the *Encyclopedia Britannica*.

2. This and subsequent quotations from Maurice Valency are sequentially from p. 25, p. 33, p. 150, p. 24, and p. 150 of his book, *In Praise of Love* (1961).

3. Troubadour historical references are taken from Valency (1961); from F. W. Locke's edition (1957) of the twelfth century book, *The Art of Courtly Love*, by Andreas Capellanus; and from M. H. Levine's 1976 edition of *Falaquera's Book of the Seeker (Sefer Ha-Mebaqqesh)*.

4. R. Colp, Jr., 1981.

5. Locke, p. 25.

CHAPTER
5

The Dictatorship of Renunciation

The Fires of the Inquisition Are Lighted

Listening to the troubadours, the church heard more than love songs. It heard a behind-the-scenes challenge to the authority of its own dominion. It heard an allegiance to the old Gnostic doctrines that had lingered on in the teaching of Manes (216-276). These teachings had been branded by the church as the Manichean heresy and had long been outlawed. Now this heresy was spreading again, out in the open, in defiance of the church.[1]

By the middle of the eleventh century, a group of religious dissidents at Albi, near Toulouse and the troubadour country of southern France, had become adherents of Catharism (meaning Purism), a version of the Manichean heresy believed to have been imported from the Bulgarian region. After the name of their town, their heresy became known as the Albigensian heresy.

In 1209, the Pope ordered a crusade against the Albigenses. By 1229 the power of their governing princes had been completely destroyed and the brilliant flowering of troubadour culture in Provence was doomed. The heresy, however, had not been extinguished among the people.

After 1233, the religious officials of the Inquisition took unrelenting action against the Albigenses and against all other inhabitants of the region suspected of the Catharist heresy. They tortured them to make confessions and to denounce their fellow believers, imprisoned them, and burned them at the stake. In 1245, two hundred Cathari were burned in one day.

The Inquisitors confiscated the property of heretics. They kept half of their wealth and lands for themselves and gave half to those secular rulers who supported them. It was a profitable business for the prosecutors. It went on relentlessly for a century or more, laying waste the countryside and depopulating it. It entrapped the survivors in an agony of mistrust and suspicion.

43

In the eradication of the Albigensian heresy, the Inquisition was more concerned with eradicating ecclesiastical competition than with suppressing love songs and the heresy of sexual passion that they represented. By the middle of the fourteen hundreds, the table had been turned: the heresy of sexual passion became evidence and proof of the heresy of witchcraft.

The word *witch* had the same origin as wise, witness, and wit (as in having your wits about you). The special wisdom or knowledge of a witch is of things pertaining to the pagan religion of the dead who had lived before the spread of Christianity. For the church it was the religion of the devil.

The word *devil* had the same origin as divine, and signifies a fallen god. In the Europe of the Middle Ages, the fallen gods of the peoples of the pre-Roman and pre-Christian period had no organized priesthood. Their religious doctrine had been lost, as had most of their religious ritual. What little remained amounted to a few folk customs and superstitions. For example, their gods were believed to appear to their worshippers in animal form, or wearing animal skins, and to have sexual intercourse with them. All the sexual sins of Christianity were projected onto the pre-Christian devils and their worshippers, the witches.

There is substantial historical evidence that the Cathar religion had a large enough following in France, with enough political power to challenge their Christian competition. But there is no corresponding evidence of a powerful organization of witchery that threatened the power of the fifteenth-century church anywhere in Europe. The charges of the church against witches read like a kind of science fiction. To a significant degree, the justification of the witchcraft fiction had its genesis in the scholastic doctrines of St. Thomas Aquinas.

Women Become Witches

These charges were set forth in 1484 by the Pope (Innocent VIII): "It has come to our ears that members of both sexes do not avoid having intercourse with demons, incubi and succubi; and that by their sorceries and by their incantations, charms and conjurations, they suffocate, extinguish and cause to perish the births of women, the increase of animals, the corn of the ground, the grapes of the vineyard and the fruit of the trees, as well as men, women, flocks, herds and other various kinds of animals, vines and apple trees, corn and other fruits of the earth; making and procuring that men and women, flocks and herds and other animals shall suffer and be tormented both from within and without so that men beget not nor women conceive; and they impede the conjugal action of men and women."

This statement is extracted from a document, a papal bull, which was issued in support of the witch-hunting mania of Jakob Sprenger (1436-1495) and Heinrich Kramer (1430-1505) in Germany. They published it in their infamous *Malleus Maleficarum* (Witches' Hammer), the Inquisition's textbook on how to find, torture, and dispose of witches.[2]

Sprenger and Kramer abominated witchcraft above all other heresies, and identified it with renunciation of Christianity; sacrificing unbaptized infants to Satan; dedication of body and soul to evil; and cohabiting sexually with a demon, a male incubus, or a female succubus. Either an incubus or a succubus could to its demonic work by possessing, respectively, an actual man or woman.

Because incubi and succubi were not human, sexual intercourse with them was likened to bestiality, intercourse with animals. For good measure, it was equated also with sodomy, adultery, and incest, and was also a malice against religion.

One could be the victim of the little demons without actually copulating with them. They were said to be able to collect semen from nocturnal emissions or masturbation and use it to create new bodies for themselves. St. Thomas Aquinas, however, thought it more likely that a succubus would seduce a male in order to get his semen, and then changing into an incubus, transmit the semen to a female. Monsters and birth defects were proof that a succubus or incubus had been involved. In disguise as an animal, it could produce an offspring that was half-animal and half-human.

Women were identified as being more licentious than men. Therefore, they were more often accused of entertaining demons than men were. It was actually estimated that male incubi copulated with women nine times more often than female succubi did with men, according to one reckoning.

A woman's traffic with demons endowed her with the power to make a man's penis disappear. Then she alone could bring it back again. The same demons gave her the power to make another woman miscarry or be barren, and to make a man's penis impotent. A ligature or knot found tied in a cord or strip of leather could be proof of a spell cast to cause impotence.

The persecution of witches gained momentum in the fifteen hundreds and reached its peak early in the sixteen hundreds. There is no record of how many women died by burning, strangulation, or beheading, by being beaten and whipped to death, or by other means. The figure could be in the millions and, at a minimum, not less than a million. In two German–Swiss villages, it is said that every living female, regardless of age, was burned as a witch. From three villages, comprising three hundred households, at least one hundred twenty-five persons were executed between 1631 and 1676, according to records of the Archbishopric of Cologne. In Como, Italy, one Inquisitor recorded burning a thousand witches in one year (1523).

In Scotland, the last witch-burning was in 1728. The last legal execution of a witch is said to have been in Switzerland in 1782, though an illegal burning took place in Poland in 1793. Even though the fires were extinguished, the office of the Inquisition remained part of the ecclesiastical dictatorship of Spain until late in the nineteenth century.

Kramer and Sprenger may have been power-crazy lust murderers in clerical disguise, but that does not explain why the church endorsed them, nor why their antiheretical witch-hunting mania took hold in Europe for three centuries. Nor does it explain why witch-hunting reached across the Atlantic to colonial America, English-speaking as well as Spanish, Protestant as well as Catholic.

It is possible to make a case for the explanation that the church, having been the victim of its pagan adversaries in its early days, had become locked into a strategy of being dependent on having an adversary in order to maintain cohesive orthodoxy and to prevent doctrinal dissidence. Victorious over its pagan adversaries, it turned to establishing an ecclesiastical bureaucracy, the Inquisition, with power equivalent to that of a secret police, to eradicate all dissidence as heretical.

All bureaucracies have a vested interest in being self-perpetuating. Otherwise they have no income and no means of support. If their mission is completed, they discover a new one. The Inquisition may, then, have been so thorough in eradicating its heretical rivals by the end of the fourteen hundreds that it needed a Kramer and a Sprenger to think up and define a new class of heretics. These new heretics were within the ranks. They infiltrated Christian places of worship as secret agents of Satan. The age-old accusation of spying from within is the same one that characterized McCarthyism in the America of the 1950s, though the heretics then were not witches, but communists. Today's heretics, according to the New Right, are homosexuals and pornographers, child-molesters and those in favor of legal abortion.

There was no chance that witch-hunters would return empty-handed, for guilt was proved by accusation. A woman accused of witchcraft was brain-washed and tortured in secret until she falsely confessed to having had sexual intercourse with a demon in a dream which, in fact, she had never dreamed. Then she was sentenced to death.

Small wonder that sexual imagery and its publication or disclosure is still an ever-present danger in the criminal justice system today. Law took up where religion left off.

In the fifteen hundreds, the hysteria of demon-possession became a social contagion that spread to extend the ranks not only of informants and accusers but also of victims who came forward to incriminate themselves. Their demon-possession was imitative, theatrical, and on public display, consequences notwithstanding.

What brought the witch-hunting of the Inquisition eventually to its conclusion? It was not the shrieks of the tortured, nor the stench of burning flesh, for human beings become addicted to cruelty. More likely, it was a late outcome of the heresy of the Protestant Reformation of Martin Luther (1483-1546) and Henry VIII (1491-1547). This was a more explicit heresy and much more readily proved than the sexual phantasmagoria of witchcraft. The church fought this new heresy, but the battle left it permanently divided into Protestant and Roman.

Contemporaneous with the Reformation, there emerged also the challenge to the church of the beginnings of the new learning that would become the Renaissance, which would be followed by the rational and empirical method of the Enlightenment and the dawning of the age of modern science.

Dissent and Dictatorship

In sheer horror and magnitude, the Inquisition matches Stalin's purges, Hitler's holocaust, Mao's cultural revolution, and Khomeini's revolutionary guards. In duration no other persecution can match it.

For the church and its Inquisitors there has at no time been a Nuremburg Trial as there was for the Nazi criminals of Hitler's holocaust. The church has never been required to examine its conscience and reveal its guilt. There has been no public or ecclesiastical soul-searching as to what aspects of people's lives the church has historically dictated or the criteria of justification for its having done so.

The church still operates with the conviction of absolute moral authority in matters of sex. Its doctrines are subject neither to review nor to appeal, regardless of dissent. The only effective means of individual dissent is to disobey or to defect. It would be different if the organization of church governance were designed to ensure democratic self-examination, self-criticism, and self-correction in the face of error.

The errors of the Inquisition still haunt the church's sexual policies. They hinder the church's adaptation to the sexuality of its people in the new era since the invention of birth control. There are exceptions, to be sure, especially under Protestantism. They are variable in nature and extent. Nonetheless, for the most part the church is extremely cautious, if not downright unyielding, with respect to sexual change in the beliefs and practices of its people—on such issues as, for example, contraception, sexual life in teen age, masturbation, homosexuality, pregnancy termination, donor insemination, and laboratory fertilization of the egg outside the womb.

Reference Notes

1. The historical material in this chapter is documented in John Boswell (1980); Vern L. Bullough (1976); Emmanuel Le Roy Ladurie (1978); and the *Encyclopaedia Britannica*.

2. Heinrich Kramer was known in the Dominican register as Father Henricus Institoris de Sletstat, and this name was used in the Reverend Montague Sommers's translation of the *Malleus Maleficarum* in 1928, reprinted in 1948.

CHAPTER
6

From Demons to Degeneracy

The Death of Demon Possession

Demon-possession theory was a jack-of-all-trades that could explain all human afflictions, including the epidemics and plagues that swept Europe in the Middle Ages. They were interpreted as God's penitential warnings of worse to come, in the hereafter, if heresy were not eradicated.

The body of medical knowledge that had been passed on from Hippocrates and Galen to physicians of the fifteen hundreds was not itself on a firm enough theoretical foundation to be able to challenge the demon-possession theory of the church. On the contrary, medical theory and demon possession theory accommodated one another fairly comfortably, for the evils and afflictions that each claimed to explain, and attempted to deal with, had little overlap. There were, in fact, very few sufferings that medicine could effectively relieve with its apothecary jars and concoctions, its blood-letting, and its primitive knowledge of anatomy and surgery in the era predating anesthesia, first used in 1846. Doctors, being themselves the product of religious indoctrination, had no qualms about agreeing with the theory of demon-possession as offering a suitable explanation of evils and ills that lay beyond their professional competence to relieve.

The year 1543 is as good a one as any to mark as the birth year of modern scientific medicine. It was then that Vesalius (1514-1564) published the first textbook of anatomy. It was a book that vexed the church, insofar as it was based on the dissection of the human corpse, a practice forbidden to priests. For the devout, dissection was a sacrilege, just as an autopsy is for many people today. In the mystical teaching of the church, the body would be needed again on the day of resurrection and final judgment, at the end of the world.

In the sixteen hundreds, while the new scientific theories of medicine developed from their infancy to the stage of learning to walk, the theory of demon-possession grew more decrepit and senile. It died a lingering death at some time before the early seventeen hundreds. As it was dying, medi-

49

cal science grew rapidly toward a vigorous, if sometimes theoretically overconfident, adolescence.

The death of demon-possession theory left a large gap, too big to be filled by the rational and scientific explanations of the times. The obvious deficiency, after so many years of sexual persecution, was a lack of any scientific substitute for the sexual foundation of the theory of demon-possession.

The Demon Named Masturbation

Early in the seventeen hundreds, an unidentified English clergyman, a Dr. Bekkers of London, according to Tissot (see below), came to the rescue with a replacement for Kramer and Sprenger's fantasy that having sexual intercourse with the devil could be a cause of social or individual evils and afflictions.[1] He revived and revised the ancient theory that the loss of semen causes loss of strength. Referring to the testicles and their spermatic tubules, he wrote: "The blood is made into Seed, which is further elaborated and purify'd in the Epidydimides . . . the oftner the Vesiculae Seminales are emptied, the more work is made for the Testicles, and consequently the Confumption of the fineft and moft Balfamick part of the blood" (*Onania*, pp. 111-112). This was good science-fiction for the early seventeen hundreds, but when the time was ripe, much later on, to put it to the uncompromising tests of genuine science, it proved to be a physiological fairy-tale.

The tract, or sermon, from which the foregoing quotation is taken was printed first in London. The first American reprinting was in Boston in 1724. Its lengthy title is: *Onania; or, the Heinous Sin of Self-Pollution, and All its Frightful Confequences, in both Sexes, Confidered. With Spiritual and Phyfical Advice to thofe, who have already injur'd themfelves by this Abominable Practice. And Seafonable Admonition to the Youth (of both SEXES) and thofe whofe Tuition they are under, whether Parents, Guardians, Mafters, or Miftreffes. To which is Added, A Letter from a Lady (very curious) Concerning the Ufe and Abufe of the Marriage-Bed. With the Author's Anfwer thereto.*[2]

"Self-pollution," began *Onania*, "is that unnatural Practice, by which Perfons of either Sex, may defile their own Bodies, without the Affiftance of others, whilft yielding to filthy Imaginations, they endeavour to imitate and procure to themfelves that Senfation, which God has order'd to attend the carnal Commerce of the two Sexes, for the Continuance of our Species."

There was no specified limit to the list of the corruptions of the body attributable to self-pollution, according to *Onania.* Palsies, distempers, consumptions, gleets, fluxes, ulcers, fits, madness, childlessness—all the syndromes of the day were included, even death itself. The common denominator was debility, brought on by the loss of semen. It could affect offspring. They were born sickly and ailing and died or became a dishonor to the human race.

Onania reincarnated the heresy of witchcraft as the heresy of masturbation. The mania of witch-hunting became the mania of masturbation hunting. The change was more humane in one sense: The body of the masturbator was not burned alive in order to save its immortal soul from the dire consequences of its heresy. Instead, the body of the masturbator was consumed by self-induced debility and disease. It would destroy itself, according to the *Onania* doctrine, unless the sinner ceased his sin. Hence, dire warnings and threats, and disciplinary cruelty, abuse, and deprivation were preached with fanatical fervor for the next two hundred years. Even today they have not entirely disappeared.

The author of *Onania* wrote with unwavering certainty his dogma of masturbatory debility and disease. He propped up his argument by quoting well-known authorities, by telling of cases he had known, and by reproducing and commenting on dozens of testimonials, confessions, and pleas for help that he had received in writing. For him the individual illustration constituted proof of a moral principle, in much the same way as a fable or story proves a moral principle in a sermon.

He did not require proof in numbers. His was the prescientific way. He did not require being able to replicate findings many times before considering that a theory had been proved. There would be generations of his followers who would copy his method, even after it had become hopelessly out of date. They claimed to be authoritative, simply because they had the rank and authority, either religious or medical, to impose their dictates on others.

Masturbation Goes to Medical School

One of these followers was a Swiss physician, Simon André Tissot (1728-1797). Expanding the relatively minor significance of debility in *Onania,* Tissot gave great prominence to the idea of debility in medical theory. In the 1750s, he developed it into a theory of degeneracy (*dégénérescence*). The early editions of his work were in Latin and French. The first English translation was published in London in 1776. The first American translation ("from a new edition of the French") was published in New York in 1832, under the title: *Treatise on the Diseases Produced by Onanism.*

In the tradition of his day, and like the author of *Onania* before him, Tissot relied on citing authority rather than empirical evidence. Thus he quoted "one of the greatest men of the age" (unidentified) on the power of semen retained in the seminal vesicles: ". . . it excites the sexual desires of the animal; but the greatest part, the most volatile, the most odorous, that which has the most power, is resumed by the blood, and produces on entering it, remarkable changes, the hairs and the beard; it alters the voice and the manners, for age does not produce these changes in animals; they are caused by the semen alone, as they never occur in eunuchs." By drawing on every farmer's knowledge of the effects of castration, Tissot gave plausibility to his argument. But the plausibility was based on guesswork. It would be proved totally wrong when the science of sex hormones came into existence in the laboratories of the early nineteen hundreds. The testicles do indeed produce the masculinization of puberty and adulthood, but not by way of the semen. They do it by secreting the male hormone testosterone, which seeps out of the hormone cells into the neighboring minuscule blood vessels, and then is pumped in the bloodstream to all other parts of the body. Semen and sex hormone, athough they are both under the control of the testicles, are entirely different substances.

To be logically systematic, Tissot needed to fit women into onanistic degeneracy theory. "The symptoms which supervene in females, are explained like those in men," he wrote. "The secretion which they lose, being less valuable and less matured than the semen of the male, its loss does not enfeeble so promptly, but when they indulge in it to excess, as their nervous system is naturally weaker and more disposed to spasms, the symptoms are more violent. Sudden excesses produce symptoms similar to those of the young man mentioned above, and we have seen a case of this kind. In 1746, a prostitute, twenty-three years of age, had connection in a single night with six Spanish dragoons near Montpelier. The next morning she was brought into the city in a dying state; she expired in the evening bathed in uterine hemorrhage which flowed in a constant stream" (p. 45).

Tissot found reasons for seminal loss in masturbation being more pernicious than in coition. He attributed to Sanctorius (1561-1636) the idea that, when the seminal vesicles were not semen filled, imagination and habit could more easily excite masturbation and thereby not only deprive nature of what was necessary for her healthful operations in coition, but also enfeeble all the faculties of the mind, particularly the memory—which imagination was believed always to do.

His most irrefutable argument, however, relied upon the *torrens invisibles.* "The exhalant vessels of the skin," he wrote, exhale at every instant an extremely thin fluid . . . at the same time another kind of vessels admit a part of the fluids which surround the body and carry them into the other vessels . . . These observations explain how the young woman with whom David slept, gave him strength . . . A person perspires more during coition than at any other time. This perspiration is perhaps more active and more volatile than at any other time: it is a real loss, and occurs whenever emissions of semen take place, from whatever cause, since it depends on the agitation attending it. In coition it is reciprocal, and the one inspires, what the other expires. This exchange has been verified by certain observations. In masturbation there is a loss without this reciprocal benefit" (pp. 50-51).

Tissot did not face up to the defects that would be revealed in his theory had he tried to apply logic to the effects of losing semen in oral or anal sex, mutual masturbation, or sex between two men or two women. He by-passed such complications by the simple expedient of having two kinds of sex. One was onanism, which signified that procreation was defeated because the semen was denied entry into the womb. The other was sexual intercourse with the penis in the vagina. Even within the legitimacy of marriage, however, husband and wife were recommended to observe long periods of abstinence as a health measure. Thus did the ancient theological doctrine of abstinence from sexual passion, and of copulating for procreation only, become medicalized.

The medicalization of abstinence, and its rationalization in accordance with degeneracy theory, allowed medical practitioners of the day to lay claim to being learned. It also provided them with a newfound power over their patients for whose afflictions they promised relief by first inflicting a cure of masturbation. Before long, masturbation itself became a disease. It was of such high prevalence that the lucrativeness of promised cures was guaranteed. This guarantee of wealth surreptitiously ensured that the disease of masturbation would remain in the textbooks of medicine for close on two centuries. So also did the theory of degeneracy.

The Vice of Venery

Tissot did not spell out in his *Treatise* what experiences he had as a doctor that made him decide to write it. It is likely that he became concerned with preventing the ravages of what, today, we would call the venereal diseases. Tissot might have recognized them only as diseases that begin in the sex organs, or are harbored in them, or spread from them, perhaps to afflict a pregnant mother's baby, and perhaps to end in death. He did not tell us about the prevalence of these diseases in his time.

However, it is known that syphilis spread in Europe rather like a plague some time after Columbus's sailors returned from their voyages of discovery in the New World, in the late fourteen-nineties and early fifteen hundreds. It is possible that Europeans had no resistance to the American form of the disease, just as, at a later time, Polynesians would die by the hundreds of thousands from lack of resistance to European measles and tuberculosis.

In Tissot's day, it was known that the clap (gonorrhea) and the pox (syphilis) were diseases related to sex. It was known also that they could be spread by contagion. There was no germ theory to explain how contagion could spread from one person to another. Contagion was, instead, attributed to putrefaction and pollution, especially of the air. Vice and immorality were also blamed. The sexual vices of whoring and adultery could bring on disease because they led to the depravity of excess. Too much sex, in Tissot's view, was what made people sick. It drained away their strength and debilitated them.

Tissot went beyond the social vice (prostitution) and lent the support of his authority to the idea that sexual excess from the secret vice (masturbation) was equally powerful in causing sexual disease. Then he went beyond sexual disease to any disease. Masturbation, he said, causes degeneracy, and degeneracy causes all manner of infirmities and death.

Tissot probably did get the watery discharge of diseases of the urethra confused with the clear discharge that may precede orgasm in masturbation: and he may actually have mistaken the white pus discharge of gonorrhea for the milky semen discharge of ejaculation. Even in the eighteenth century, a meticulous observer who knew about Leeuwenhoek's report (1677) of viewing sperm under the microscope should not have made such a mistake. Tissot, however, was so convinced that his masturbation theory was not a theory but an absolute truth that he needed only to illustrate it with examples, not to find proof by accurately enumerating and comparing both positive and negative evidence. He used any and all symptoms of disease, not only those of the sex organs, to illustrate the certainty of the truth he so ardently believed.

In Tissot's day, there was no clear separation between gonorrhea and syphilis as two diseases. Some experts claimed them to be different manifestations of one and the same vice—the vice of venery. Others argued that they were independent infections. John Hunter (1728-1793), British anatomist and surgeon, infected himself with the discharge of pus from a patient with gonorrhea in order to demonstrate that it would cause only gonorrhea. He did not reckon with the possibility that his patient might have been infected simultaneously with the infectious stage of syphilis, which was, indeed, the case. Thus Hunter caught both diseases, and thought that they were one. When he died of heart disease, he did not know that his heart had become defective as a third-stage result of being infected with syphilis.

In addition to heart disease, syphilis in its third stage can produce disease, both chronic and fatal, of other organs of the body. In its early contagious stage, a pregnant mother's syphilis can also produce deformity of the baby or cause it to be stillborn. For these reasons, syphilis has earned the reputation of being the disease that is the great deceiver. Though Rickard had by 1860 traced the course of the disease, the full range of what syphilis could produce would not be finalized until early in the nineteen hundreds, for it was not until 1906 that the organism, the spirochete, that causes syphilis was, at last, seen under the microscope. However, by observing the disease in individual patients, Tissot may have had some idea of the long-range havoc of which it is capable.

Thus there exists the possibility that Tissot, following in the footsteps of *Onania*, laid the blame for the havoc of syphilis—and much else besides—on the secret vice of masturbation instead of on venereal infection caught from a sexual partner. If that is the case, then the error represents one of the epic blunders of the human intellect as it tried to figure out cause and effect.

The consequences of this blunder were of incalculable enormity, for the blunder was reiterated, again and again, long after there were facts available with which to expose its fallacy.

Reference Notes

1. The quotations in this chapter, and the references to masturbation, debility, and degeneracy theory, are from *Onania* and from Tissot's *Treatise*.

2. The original spelling, with ƒ the letter for s in some words, corresponds with the out-datedness of the text, and so is retained in the quotations.

Degeneracy Migrates to America

Excitement and Debility

The principle of sexual degeneracy became widely accepted. By the early eighteen hundreds, it had diffused its way into general medical thinking. As a theory of the cause of disease, it belonged in the general category of vitalism. Part of its appeal was its ready compatibility with other vitalist principles and theories of the day.

Vital forces and vital spirits have a long history that goes all the way back to Aristotle (384-322 B.C.) and Galen (A.D. 130-200),[1] and reaches to the present in some of the concepts of holistic medicine and spiritual healing.

Aristotle's three-way division of the human soul into vegetative, sensitive, and rational was incorporated into the medical thinking of ensuing centuries. The soul, it was said, kept in communication with the body by way of a spirit or vapor, which itself had three components, natural spirit, vital spirit, and animal spirit, corresponding to vegetative, sensitive, and rational, respectively.

In Galen's teachings, derived from Aristotle, natural spirit was produced in the liver. From there it ascended to the heart, where it was refined into vital spirit. Vital spirit from the heart next reached the ventricles of the brain and was refined into animal, or animating, spirit. Animal spirit furnished the soul with the faculties of sense, memory, and intellect. Vital spirit from the heart furnished the soul with emotions.

Though the humors and spirits of Galen and his era are now museum pieces, some of the concepts and terms have refused to die, especially in everyday expressions, like "straight from the heart." The idea of vital spirits that allow parts and organs of the body to communicate with one another has never become extinct, but the terminology has changed. By the seventeen hundreds, sympathies had been added to humors, vapors, and vital spirits. From sympathies, the term *sympathetic nervous system* is still retained. Another change in terminology, early in the nineteen hundreds, was the branching off of *hormones*, and, more recently, *phero-mones*, from the trunk of the sympathy tree. The very newest branching off is that of *neurohormones, neurotransmitters,* and *neuromodulators.*

The age of sympathies was also the age of increased scientific under-standing of the nervous system as a system of communication throughout the body. The life-regulating function of the nervous system was a promi-nent principle in the physiology of the famous teacher William Cullen (1712-1790), in Edinburgh. His influence was brought to America by his pupil Benjamin Rush (1745-1813) when he returned to Philadelphia.[2]

Rush was influenced also by two French physicians, Xavier Bichat (1771-1802) and his colleague, François Broussais (1772-1832), who sur-vived him. These two men developed a physiological theory that postulated two nervous systems. One regulated the person's external life within the world; the other regulated his / her internal life within the self. The former is nowadays known as the central nervous system (CNS), but Bichat and Broussais named it the "animal (i.e., animating) nervous system," harking back to Aristotle and the terminology of Erasistratus, of the third century B.C. The latter is nowadays known as the autonomic nervous system. For Bichat and Broussais, it was the "organic" or "vegetative nervous sys-tem"—again harking back to Aristotle.

The animal nervous system belonged to the special senses and to movement of the muscles and limbs. The organic nervous system be-longed to regulation of the internal organs. Broussais put forward the idea that the "great sympathetic nerve" of the organic nervous system bore a relationship to the gut (and hence to nutritional health) that was paralleled by the relationship of the CNS to the spinal cord.

These new French teachings were of value to Rush in formulating a theory of disease that would be an improvement over the theory of releasing bad humors by blood-letting that was still in vogue. Rush taught that there was only one disease and that it took many different forms. The basic disease was morbid excitement or irritability of an organ or part of the body. The idea of irritability of a nerve or muscle traces back to experiments done by the great Swiss scientist-physician Albrecht von Haller (1708-1777).

Rush gave up the idea that the opposite of irritability is debility. Instead, he said that irritability becomes worse if the part has first been worn out or debilitated. Debility, he taught, increases the susceptibility to morbid excitement, known in physiology as erethism. So far so good, except that Rush's theory began to eat its own tail when he had to allow that too much irritation, excitement, or stimulation could cause debility; and so could too little of them. Too much caused indirect debility; and too little, direct debility. Either too much or too little was a kind of intemperance, and all intemperance was unhealthy.

There were, in Rush's system, many ways of being intemperate, all of them subsumed under the principles of nutrition, exercise, and sex. Tissot, before him, and the author of *Onania*, also had borrowed these three principles of health theory from their forebears. They added their own doctrines of dietetic and exercise prescriptions and prohibitions, especially as they related to the cure of self-abuse and sexual excess.

Benjamin Rush put an absolute exclusion on alcoholic spirits and tobacco, adding them to the list of spices and condiments that had been condemned for centuries. Tea and coffee were also condemned. Rush considered all of them too stimulating.

He endorsed physical exercise outdoors and fresh air while sleeping as well as working. Fresh air was widely considered to be an antidote to disease, because diseases were believed to spread in putrefactions and other foul substances and vapors that polluted the air.

There is no argument about the validity of nutrition, exercise, and sex as principles of health and well-being. The criteria of what constitutes healthy nutrition, healthy exercise, and healthy sex are what provoke argument. Almost anyone can claim the right of authority.

Rush himself, in prescribing proper diet, proper exercise, and proper sex did not stray far from the path of accepted authority. For example, his ideas of proper sex were sufficiently compatible with those of Tissot that in the "Notes and an Appendix" to the American translation of Tissot's *Treatise*, a "Physician of the Medical Society of the city and county of New York" was able to quote him in justification of having made the work available in English.

"This appetite, which was implanted in our natures for the purpose of propagating our species, when excessive, becomes a disease of both the body and the mind," Rush had written. "When restrained, it produces tremors, a flushing of the face, sighing, nocturnal pollutions, hysteria, hypochondriasis, and in women the furor uterinus. When indulged in an undue or a promiscuous intercourse with the female sex, or in onanism, it produces seminal weakness, impotence, dysury, tabes dorsalis, pulmonary consumption, dyspepsia, dimness of sight, vertigo, epilepsy, hypochondriasis, loss of memory, manalgia, fatuity and death" (Tissot, p. 109).

Rush did not add anything fundamentally new to early-nineteenth-century sexual theory in America. His innovation was his general theory of health and disease. It provided a creed, so to speak, ready-made for the health-reform crusaders of the next part of the century. They would provide their own definitions of proper diet, proper exercise, and proper sex.

Sylvester Graham was one of the earliest beneficiaries. He began his crusade with brown bread and intolerance for alcohol, tobacco, coffee, tea, salt, spices, and condiments. After he arrived in Philadelphia, he rapidly assimilated the basic tenets of Rush's medical system. They gave his lectures an aura of erudition, and they enabled him to expand the scope of his crusade to include the virtues of fitness and sexual abstinence.

It was Graham's teaching more than Rush's that initiated America's fight against degeneracy and influenced its food, fitness, and sexual habits. He set a fashion that would be adopted and adapted by others who would extend his influence over the next one hundred and fifty years throughout the English-speaking world.

Reference Notes

1. The heritage of Aristotelian and Galenic concepts of spirits and humors in Western thought is here adapted from Valency (1961) and from the *Encyclopaedia Britannica*'s survey of medical history.

2. Nissenbaum (1980) relates Benjamin Rush's conceptions of health and illness to those of his teacher and French contemporaries and traces their influence on Sylvester Graham.

Sylvester Graham's Concupiscence Disease

Hygiene for Beginners

Graham's small book, *A Lecture to Young Men,* was published in Providence, in 1834. It contained the elements of his later, larger work, the *Science of Human Life,* but in the long run it was more influential because its claims became repeated and expanded in uncounted scores of sex-information manuals of the eighteen and early nineteen hundreds. They all treated sexual desire as a Frankenstein monster, and as a source of disease, terror, and doom in young people's lives.[1]

At the outset, Graham entrapped the attention of his audience by entrusting them with medical scholarship that pandered to their lack of higher education. It was beguilingly simplified and, in the knowledge of hindsight, pure physiological fable.

"Constituted as man is," Graham began, "two grand FUNCTIONS of his system are necessary for his existence as an individual and as a species. The first is NUTRITION:—the second is REPRODUCTION.

"Nutrition is the general function by which the body is nourished and sustained; and includes, in its detail, digestion, absorption, circulation, respiration, secretion, excretion &c. Reproduction is the function by which an organized being propagates its kind. The first is necessary for man's individual, bodily existence. The second is necessary for the continuation of his species. Man is accordingly furnished with organs fitted for these great functions of life. . . .

"The function of reproduction is not necessary for man's individual existence, and therefore its final cause, or constitutional purpose, does not require its constant exercise: and accordingly, the organs, constituting the apparatus necessary for this function, are not all complete until many years after birth. . . ."

With the lesson in physiology hardly begun, Graham digressed into moralizing about sexual excess. He compared the purity of the control of sex in animals by instinct with its control in man by his rational powers.

"In a pure state of nature," he declared, "man would have no disposition to exercise this function to any injurious excess. . . ." Then becoming excited and ungrammatical, he continued: "It is by abusing his organs, and depraving his instinctive appetites, through the devices of his rational powers, that the body of man has become a living volcano of unclean propensities and passions . . . he sinks himself in degeneracy, below the brutes."

The volcano could erupt not only in masturbation but in too much sexual intercourse in marriage also. At this point Graham addressed himself simply to sex in general. Then he returned to physiology, and the new French theory of the two nervous systems, upon which hinged the plausibility of all his arguments:

> The functions of nutrition and reproduction depend on the vital properties of the tissues which form the organs of the system—particularly the muscular and nervous tissues; and more especially the nervous. The nerves belonging to the human body, are divided into two classes.
>
> First; the BRAIN and SPINAL MARROW, with their various cords, branches, fibres and filaments. These nerves appertain to what is called *Animal Life,* and are the organs of sensation, perception, intellection, volition; and are connected with the muscles of voluntary motion.
>
> Second; the GANGLIONS and PLEXUSES with their various cords, branches, fibres and filaments. These nerves appertain to what is called *Organic Life.* They are distributed to the various internal organs, and preside over all the processes of vital chemistry:—or, in other words, they are the immediate instruments or conductors of that vital energy by which the living body converts food into chyme, and chyme into chyle, and chyle into blood, and blood into the various solids and fluids of the whole system. . . .

"The function of reproduction depends on both classes of nerves," Graham says, quite correctly, but then goes on repeating Tissot's error that blood is turned into semen:

> The power of the male organs of generation to convert a portion of the arterial blood into semen, and to deposit that semen in its appropriate receptacles, and finally to eject it with peculiar convulsions, depends on the nerves of organic life: but the power to exercise the organs of generation in the fulfilment of the function of reproduction, depends on the nerves of animal life. Hence the genital organs hold important relations, both with the organs of nutrition, and with the brain and spinal marrow, and with the parts supplied by them with nervous power. . . . Hence the influences of the brain may act directly on the genital organs; and of

these latter on the brain. Lascivious thoughts and imaginations will excite and stimulate the genital organs; cause an increased quantity of blood to flow into them; and augment their secretions and peculiar sensibilities:—and, on the other hand, an excited state of the genital organs, either from the stimulations of semen, or from diseased action in the system, will throw its influence upon the brain, and force lascivious thoughts and imaginations upon the mind.

Here again Graham is echoing Tissot. He was absolute and unequivocal in placing the responsibility for degeneracy not on the fluid mechanics of semen loss but on the lascivious thoughts and imaginations, and the "peculiar excitement of the nervous system" that stimulated the genital organs into losing semen. By using this logic, Graham painted himself into a corner from which there was no escape when he tried to deal with the prevention of nocturnal emission, the loss of semen during sleep in a wet dream. By contrast, the same logic enabled him to put loss of semen by either two-person copulation or one-person masturbation in the same class and to dictate abstinence from both. It also enabled him to apply all of his arguments to females as well as males, and to children before as well as after the sexual development of puberty. In consequence, he had the entire human race under indictment for failing to eradicate its lascivious thoughts and imaginations. His power of condemnation was unlimited and intoxicating. He explained:

All extraordinary and undue excitements, whether caused by mental, moral or physical stimuli, increase the excitability and unhealthy activity of the nerves of organic life; and tend to induce diseased irritability and sensibility in them, which is more or less diffused over the whole domain; and affects all the particular organs and functions. A frequent repetition of these excitements, always induces a greater or less degree of debility and diseased irritability in the nerves of organic life:—disordering and deranging the functions, and often causing excessive morbid irritability and sensibility and inflammation, and even disorganization or change of structure in the viscera—such as the brain, stomach, lungs, liver, kidneys, heart, &c. . . . .

The nerves of the genital organs partake, in common with those of the other organs, of this general debility and diseased excitability, and become exceedingly susceptible of irritation; sympathizing powerfully with all the disturbances of the system, and especially of the brain, and alimentary canal. Their peculiar sensibilities are augmented to a morbid or preternatural state, of a chronic character; and thus a diseased prurience, or concupiscence, is permanently established,—forcing the sufferer into excessive desires, and unclean thoughts, almost incessantly. Hence, hypochondriacs, and those who are afflicted with nervous melancholy, are generally morbidly lecherous; and hence, also, insanity, resulting from the morbid condition of the nerves of organic life, is generally attended with excessive sexual desire, and the mind becomes filled with unclean images. This is the reason why many people, who were perfectly modest while in health, become exceedingly obscene in their conduct and talk, when insane; and often, if they are not prevented, give themselves up to self-pollution, and thus exceedingly aggravate and confirm their disorders.

Graham's listeners, like his readers, have now been given fair warning of where their lascivious thoughts and imaginations will lead them, and by implication they have no one to blame but themselves for the tragic consequences of their lack of foresight and will-power. This is the point at which Graham pulls them back from the brink of despair, and he does so by blaming something that they can change. Diet is the culprit: "All kinds of stimulating and heating substances; high-seasoned food; rich dishes; the free use of flesh; and even the excess of aliment; all, more or less,— and some to a very great degree—increase the concupiscent excitability and sensibility of the genital organs, and augment their influence on the functions of organic life, and on the intellectual and moral faculties. . . ."
Overstimulated by wrong food and lascivious thoughts and imaginations, sexual desire spreads health-destroying effects through all the nerves of all the organs of the body:

The convulsive paroxysms attending venereal indulgence, are connected with the most intense excitement, and cause the most powerful agitation to the whole system, that it is ever subject to. The brain, stomach, heart, lungs, liver, skin—and the other organs—feel it sweeping over them, with the tremendous violence of a tornado. The powerfully excited and convulsed heart drives the blood, in fearful congestion, to the principal viscera,—producing oppression, irritation, debility, rupture, inflammation, and sometimes disorganization;—and this violent paroxysm is generally succeeded by great exhaustion, relaxation, lassitude, and even prostration. . . . All the organs and vessels of the body, even to the smallest capillaries, become extremely debilitated; and their functional power exceedingly feeble.

Graham knew the stratagems of the preacher's trade. So he eased up on direct threats of doom. With the self-righteousness of today's crusaders against childhood sexuality, he appealed to his audience to protect their young against bad diet, effeminate inactivity, and sexual stimulation:

If we will train our offspring into the early and free use of flesh-meat, and accustom them to high-seasoned food, and richly prepared dishes, and learn them to drink tea, and coffee, and wine; and to indulge in various other stimulants, with which civic life is universally cursed,—and effeminate their bodies with feather beds, and enervating dress,—in short, if we will sedulously educate them, to all the degenerating habits of luxury, indolence, voluptuousness and sensuality, we shall be more indebted to their want of *opportunity to sin,* than to any other cause, for the preservation of their bodily chastity,—if, indeed, we escape the heart-rending anguish, of seeing them the early victims of passions, which we have been instrumental in developing to an irresistible power! For these lascivious, and exceedingly pernicious day-dreams of the young, are but the first buddings of a depraved instinct, which will not be satisfied with the passive reveries of the mind and affections of the body. The delicate susceptibilities of youth being constantly tortured, and their young blood continually heated, by a stimulating and depraving diet, their animal propensities are much more rapidly developed than are their rational and moral powers; and a preternatural excitability of the nerves of organic life, is inevitably induced; while other habits of luxury and effeminacy, serve to increase the general debility of their system, and assist in throwing a common anarchical depravity over the whole domain of instinct. . . .

A "disproportionate exercise of the brain," caused by schooling, is also on Graham's list of dangers, for it "leads to a general debility of the nervous system, involving the genital organs."

Concupiscence, the Disease of Lust

After this admonition on behalf of children, Graham admonishes those in his audience who engage in "illicit commerce between the sexes. . . . Their imagination is wrought up," he says, "and presents lewd and exciting images . . . the genital organs are almost continuously stimulated by the mind . . . which produces the most ruinous consequences."[2]

The provocation of lust distinguishes illicit commerce from marriage: "Between the husband and the wife, where there is a proper degree of chastity, all these causes either entirely lose, or are exceedingly diminished in their effect. They become accustomed to each other's body, and their parts no longer excite an impure imagination, and their sexual intercourse is the result of the more natural and instinctive excitements of the organs themselves;—and when the dietetic, and other habits are much as they should be, this intercourse is very seldom. . . ."

Graham updated the list of infirmities attributed to sexual excess within the precincts of wedlock:

> Languor, lassitude, muscular relaxation, general debility and heaviness, depression of spirits, loss of appetite, indigestion, faintness and sinking at the pit of the stomach, increased susceptibilities of the skin and lungs to all the atmospheric changes, feebleness of circulation, chilliness, headache, melancholy, hypochondria, hysterics, feebleness of all the senses, impaired vision, loss of sight, weakness of the lungs, nervous cough, pulmonary consumption, disorders of the liver and kidneys, urinary difficulties, disorders of the genital organs, weakness of the brain, loss of memory, epilepsy, insanity, apoplexy,—and extreme feebleness and early death of offspring,—are among the too common evils which are caused by sexual excesses between husband and wife. . . . Pulmonary consumption is always more speedily developed and terminated in death, by venereal pleasures. Organic diseases of every kind, are always aggravated by this cause; and many of them cannot be cured, unless such pleasures are entirely suspended. Epilepsy, for instance, which is often induced by venereal excess, frequently defies all remedial agents and measures, until sexual pleasures are wholly abandoned. . . .

There was no escape from these diseases of sexual excess on the pretext of having been implanted by nature with a high degree of the propensity for concupiscence (there was no libido or sex drive in the dictionary of Graham's era):

> I have known married gentlemen who were so much troubled with habitual concupiscence, that they were inclined to consider themselves peculiarly constituted; and were sometimes disposed to reason themselves into the belief, that, being thus tempered by NATURE, they would be justifiable in acts of incontinence. But these same gentlemen, by adopting a proper system of diet and general regimen, have not only improved their health, exceedingly, in every respect, but so subdued their sexual propensity, as to be able to abstain from connubial commerce, and preserve entire chastity of body, for several months in succession, without the least inconvenience, and without any separation from their companions. . . .

Graham made no special mention of women with habitual concupiscence.

Graham was an expert on the wages of sin, when the sin was sexual excess, but not on the definition of sexual excess. In fact, like many experts today, he was something of a copout. Addressing himself "to the healthy and robust," he advised:

> It were better for you, not to exceed in the frequency of your indulgencies, the number of months in the year; and you cannot exceed the

number of weeks in the year, without impairing your constitutional powers, shortening your lives, and increasing your liability to disease and suffering; if indeed, you do not thereby actually induce disease of the worst and most painful kind; and at the same time transmit to your offspring an impaired constitution, with strong and unhappy predispositions. . . .

Though it had not been Graham's stated purpose to make concupiscence, the thoughts and voluptuous imaginations of sex, into a disease, his *Lecture* did, in effect, achieve just that. It was a disease modeled after the example of sin: it was self-induced by voluntary choice and self-cured by voluntary renunciation and will-power. Thus, in today's medical terminology, it would be called an addiction. The victim was addicted to the targets or recipients of concupiscence.

Concupiscence manifesting itself in the imaginations of a dream and seminal emission while asleep tests Graham's voluntary-choice explanation to the breaking point. Small wonder, then, that he postponed consideration of this topic until, as an afterthought, he added a couple of paragraphs to his already finished *Lecture*. They form a bridge to the second half of his book, an essay called *Self-Pollution*.

Self-pollution is the word for masturbation that is borrowed from the prescientific idea of illness being caused by the vapors of putrefaction that pollute the air. Polluted air could be breathed in from the vapors of sick and dying people, as well as from swamps, cesspools, rotting carcasses, and the like. Pollution could be also moral pollution, caused by iniquity, sin, and vice. Hence self-pollution was known also as the secret or solitary vice. Self-abuse was still another name.

Reference Notes

1. All the quotations in this chapter are taken from Graham's *A Lecture to Young Men;* those in this first section, "Hygiene for Beginners," are from pp. 12-26.
2. The quotations in this second section are from Graham's *Lecture*, pp. 33-37.

Sylvester Graham:
Doctor of the Self-Polluted

The Nighttime Disease: Nocturnal Pollution

"There is," Graham wrote, "a common error of opinion among young men, which is, perhaps, not wholly confined to the young,—that health requires an emission of semen at stated periods, and that frequent nocturnal emissions in sleep, are not incompatible with health. All this is wrong,—entirely, dangerously, wrong! Health does not absolutely require that there should ever be an emission of semen, from puberty, to death, though the individual live an hundred years:—and the frequency of involuntary, nocturnal emissions, is a certain demonstration, that the parts at least, are suffering under a debility, and morbid irritability, utterly incompatible with the general welfare of the system."[1]

With this statement, Graham goes beyond defining concupiscence as a disease and defines the involuntary nocturnal emission of sleep as itself a disease. Not unexpectedly, given Graham's three-way system of diet, exercise, and sex, the cure for the disease of spermatorrhea, as involuntary emission would later come to be known, was through diet and exercise. Graham's cure came by a direct line of descent from Tissot.

The right means of cure is spelled out in complicated and self-contradictory detail by Graham, beginning as follows:

If, therefore, you are very much reduced, and afflicted with involuntary nocturnal emissions; and distressed with pains, and impaired senses, and enfeebled mind, and cheerless melancholy, tending to despair and madness; remember the general and special sympathies and reciprocities which I have pointed out,—and particularly those which exist between the genital organs and the alimentary canal and the brain. . . .

Every irritation and undue excitement of the brain and stomach and intestines, are calculated to continue the involuntary emissions,—while these, in turn, keep up and increase the morbid irritability of those organs. Improper kinds of food in the stomach and intestines, will, in this excessively irritable state of the system, cause nocturnal emissions.

Improper quantities of the best aliment in nature, will produce the same effect; and so will, also, the presence of food in the stomach, duodenum, &c, at improper times; an over-fulness, or late supper, will almost invariably cause nocturnal emissions, in those who are liable to such an affliction; and while those emissions continue, it is impossible for the system to recover strength and health. Costiveness of the bowels, is also sure to keep up the nightly discharges; and if recourse be had to medicine, for the purpose of keeping the bowels open, it is sure to perpetuate the mischief, by irritating and debilitating still more the tissues of the alimentary canal, and through them, the whole system. The food, therefore, must be of such a character as will pass through the stomach and intestines with the least irritation and oppression; while, at the same time, it affords a sufficient supply of nourishment, and keeps up, in the most natural and healthful manner, a regular and free peristaltic action of the bowels. A person laboring under the difficulties which we are contemplating, must likewise avoid with great care, every crude and cold article of diet.

The recommended nutrition, not surprisingly, is Graham's own cereal diet:

Farinaceous food, properly prepared, is incomparably the best aliment for such a sufferer; and good bread, made of coarsely-ground, unbolted wheat, or rye-meal, and hominy, made of cracked wheat, or rye, or Indian corn, are among the very best articles of diet that such a person can use. These, taken with a little molasses or sugar, at proper times, and freely masticated, will digest easily and pleasantly; and will be sure to keep up a regular and healthy motion of the bowels.

When the night emissions are frequent, and the system extremely irritable, the patient should confine himself to a very few articles of diet, and eat but little, and be very uniform in all his habits: always very carefully avoiding full and late suppers. Milk will be found too heating and too oppressive for such persons. No animal food, therefore, should be used, in any quantity, by the patient; and no other liquid but pure, soft water, or toast water, should ever be drank by him. . . .

The patient cannot be too careful to observe a strictly correct and undeviating regimen:—nor too scrupulously avoid spirits, and wine, and malt-liquors; and every other kind of alcoholic drinks—even in the smallest quantity; and opium, and tobacco, and coffee, and tea, and all other narcotics;—and pepper, and ginger, and mustard, and horse-radish, and peppermint;—in short, every kind of stimulating and heating substances. . . .

Let the patient, like a rational and intelligent being, promote the tone and action of his organs, and general vigor of his system, by active exercise; and let him exhilarate himself, by free and copious draughts of the pure air of heaven! Let him go to the gymnasium, and with moderate beginning, and gradual increase of effort, let him swing upon, and climb the poles, and ropes, and ladders, and vault upon the wooden horse, and practice all the other feats of that admirable institution:—or let him ride on horse-back, and walk and run and jump: or labor on the farm; and avoid sedentary habits, and all anxieties and excitements of the mind: and most strictly shun all dalliance with females, and all lewd books, and obscene conversation, and lascivious images and thoughts:—let him sleep on a hard bed, and rise early in the morning, and take a shower-bath of cold water; or plunge into cold water; or sponge his body all over with it,—and, in either case, rub himself off briskly and freely with a coarse towel, and follow that freely with a good, stiff flesh-brush, and then exercise vigorously in the open air or in the gymnasium, for an hour before breakfast. Let him exercise as much as he can through the day:—let him take an early, light supper, and take a good deal of active exercise before going to bed: and, if his nocturnal emissions still continue, let him, just before getting into bed, repeat his shower, or sponge-bath, and follow it freely with the coarse towel and flesh-brush. . . .

Even when improvement permits some relaxation of the regimen, the patient "must not go beyond the vegetable kingdom and pure water for his aliment."

Graham's long-windedness on the cure of nocturnal self-pollution while asleep was inevitable. He rated self-pollution, whether sleeping or waking, as "by far the worst form of venereal indulgence." Yet he knew that threats and admonitions directed at stopping waking masturbation were ineffectual at bringing wet dreams under voluntary control.

Graham's cure for waking masturbation was not diet or exercise, but terrorization. He anticipated the strategy of what would long after him become the bastard science of victimology by sounding the alarm against the corruption of children: "The habit has in some instances begun as early as the fifth or sixth year; and shocking as it may seem, nurses, and even parents, have been the teachers of the abominable vice. . . . It is, however, more frequently communicated from one boy to another; and sometimes a single boy will corrupt many others." A victim grows up "with a body full of disease, and with a mind in ruins, the loathsome habit still tyrannizing over him, with the inexorable imperiousness of a fiend of darkness. . . ."

Again and again, Graham gets carried away with the extravagance of his own words. He was like the producer of a horror movie, getting his own payoff by terrifying his audience. He was mindless of the fact that some of his listeners might be able to contradict him by drawing on their own personal experience. Likewise, he was mindless of the deleterious effect his censure and reviling might have on susceptible listeners. For page after page it continues, as he describes what self-pollution does, organ by organ, to the body. The hapless teenager, stigmatized with acne, is publicly revealed: "Pimples of a livid hue, come out upon the forehead and about the nose, and sometimess over the whole face,—and even ulcerous sores, in some cases, break out upon the head, breast, back and thighs; and these sometimes enlarge into permanent fistulas, of a cancerous character, and continue, perhaps for years, to discharge great quantities of foetid, loathsome pus; and not unfrequently terminate in death. . . ."

All the senses degenerate, but "the eyes, more generally, are the greatest sufferers from venereal abuses. They become languid and dull, and lose their brightness and liveliness of expression, and assume a glassy and vacant appearance; and fall back into their sockets, and sometimes become red and inflamed, and weak and excessively sensible; so that wind, light, &c., irritate and distress them. The sight becomes feeble, obscure, cloudy, confused, and often is entirely lost; and utter blindness fills the rest of life with darkness and unavailing regret. . . ." Graham might have been describing tertiary syphilis, but ordinary masturbation—no!

Wrong Diagnosis

Like Tissot before him, Graham erroneously attributed to masturbation afflictions that were undoubtedly long-range symptoms of gonorrhea and of the final stage of syphilis, which was already known to be a venereally transmitted disease. Graham wrote:

> The spinal marrow sometimes becomes the focal point of mischief, from these filthy outrages on nature; and with its consumption, accelerates the general work of ruin, to a most loathsome termination in death!
>
> The brain is neither last nor least in these terrible sufferings . . . epilepsy is often induced . . . paralysis, partial and general, often occurs. . . . Apoplexy is also a legitimate, and not unfrequent effect of these causes, which increases with terrible efficacy, the fearfulness of the general anarchy of the system, and sometimes, forecloses the whole, by sudden death, even in the very act of venereal indulgence; and thrusts the filthy transgressor with all his abominable pollutions upon him, uncovered, into the presence of God, where perhaps the only utterance which will greet his ear, will be—"He that is filthy, let him be filthy still!"
>
> Sometimes, general mental decay continues with the continued

abuses, till the wretched transgressor sinks into a miserable fatuity, and finally becomes a confirmed and degraded idiot, whose deeply sunken and vacant, glossy eye, and livid, shrivelled countenance, and ulcerous, toothless gums, and foetid breath, and feeble, broken voice, and emaciated and dwarfish and crooked body, and almost hairless head—covered, perhaps, with suppurating blisters and running sores—denote a premature old age! a blighted body—and a ruined soul!—and he drags out the remnant of his loathsome existence, in exclusive devotion to his horridly abominable sensuality. . . . Even when he attempts to pray to the omniscient and holy God, these filthy harpies of his imagination will often flit between his soul and Heaven, and shake pollution on him from their horrid wings! . . .

The genital organs, themselves, often suffer in the most extreme degree. Their peculiar susceptibilities and sensibilities become morbidly excessive,—an undue quantity of blood is received and retained in them,—the secretion of the parts become unhealthy and excessive, and extremely irritating and debilitating,—tending always to turgescence, inflammation and change of structure. Heat and burning of the parts—shocking enlargement of the spermatic cords—swelling—inflammation—intense sensibility—excruciating pain—induration—scirrhus and ulceration of the testicles, are among the terrible evils which result from venereal excess. In other cases, a general withering, and impotence and decay of the parts, commences and continues on, till almost every vestige of the *insignia,* and all the power of virility are gone. But before this shocking result of continued outrage has taken place, the extremely debilitated, and excessively irritable parts, sympathizing with all the disturbances of the brain and alimentary canal; and, in fact, with those of every part of the system, become excited on every slight occasion, and an involuntary emission of crude and watery, and sometimes bloody semen occurs; and in many instances, a continual gonorrhea, or constant dribbling of thin purulent matter from the penis, is experienced.

Once again, Graham was wrongly blaming masturbation as the cause of various other diseases. Later writers would correct some such errors, though keeping masturbation as the cause of some afflictions, especially those mental and sexual afflictions for which no other cause had yet been found.

Graham warned the self-polluted victim could become incurable, so that "Nothing but constant watching, and pinions, and manacles, could prevent the continuance of the shocking habit—even in utter insanity."

The fate of the victim was morally transcended, however, by the curse of "begetting puny offspring, which either fall abortive to the grave, or come forth to individual existence, weak and delicate, and full of predisposition to disease, and drag out a miserable period of suffering; covered with sores and ulcers, and deformed with rickets and distortions, and

finally perish, infant Lazaruses, on whom are fearfully visited the iniquities of the father! . . ."

There was nothing original or unique in Graham's teaching on self-
pollution. Most of it can be found in Tissot's *Treatise*. What Graham did
was to exaggerate, modernize, and Americanize what Tissot had written
eighty years earlier, and to set a religious and medical vogue for antisexualism—no small achievement for a demagogue who had never seen a
patient!

John Wesley's Household Doctor Book

Graham preached his gospel of health through hygiene in diet, exercise,
and sex to an America that, in the century before him, had welcomed
Europe's persecuted nonconformist and heretical sects. This America, in
the new century of its own democracy, was ready to follow its own home-
grown messiahs who would lead their own movements of the disaffected
and found their own little utopian kingdoms of heaven on earth. The
nineteenth century was a religion-making century in America.

The connection between religion and healing is as old as the Bible. So
it comes as no surprise that the new messiahs would preach health as well
as healing. John Wesley (1703-1791), founder of the Methodist faith, had
led the way as early as 1747 with a small volume, first published in
London, *Primitive Physic or an Easy and Natural Method of Curing
Most Diseases*. It was the first in what would become a long line of
doctors' books written for do-it-yourself household nursing and healing.
Because of its immense popularity, it went through many editions and
revisions. An American reprinting of the sixteenth edition was issued
from Trenton, New Jersey, in 1788, and more followed.

Wesley's health hints and cures omitted all reference to sexual life.
They relied on a mixture of diet, exercise, fresh air, and herbal concoctions that were, indeed, as his title announced, primitive. Most of
them were either useless or dangerous; and the how and why explanations
of illness and recovery are chiefly a collection of old wives' tales. By
comparison, Sylvester Graham's teachings were a veritable model of
logical organization and rational explanation.

Reform Survives Absurdity

For the fifty or sixty years after Graham ceased teaching, until the end of
the century, which included the antislavery and the Civil War years,

eastern America went through a ferment of new ideals, movements, religions, and cults. The big issues of the era were emancipation, temperance, woman's suffrage, and birth control. It was an era of ferment not unlike the ferment, especially in western America, of the counterculture movements of the recent past, which included antiracism and another divisive war, Vietnam.

Each in its own way, the nineteenth-century reform movements and their twentieth-century counterparts took up one or more of the familiar health triad: food (vegetarianism and nutritional reform); fitness (fresh-air, exercise, clothing reform, massage, hot-tubs and the water-cure); and sex (sexual reform, sex therapy, and women's rights). In both centuries, reformist zeal ran the risk of becoming extreme and absurd. The verdict of history, so far as the nineteenth century is concerned, is that the seed of absurdity housed the plant of reasonable change. Thus, in the long run, diet reform did enlarge America's menu, and that of much of the world, with ready-to-serve breakfast cereals. Orange, tomato, and other juices became standard items, and peanut butter a staple sandwich spread. Coffee substitutes made from roasted grains led to the commercialization of decaffeinated coffee, and sugar became replaced with artificial sweeteners in low-calorie drinks and diet foods.

Exercise reform brought gymnastics and physical education into the school curriculum and made outdoor sports and recreation into a cult of regional patriotism. The theory of fresh air as an antidote to contagious vapors affected the awareness of ventilation in home design. The water-cure popularized daily bathing and changed domestic architecture by making the household bathroom a necessity in every home. Dress reform released women from the constraints of laced bodices and hooped skirts into the first pants suits, known a century ago as bloomers, after Mrs. Amelia Bloomer, who popularized them in the women's movement.

Sexual reform did not abolish marriage by turning America into a nation of celibacy, as it did the colonies of the Shaker sect that had no marriage and no children. Though it may have reduced the average family size, abstinence did not depopulate the country. Its actual effect had been unforeseen: Upturned, so to speak, abstinence theory became a vehicle of women's sexual emancipation from the dominion of men, in association with both the birth-control movement and the woman's suffrage movement for political equality with men.

Reference Note

1. The Graham quotations and references in this chapter are from *A Lecture to Young Men*, pp. 39 ff.

CHAPTER

10

Some Said Sex Was Good

Aristotle's Masterpiece

The generation that read Wesley's *Primitive Physic* in the late seventeen hundreds read also another best-seller known as *Aristotle's Masterpiece*. The actual title of this book is: *The Works of Aristotle the Famous Philosopher in Four Parts*. The lengthy subtitle discloses what manner of book it is: "Containing I. His *Complete Masterpiece*; displaying the secrets of Nature in the Generation of man. To which is added *The Family Physician*; being approved remedies for the several Distempers incident to the human Body. II. His *Experienced Midwife*; absolutely necessary for Surgeons, Midwives, Nurses and Child bearing Women. III. His *Book of Problems*, containing various Questions and Answers, relative to the State of Man's Body. IV. His *Last Legacy*; unfolding the Secrets of Nature respecting the Generation of Man."

The only thing certain about the authorship of the book is that it was not written by Aristotle. A likely date for the first London edition is 1684. In America, it had by 1820 been reprinted in about thirty different editions or versions, some containing the same material in two places. Basically, it is a household manual of information about procreation in its several aspects: the sexual organs and their function, sexual intercourse, conception, childbearing, labor and delivery, midwifery skills, and birth defects. There is also information on how to judge character from appearances; home remedies for various ailments; and curiosities and absurdities of folk wisdom and old wives' tales.

Aristotle's Masterpiece is written unpretentiously from the point of view that everyone has the right to know anything and everything there is to know about sex, without moralistic restriction. There is no disputation about the pleasure of sex, either to defend or to deny it. It is stated the way it is. Here, for example, is what the reader learns about the clitoris (p. 23):

The next thing is the clitoris, which is a ſinewy and hard part of the womb, replete with ſpongy and black matter within, in the ſame manner as the ſide ligaments of the yard ſuffers erection and falling in the ſame manner, and both ſtirs up luſt and gives delight in copulation, for without this, the fair ſex neither deſire nuptial embraces nor have pleaſure in them, nor conceive by them; and according to the greatneſs or ſmallneſs of this part, they are more or leſs fond of men's embraces; ſo that it may properly be ſtyled the ſeat of luſt.

> Blowing the coals of thoſe amorous fires,
> Which youth and beauty to be quench'd requires.

And it may well be ſtiled for, for it is like a yard [i.e. penis] in ſituation, ſubſtance, compoſition, and erection, growing ſometimes out of the body two inches, but that happens not but upon ſome extraordinary accident. [p. 5].

Two or more lines of rhymed verse are inserted in many places to give poetic voice to the personal experience of the act of lovemaking and its feelings. "ſince the utmoſt intention of deſire is required in this act," the text advises (p. 23), "it may not be amiſs for the bridegroom for the more eager heightening of this joy, to delineate the ſcene of their approaching happineſs to his fair languiſhing bride in ſome ſuch amorous rapture as this,

> Now, my fair bride, now will I ſtorm the mint
> Of love and joy, and rifle all that's in't.
> Now my infranchis'd hand on every ſide,
> Shall o'er thy naked poliſh'd ivory ſlide,
> Freely ſhall now my longing eyes behold,
> Thy bared ſnow and thy undrained gold:
> Nor curtain now though of tranſparent lawn,
> Shall be before my virgin treaſure drawn.
> I will enjoy these now my faireſt come
> And fly with me to love's elyſium,
> My rudder with thy bold hand, like a try'd
> And skillful pilot, thou ſhalt ſteer, and guide,
> My bark in loves dark channel, where it ſhall
> Dance, as the bounding waves do riſe and fall.
> Whilſt my tall pinnace in the Cyprian ſtrait
> Rides ſafe at anchor and unlades the freight.

Having by theſe and other amorous acts (which love can better dictate than my pen) wound up your fancies to the higheſt ardor, and deſires,

Perform tho/e rights nature and love requires,
Till you have quench'd each other's am'rous fires

The celebration of sexual joy in *Aristotle's Masterpiece* is a flower
from the same garden that was cultivated by the poets, playwrights, and
painters of England during the reign (1660-1685) of Charles II in the
period of the Restoration. This was the period of freedom in reaction to
the puritanical dictatorship of Oliver Cromwell (1599-1658). Though the
garden was not long-lived, its blooms survived to influence posterity. The
unexpurgated joyousness of being in love and being erotic lovers, and the
candor of writing about it in *Aristotle's Masterpiece*, became expurgated
in the new wave of *Onania*, Tissot, and Graham. But the *Masterpiece*
itself did not disappear leaving no trace. Its positive message of sex was
echoed by social reformers with utopian dreams of a community of people
not deprived of their sexual birthright—reformers like François Marie
Charles Fourier (1772-1837) in France and Robert Owen (1771-1858) in
England. Owen, like John Humphrey Noyes (see Chap. 6) of Oneida,
tried to establish his utopia in the new world.

Russell Thacher Trall

Nor did the message of positive sex vanish without trace from medical
writings, though it was sentenced to house arrest, one might say. Those
who knew at first hand the positive joy of their own love-lives took action
to release the prisoner. Among them was Russell Thacher Trall, teacher
of John Harvey Kellogg.

Trall was too sophisticated in his knowledge of reproduction to justify
abstinence as a male health measure. Insofar as he paid lip-service to
abstinence, he justified it in terms of a woman's right to decide her own
pregnancy. His book, *Sexual Physiology: A Scientific and Popular Exposition of the Fundamental Problems in Sociology* appeared first in
1866. It is a professional text that begins with an anatomical description,
with diagrams, of the organs of generation. Chapter 12, "Regulation of
the Number of Offspring," begins with the section "Women's Rights."
Trall wrote:

> No truth is to my mind more self-evident, no rule of right more plain,
> no law of Nature more demonstrable, than the right of a woman to her
> own person. Nor can this right be alienated by marriage. "Life, liberty,
> and the pursuit of happiness," and also health—without which life and
> liberty are of little account, and the pursuit of happiness impossible—are
> God-given prerogatives, and inhere in the person, male or female; and

all statutes, ceremonies, creeds, institutions or usages, which in any respect contravene the fundamental law of absolute personal freedom, in all the relations of life, are in derogation of the laws of Nature, and in opposition to the best good of the human family. The great want of the age, of humanity—the great need of man as well as of woman—is, the recognition of woman's equality. Would it not excite the just indignation of a *man* to be told by any person, even though that person were his "lawful-wedded" wife, that he must beget children when he did not desire them? or that he must perform the act of sexual intercourse when he did not feel inclined to? Certainly, he would never submit to such dictation, such tyranny, nor should he. And why should woman? It ought to be understood by all men and women that the sexual embrace, when either party is averse to it—when both parties are not inclined to it—is an outrage. It is a lustful, not a love indulgence. And whether the consequences are sexual diseases of one or both parties, or personal alienation, or depraved offspring, or all, there is no possible escape from the penalties. [p. 201]

Woman's equality in all the relations of life implies her absolute supremacy in the sexual relation. It is for her to nourish and sustain the new being; it is her health and life that are directly imperiled by being compelled to bear children when she is unfitted and unwilling for the sacred office; it is her happiness that is more especially destroyed when forced to bring into the world sickly and deformed children, who can be nothing but a torment to themselves, of no use to the world, and nothing but a grief and a shame to their parents. For these reasons it is her absolute and indefeasible right to determine when she will, and when she will not, be exposed to pregnancy. [p. 202]

Trall was not a fanatic about abstinence as the only way that a woman had of regulating whether she would become pregnant or not. He even allowed that some women who had no other choice might find that "a piece of soft sponge introduced high in the vaginal canal as possible may prove efficacious." He mentioned also "articles made of caoutchouc or other soft and elastic material" that were on sale in large cities, but warned that they were liable to become displaced and thus fail to prevent "contact between the semen and the ovum." He could not condemn, he said, the thousands of women who had implored him for help against being "compelled to bear children which could not possibly be reared, and which were a constant drain upon their life forces." Then, as if to cover himself against enemy retaliation, he added the proviso: "Let it be distinctly understood that I do not approve any method for preventing pregnancy except that of abstinence, nor any means for producing abortion [which he had described], on the grounds that it is or can be in any sense physiological."

Rhythm Method, Wrong Timing

The key word here was *physiological,* for Trall did have what he thought to be a physiological theory and method of pregnancy prevention without total abstinence. It was the method of periodic abstinence, as in the rhythm method of today. Alas! Trall's timing was exactly the opposite of what it should be. His recommended safe period was, in fact, the period of maximum fertility. His error was this: "The ovum usually passes off in a few days after the cessation of the menstrual flow, and if intercourse is abstained from until ten or twelve days after the cessation of the menstrual flow, pregnancy will not occur . . . when the egg passes the os uteri there is, in most cases, a sense of weight, stricture, or bearing down, followed by instant relief."

Trall put forward his method without claiming it to be one hundred percent effective. He wanted to provide people with a way "to prevent pregnancy without interdicting sexual intercourse." Otherwise, intercourse could not be "intended as a love act, independent of reproduction," but would instead be "a mere generative act, as is the case with animals."

Trall wrote from the point of view of a sex-positive existence that life had totally denied to Sylvester Graham. Under the heading "Pleasure of Sexual Intercourse," he wrote as follows:

> Whatever may be the object of sexual intercourse—whether intended as a love embrace merely, or as a generative act—it is very clear that it should be as pleasurable as possible to both parties. Indeed, when it is otherwise to either party, unless generation is intended, it is mere lust. Nor can the offspring be as perfect as it should be unless the act is both desired and enjoyed by both parties. This rule or law, for it is a law of Nature, at once suggests the conditions which are necessary to insure this result. There must be mental harmony and congeniality between the parties. Each must be able to respond to the *whole* nature of the other—bodily, morally and intellectually, to that extent that there shall be no sense of discord, no feeling of repugnance; but, on the other hand, an utter abnegation of selfhood. [p. 245]

The harmony of the couple had a significance far beyond their own pleasure, in Trall's teaching, for it made for a perfect conception:

> There can be no question that the most perfect organization of the

offspring requires the most complete commingling of elements, or magnetism, or whatever else the parents impart or contribute in the sexual embrace, and that there should be the most perfect harmony and enjoyment with each other. There should be as much *at-one-ment* as possible, so that, at the moment of conferring life upon a new being, each should almost lose, in the intensity of pleasurable sensation, the consciousness of individual or independent existence. I can not understand how this condition can be so well acquired and maintained as by *temperate* sexual indulgence, even when offspring are not desirable nor proper.

Then Trall revealed again his humanity and disinclination to walk a moral tightrope by adding, "But what *is* temperate indulgence may not be so easily determined" (p. 232).

CHAPTER
11

Secret Vice and the Vice Squad

Captain of the Vice Squad

Like all teachers, Russell Thacher Trall could expect to influence his students, but with no guarantee that they would assimilate his precepts, or neglect them, or openly repudiate them. There is no surviving statement of John Harvey Kellogg's reaction to his teacher's sex-positive ideas in *Sexual Physiology*. The evidence of Kellogg's own writings is that, whereas he followed Trall's methodical organization of the facts of reproduction separately from the requirement of healthy living, he repudiated what his teacher taught about sexual health as being too sex-positive.

In his life, as well as in his writings, Kellogg was sex-negative.[1] He grew up in the Seventh-day Adventist faith. In the years of his adolescent idealism, Mrs. Ellen White, the Adventist prophetess, had already had a divine inspiration in which the same health principles as taught by Sylvester Graham and his follower, James Caleb Jackson, were ordained by God to be practiced by faithful Adventists. In the manner of the times, his early schooling had been a privilege, not an obligation. The world of knowledge began to open up to him when he worked, from the age of twelve onward, in the Adventist printing and publishing business in Battle Creek, Michigan. One of the publications, founded in 1866, was *The Health Reformer* (later, *Good Health*), a magazine on religion and health for church members. The manuscripts contributed to this magazine helped to keep the young Kellogg updated on such matters of healthy living as vegetarianism, fresh-air fitness, the water-cure, clothing reform, and abstinent living. In addition, the editorial office was furnished with copies of books by Graham, Jackson, Trall, and various reformers such as Joel Shew (1816-1855), an early water-curist, and William A. Alcott (1798-1859), an early vegetarianist.

It is unlikely that Kellogg got born again to sexual renunciation, but rather that he found that Graham's theories gave intellectual justification and respectability to his own already developed aversion to his own sexuality. The sources of that aversion will remain probably forever unknown, except for a wildcat speculation. As world-famous superintendent of the Battle Creek Sanitarium, John Harvey Kellogg had, after breakfast every morning, an enema personally administered by an orderly. This quirk of daily indulgence may have been purely hygienic, but it should not have been necessary according to Kellogg's own dietary rules. Thus it may have been symptomatic of klismaphilia, an anomaly of sexual and erotic functioning traceable to childhood, in which an enema substitutes for regular sexual intercourse. For the klismaphile, putting the penis in the vagina is experienced as hard work, dangerous, and possibly as repulsive.

Whatever the explanation, Kellogg did have a repulsion, or aversion, to sexual relations. He and Ella E. Eaton (1853-1920), a bright hygiene-and-nursing student at the Sanitarium, married in February 1879. On their honeymoon, he spent his time writing *Plain Facts for Old and Young*, a warning against the evils and dangers of sex. In "The Residence," the twenty-room Kellogg mansion in Battle Creek, each occupied separate apartments. Their marriage remained forever unconsummated in sexual intercourse. Kellogg left no explanation, except indirectly in referring to his disgust, in the days of his youth, with the boasting of those who equated venereal infection with proof of manhood. His ideal was to prove that sexual activity is not necessary to health. He never once wrote of lovers or of being in love.

In *Plain Facts*, he stated that "the reproductive act is the most exhausting of all vital acts. Its effect upon the undeveloped person is to retard growth, weaken the constitution, and dwarf the intellect" (p. 119). He also gave credence to the idea, attributed to "some physiologists," that sperms "are composed of a substance identical with nerve tissue, and that by absorption they play a very important part in the development and maintenance of the nervous system" (p. 56).

The Kelloggs had no offspring. Instead, John Harvey Kellogg brought under his care forty-two children who were either adopted or fostered. At one period, there were twenty of them in the home. Eventually Mrs. Kellogg became a recluse in her own apartment and exempted herself from her husband's experiment in "race betterment" by means of rearing children according to his own rules of diet, exercise, and sexual abstinence. One boy in particular, the abused and abandoned son of a big-city prostitute, defeated the efforts of race betterment bestowed on him—a not unusual outcome of early, excessive abuse and neglect. Other children turned out well, but none became an outstanding example of race betterment.

Kellogg never did question what his family of adopted and fostered children proved or disproved about his race-betterment theory. To judge a theory by its outcome was not one of his strong points. His motto could have been: Don't bother me with your facts; my mind is already made up. His conviction of being right was proof enough for him. He had no tolerance of opposition.

His conviction that he was a good industrialist was opposed by his brother, who won. His conviction that he was a great surgeon was opposed by none, and agreed with by all who knew his work. His conviction of holding the key to health reform for all was endorsed by a legion of enthusiastic, high-paying patients, but the most successful cures were for those who needed a diet for dyspepsia or for overweight, or a health resort for an expensive placebo cure. His conviction that the secret and solitary vice of self-abuse (masturbation) or any sexual indulgence was evil and the cause of all otherwise unexplained afflictions and infirmities became gospel to some and anathema to others. It was a conviction that had the power of Dracula to destroy the health and well-being of those tyrannized by it in childhood and adolescence.

Guilty Because Accused: Secret Vice, Solitary Vice, or Self-Abuse

Kellogg's conviction that the secret vice causes disease gave him a dictator's power over the lives of those who listened to or read his theory, because it could never be proved wrong. The doctor was always right. His theory allowed him to pass responsibility for an illness onto the patient's secret vice. If the illness persisted, that was proof that the secret vice persisted, that its effects were long-term and irreversible, or that its effect had been inherited from the secret vice of the parents. Kellogg attributed the responsibility for illness to secret vice in the same way that some therapists today attribute it to resistance and the unconscious.

To be always right and intolerant of correction is to be self-righteous. The clergy of the Inquisition were self-righteous. Nothing could shake their conviction that the responsibility for witchcraft lay in the witch's heresy. Secret vice, in Kellogg's system of thought, is really only another name for heresy, and its practitioners are all heretics. To be accused is to be guilty because, by definition, there is no source of evidence that will disprove a secret. No amount of protest will suffice. The protester will simply be branded a liar.

Kellogg's list of the signs and symptoms of secret vice was so long and all-inclusive that no one could escape his accusing finger. Without recognizing the omission, he never accused himself—only all of us. From his throne of righteous judgment, wearing the white garments of purity, he proclaimed the accusations and the penalties. (In his older years, in everyday life, he in fact wore all-white clothes exclusively and was accompanied by a white Australian cockatoo.)

Kellogg's self-image was that of a kindly benefactor, and not that of an avenging terrorist out to destroy youthful sexuality. The subjective danger of what might ensue from a challenge to his own personal sexual aversion apparently made him blind to the disconnection in himself between the benefactor and the terrorist.

Without such a self-protective blindspot, John Harvey Kellogg surely could not have been so oblivious to the malevolence of his influence on the sexuality of children and their parents. Woe to the young wife who read, in the *Ladies' Guide in Health and Disease: Girlhood, Maidenhood, Wifehood, Motherhood,* authored by J. H. Kellogg, M.D., the section on the "Effects of Solitary Vice in Girls." There, among the signs she would read number 9: "Ulceration about the roots of the nails, especially affecting one or both of the first two fingers of the hand, usually the right hand, is evidence of the habit which depends upon [leucorrhea], the irritation of the fingers being occasioned by the acrid vaginal discharge" (p. 152).

The entire section is written as if masturbation were a new plague, and that no adult reader of the *Ladies' Guide* would have a history of childhood masturbation. Heaven help her who did! She would know that all the ills and afflictions of her own life could be attributed to it; that her pregnancy could be endangered by it; and that her baby might inherit the debilitating effects of it. And what about her husband's history of self-abuse? He also would transmit the evil to his progeny.

Whether she worried about herself or not, the young mother would, if she heeded the advice given her, run her household as a penal colony in which the children needed constant supervision and regular checks for signs of the solitary or secret vice of self-abuse, and disciplinary abuse if ever it were discovered.

Sex Manuals for the Mass Market

The *Ladies' Guide* was one of two large volumes. The title of its companions, reminiscent of *Aristotle's Masterpiece,* is *Man the Masterpiece, or Plain Truths Plainly Told About Boyhood, Youth, and Manhood.* Both are large volumes of approximately 650 pages, and both were first published in the early 1880s. They went through many reprintings with some revisions, but the basic message was not changed. As late as in the Australian editions of 1906 and 1908 it remained the same.

In rural areas these two books were sold by itinerant salesmen as "subscription books," with gold embossed covers. They were respected as important household doctor's books of knowledge. They were partly manuals of good health through vegetarian diet, exercise, fresh air, loose-fitting clothes, and avoidance of tea, coffee, tobacco, alcohol, spices, and condiments; partly manuals of common ailments and their treatment; and partly manuals of advice on marriage, sexual sins and their consequences, reproductive function, and disorders of the reproductive organs. Because of their sexual content, they were considered suitable only for married people and were kept away from children.

Kellogg wrote for a mass market. He took advantage of the existence of an adult population with a high prevalence of readers—a product of the spread of compulsory grade-school education after the Civil War. It was not a scholarly readership, and so Kellogg wrote for popular appeal.

His method of work was to cannibalize material from his earlier writing for reuse in a new book, to meet the needs of a new market. Thus, *Man the Masterpiece* and the *Ladies' Guide* not only overlap each other but also overlap their predecessor, the book that Kellogg wrote on his honeymoon, *Plain Facts for Old and Young Embracing the Natural History and Hygiene of Organic Life.* (A "New Edition, Revised and Enlarged" was published in Burlington, Iowa, in 1888.)

This 1888 revision has the peculiar quality of containing a book within a book, namely "A Chapter for Boys" and "A Chapter for Girls." Together they restate the teaching of the adult chapters, but in a childish way that, even for juveniles, sounds condescending.

One presumes that the boys and girls who might lay hands on the book would look at the other chapters too, including the one on the "Social Evil" prostitution. Kellogg got so scandalized by the luridness of the social evil that he failed to recognize that, by giving all the details, as in a scandal tabloid, he was having his cake and eating it too—and that his readers might be doing the same. It is a far cry from Kellogg's professed intention to associate the sexual function "with the innocence of animal life and the chaste loveliness of flowers" (p. 22).

This lapse makes the criticism he applied to other sex manuals sound pretentiously pious: "To add to their power for evil, many of them abound with pictorial illustrations which are in no way conducive to virtue or morality, but rather stimulate the animal propensities, and excite lewd imaginations" (p. 21). That kind of piety leads, as it does in the law, to euphemisms like "the unspeakable crime against nature," which allow the court, in the State of Maryland, as well as elsewhere, even today to accuse a man without telling him what he is accused of. The same piety also absolutely closes the door to impartial scientific study and research.

There are 644 pages in *Plain Facts,* of which 159 are given to the chapter on "Unchastity," and 97 of these are about "Secret Vice (Solitary Vice or Self-Abuse)" and its results and treatment.

Positive Signs and Suspicious Signs

The "Positive Signs" of secret vice are few and difficult to detect because "the devotees of Moloch pursue their debasing practice with consummate cunning." Therefore, parents are advised, "if the suspected one becomes very quickly quiet after retiring . . . the bedclothes should be quickly thrown off under some pretence. If, in the case of a boy, the penis is found in a state of erection, with the hands near the genitals, he may certainly be treated as a masturbator without any error . . . If the same course is pursued with girls . . . the clitoris will be found congested, with the other genital organs, which will also be moist from increased secretion" (p. 260).

Dr. Kellogg does not tell us the source of the foregoing information, but leaves us to suppose that he observed it for himself, which leaves him open to suspicion of having, perhaps, too morbid an interest in his adopted and foster children's genitals. Even if he was not guilty, he was ignorant of what his wife could have told him had he slept with her naked—that he, like all males from infancy to old age, had three or more spontaneous erections nightly while asleep. Girls have a corresponding change in blood flow in their sexual organs.

The doctor was again wrong when he claimed that the vice in young boys before they reach puberty is revealed by stains on the nightshirt or sheet and that the only other similar stain that so resembles the stain of seminal fluid is rare and comes from piles. They are not urine stains, he said, and they may occur also after puberty, and also may result from a somewhat similar discharge in girls. Oddly enough, he omits specific mention of semen stains from masturbation or nocturnal emissions after puberty.

Compounding his errors and medical foolishness, he goes on to pronounce that the vice causes an unnatural development of the sexual organs before puberty in both sexes. In boys, after puberty, "the organs often diminish in size, and become unnaturally lax and shrunken" (p. 261), he adds.

As compared with "Positive Signs," the "Suspicious Signs" of secret vice are far more plentiful. One alone is not conclusive, but it "should arouse suspicion and watchfulness . . . though it is of course necessary to give the individual no suspicion of being watched, as that would put him so effectively on his guard as, possibly, to defy detection" (pp. 259-260). Kellogg listed thirty-nine suspicious signs.

Reference Note

1. Biographical material on John Harvey Kellogg in this chapter is drawn from Carson (1957) and Schwarz (1970).

None Shall Escape

Thirty-Nine Signs for the Vice Squad

There is no way to expose the utter wrongness of Kellogg's thirty-nine signs of the secret vice of self-abuse other than to reproduce them in their full absurdity.[1] If taken seriously, they would set parents against their children, spying on them, persecuting them, and abusing them, like victims of the secret police. Doctors would make misdiagnoses and be liable for malpractice charges. Kellogg's thirty-nine signs are:

1. *General debility*, coming upon a previously healthy child, marked by emaciation, weakness, an unnatural paleness, colorless lips and gums, and the general symptoms of exhaustion, when it cannot be traced to any other legitimate cause, as internal disease, worms, grief, overwork, poor air, or poor food, and when it is not speedily removed by change of air or appropriate remedial measure, may be safely attributed to solitary vice, no matter how far above natural suspicion the individual may be. Mistakes will be rare indeed when such a judgment is pronounced under the circumstances named.

2. *Early symptoms of consumption*, or what are supposed to be such, as cough, and decrease in flesh, with short breathing and soreness of the lungs or muscles of the chest, are often solely the result of this vice. That such is the case may be considered pretty surely determined if physical examination of the lungs reveals no organic disease of those organs. But it should be remembered that solitary vice is one of the most frequent causes of early consumption. Several cases which strikingly prove this, have fallen under our own observation.

3. *Premature and defective development* is a symptom closely allied to the two preceding. When it cannot be traced to such natural causes as overstudy, overwork, lack of exercise, and other influences of a similar nature, it should be charged to self-abuse. The early exercise of the genital organs hastens the attainment of puberty in many cases, especially when the habit is acquired early; but at the same time it saps the vital energies so that the system is unable to manifest that increased

energy in growth and development which usually occurs at this period. In consequence, the body remains small, or does not attain that development which it otherwise would. The mind is dwarfed as well as the body. Sometimes the mind suffers more than the body in lack of development, and sometimes the reverse is true. This defective development is shown in the physical organization of males, in the failure of the voice to increase in volume and depth of tone as it should, in deficient growth of the beard, and in failure of the chest to become full and the shoulders broad. The mind and character show the dwarfing influence by failure to develop those qualities which especially distinguish a noble manhood. In the female, defective development is shown by menstrual derangements, by defective growth either in stature, or as shown in unnatural slimness, and in a failure to develop the graces and pleasing character which should distinguish early womanhood. Such signs deserve careful investigation; for they can only result from some powerfully blighting influence.

4. *Sudden change in disposition* is a sign which may well arouse suspicion. If a boy who has previously been cheerful, pleasant, dutiful, and gentle, suddenly becomes morose, cross, peevish, irritable, and disobedient, be sure that some foul influence is at work with him. When a girl, naturally joyous, happy, confiding, and amiable, becomes unaccountably gloomy, sad, fretful, dissatisfied, and unconfiding, be certain that a blight of no insignificant character is resting upon her. Make a careful study of the habits of such children; and if there is no sudden illness to account for the change in their character, it need not require long deliberation to arrive at the true cause; for it will rarely be found to be anything other than solitary indulgence.

5. *Lassitude* is as unnatural for a child as for a young kitten. A healthy child will be active, playful, full of life and animal spirits. If a young child manifests indisposition to activity, a dislike for play, lifelessness and languor, suspect his habits, if there is no other reasonable cause to which to attribute his unnatural want of childish sprightliness.

6. In connection with the preceding symptom will generally be found, instead of that natural brilliancy of expression in the eyes and countenance, an unnatural dullness and vacantness altogether foreign to childhood. This is a just ground for suspicion.

7. *Sleeplessness* is another symptom of significance. Sound sleep is natural for childhood; and if sleeplessness be not occasioned by dietetic errors, as eating indigestible food, eating between meals, or eating late suppers, it may justly be a cause for suspicion of evil habits.

8. *Failure of mental capacity* without apparent cause, should occasion suspicion of evil practices. When a child who has previously learned readily, mastered his lessons easily, and possessed a retentive memory, shows a manifest decline in these directions, fails to get his lessons, becomes stupid, forgetful, and inattentive, he has probably become the victim of a terrible vice, and is on the road to speedy mental as well as

physical ruin. Watch him.

9. *Fickleness* is another evidence of the working of some deteriorating influence; for only a weak mind is fickle.

10. *Untrustworthiness* appearing in a child should attract attention to his habits. If he has suddenly become heedless, listless, and forgetful, so that he cannot be depended upon, though previously not so, lay the blame upon solitary indulgence. This vice has a wonderful influence in developing untruthfulness. A child previously honest, will soon become an inveterate liar under its baneful influence.

11. *Love of solitude* is a very suspicious sign. Children are naturally sociable, almost without exception. They have a natural dread of being alone. When a child habitually seeks seclusion without a sufficient cause, there are good grounds for suspecting him of sinful habits. The barn, the garret, the water-closet, and sometimes secluded places in the woods are favorite resorts of masturbators. They should be carefully followed and watched, unobserved.

12. *Bashfulness* is not infrequently dependent upon this cause. It would be far from right to say that every person who is excessively modest or timid is a masturbator; but there is a certain timorousness which seems to arise from a sense of shame or fear of discovery that many victims of this vice exhibit, and which may be distinguished from natural modesty by a little experience. One very common mode of manifestation of this timidity is the inability to look a superior, or any person who is esteemed pure, in the eye. If spoken to, instead of looking directly at the person to whom he addresses an answer, the masturbator looks to one side, or lets his eyes fall upon the ground, seemingly conscious that the eye is a wonderful tell-tale of the secrets of the mind.

13. *Unnatural boldness*, in marked contrast with the preceding sign, is manifested by a certain class of victims. It can be as easily distinguished, however, as unnatural timidity. The individual seems to have not the slightest appreciation of propriety. He commits openly the most uncouth acts, if he does not manifest the most indecent unchastity of manner. When spoken to, he stares rudely at the person addressing him, often with a very unpleasant lear upon his countenance. In some few cases there seems to be a curious combination of conditions. While mentally fearful, timid, and hesitating, the individual finds himself, upon addressing a person, staring at him in the most ungainly manner. He is conscious of his ill manners, but is powerless to control himself. This sign is one which could hardly be of use to any except a very close observer, however, as few can read upon the countenance the operations of the mind.

14. *Mock piety*—or perhaps we should more properly designate it as mistaken piety—is another peculiar manifestation of the effects of this vicious practice. The victim is observed to become transformed, by degrees, from a romping laughing child, full of hilarity and frolic, to a sober and very sedate little—Christian, the friends think, and they are

highly gratified with the piety of the child. Little do they suspect the real cause of the solemn face; not the slightest suspicion have they of the foul orgies practiced by the little sinner. By the aid of friends, he may soon add hypocrisy to his other crimes, and find in assumed devotion a ready pretense for seeking solitude. Parents will do well to investigate the origin of this kind of religion in their children.

15. *Easily frightened* children are abundant among young masturbators, though all easily frightened persons are not vicious. It is certain, however, that the vice greatly exaggerates natural fear, and creates an unnatural apprehensiveness. The victim's mind is constantly filled with vague forebodings of evil. He often looks behind him, looks into all the closets, peeps under the bed, and is constantly expressing fears of impending evil. Such movements are the result of a diseased imagination, and they may justly give rise to suspicion.

16. *Confusion of ideas* is another characteristic of the devotee of this artful vice. If he attempts to argue, his points are not clearly made. He may be superficially quick and acute, but is incapable of deep thought or abstruse reasoning, and is often very full of apprehension. Ideas are not presented in logical order, but seem to fall out promiscuously, and fairly represent the condition of a disordered brain. Attempts at joking are generally failures, as the jest is sure to be inappropriate or vulgar, and no one but himself sees any occasion for laughter, except at his stupidity. Such individuals are not scarce.

17. Boys in whom the habit has become well developed, sometimes manifest a decided aversion to the society of girls; but this is not nearly so often the case as some authors seem to indicate. It would rather appear that the opposite is more often true. Girls usually show an increasing fondness for the society of boys, and are very prone to exhibit marked evidences of real wantonness.

18. *Round shoulders* and a stooping posture in sitting are characteristics of young masturbators of both sexes. Whenever a child seats himself, the head and shoulders droop forward, giving to the spine a curved appearance.

19. *Weak backs, pains in the limbs, and stiffness of the joints*, in children, are familiar signs of the habit. To the first of these conditions is due the habitual stooping posture assumed by these children. The habit referred to is not the only cause of these conditions; but its causative occurrence is sufficiently frequent to give it no small importance as a suspicious indication.

20. *Paralysis* of the lower extremities, coming on without apparent cause, is not infrequently the result of solitary indulgence, even in very small children. We have seen several cases in which this condition was traced to the habit of masturbation, in children under six years of age.

21. The *gait* of a person addicted to this vice will usually betray him to one who has learned to distinguish the peculiarities which almost always mark the walk of such persons. In a child, a dragging, shuffling

walk is to be suspected. Boys, in walking rapidly, show none of that elasticity which characterizes a natural gait, but walk as if they had been stiffened in the hips, and as though their legs were pegs attached to the body by hinges. The girl wriggles along in a style quite as characteristic, though more difficult to detect with certainty, as girls are often so "affected" in their walk. Unsteadiness of gait is an evidence seen in both sexes, especially in advanced cases.

22. *Bad positions* in bed are evidences which should be noticed. If a child lies constantly upon its abdomen, or is often found with its hands about the genitals, it may be at least considered in a fair way to acquire the habit, if it has not already done so.

23. *Lack of development of the breasts* in females, after puberty, is a common result of self-pollution. Still it would be entirely unsafe to say that every female with small mammary glands had been addicted to this vice, especially at the present time, when a fair natural development is often destroyed by the constant pressure and heat of "pads." But this sign may well be given a due bearing.

24. *Capricious appetite* particularly characterizes children addicted to secret vice. At the commencement of the practice, they almost invariably manifest great voracity for food, gorging themselves in the most gluttonous manner. As the habit becomes fixed, digestion becomes impaired, and the appetite is sometimes almost wanting, and at other times almost unappeasable.

25. One very constant peculiarity of such children is their extreme fondness for unnatural, hurtful, and irritating foods. Nearly all are greatly attached to salt, pepper, spices, cinnamon, cloves, vinegar, mustard, horseradish, and similar articles, and use them in most inordinate quantities. A boy or girl who is constantly eating cloves or cinnamon, or who will eat salt in quantities without other food, gives good occasion for suspicion.

26. *Eating clay, slate-pencils, plaster, chalk,* and other indigestible articles is a practice to which girls who abuse themselves are especially addicted. The habit sometimes becomes developed to such a wonderful extent that the victims almost rival the clay-eaters of the Amazon in gratifying their propensity.

27. Disgust for simple food is one of the traits which a victim of this vice is likely to possess. He seems to loathe any food which is not rendered hot and stimulating with spices and other condiments, and cannot be induced to eat it.

28. *The use of tobacco* is good presumptive evidence that a boy is also addicted to a practice still more filthy. Exceptions to this rule are very rare indeed, if they exist, which we somewhat doubt. The same influences which would lead a boy to the use of tobacco, would also lead him to solitary vice, and each sin would serve to exaggerate the other

29. *Unnatural paleness* and colorless lips, unless they can be other-

wise accounted for, may be attributed to secret sin. The face is a great tell-tale against this class of sinners. Justice demands, however, that an individual should be given the benefit of a doubt so long as there is a chance for the production of these symptoms by any other known cause, as overwork, mental anxiety, or dyspepsia.

30. *Acne*, or *pimples* on the face, is also among the suspicious signs, especially when it appears upon the forehead as well as upon other portions of the face. Occasional pimples upon the chin are very common in both sexes at puberty and for a few years afterward but are without significance, except that the blood may be somewhat gross from unwholesome diet or lack of exercise.

31. *Biting the finger nails* is a practice very common in girls addicted to this vice. In such persons there will also be found, not infrequently, slight soreness or ulceration at the roots of the nails, and warts, one or more, upon one or both the first two fingers of the hand, usually the right.

32. The eyes often betray much. If, in addition to want of lustre and natural brilliancy, they are sunken, present red edges, are somewhat sore, perhaps, and are surrounded by a dark ring, the patient, especially if a child, should be suspected and carefully watched. It should be observed, however, that dyspepsia, debility from any cause, and especially loss of sleep, will produce some or all of these signs, and no one should be accused of the vice upon the evidence of these indications alone; neither could he be justly suspected so long as his symptoms could be accounted for by legitimate causes.

33. An habitually moist, cold hand, is a suspicious circumstance in a young person who is not known to be suffering from some constitutional disease.

34. *Palpitation of the heart*, frequently occurring, denotes a condition of nervous disturbance which has some powerful cause, and which may often be found to be the vice in question.

35. *Hysteria* in females may be regarded as a suspicious circumstance when frequently occurring on very slight occasions, and especially if there is no hereditary tendency to the disease.

36. *Chlorosis*, or *green sickness*, is very often caused by the unholy practice under consideration. It is very commonly attributed, when occurring in young women, to menstrual derangements; but it is only necessary to remember that these menstrual irregularities are in many cases the result of the same habit, as has been already pointed out.

37. *Epileptic fits* in children are not infrequently the result of vicious habits.

38. *Wetting the bed* is an evidence of irritation which may be connected with the practice; it should be looked after.

39. *Unchastity of speech* and fondness for obscene stories betray a condition of mind which does not often exist in youth who are not addicted to this vice.

Vanity Admits No Error

Kellogg's debt to Sylvester Graham is clearly evident in his list of the "Results of Secret Vice" (pp. 262-289). They include a variety of disorders of the reproductive organs in both sexes. In addition, males may get spermatorrhea (nocturnal pollutions), internal emission, impotence, and atrophy of the testes. Females may get leucorrhea, uterine disease, atrophy of the breasts, sterility, genital pruritus, nocturnal ejaculation with erotic dreaming, and hysteria. Both sexes are liable to general debility, consumption, dyspepsia, heart disease, throat infections, nervous diseases, epilepsy, blindness, deafness, spinal irritation, idiocy, and insanity.

It is remarkable enough that Kellogg had to be so totally wrong in 1888, when he claimed that all these ailments are the result of masturbation. What is more remarkable is that he lived until 1943 and did not, with age, have the professional courage to admit that formerly he had been wrong. It would have been a common decency had he done so, and it would have saved uncounted hundreds of thousands of boys and girls from fear, guilt, abuse, and punishment for the phony diseases of self-abuse and nocturnal emission (self-pollution).

Those who, in adulthood, did not learn that Kellogg's teaching was wrong were trapped in a prison of guilt and anxiety if they became sick with any of Kellogg's "results of secret vice." If they did, indeed, have a history of masturbation, then they could not go to a doctor, for their suffering itself was evidence of guilt. The consequences could be disastrous in the case of, for example, tuberculosis (consumption), for the longer the sick person stayed in hiding, at home, the more members of the household were likely to be infected with the disease. Even until the present day, there are some people who avoid going to a doctor for fear that he will blame their suffering on the sin of masturbation. People with sexual problems are particularly likely to fall into this category. There continue to be many people who believe, for example, the erroneous idea that premature ejaculation is the product of a history of masturbation. There are some also who falsely believe that masturbation still can cause homosexuality, nervous breakdown, and insanity.

Kellogg's listing of suspicious signs has been given a new lease on life currently by the professional detectives of sexual child-abuse. Here is an example of those who have not learned from history being condemned to repeat it, replete with all its dreadful consequences.

Reference Note

1. The thirty-nine "Suspicious Signs" of self-abuse are quoted from pp. 249-259 of Kellogg's *Plain Facts for Old and Young.*

More Abuse for the Self-Abused

The Torture Trade

In the section on "Treatment for Self-Abuse and its Effects,"[1] Kellogg ranges over restraints, threats, and punishment; mental and moral treatment and religion; diet and exercise; wet compresses, baths, douches, and enemas; electricity; and surgery.

His recommendations for surgery qualify as professional child-abuse and are brutal:

> In younger children, with whom moral considerations will have no particular weight, other devices may be used. Bandaging the parts has been practiced with success. Tying the hands is also successful in some cases; but this will not always succeed, for they will often contrive to continue the habit in other ways, as by working the limbs, or lying upon the abdomen. Covering the organs with a cage has been practiced with entire success. A remedy which is almost always successful in small boys is circumcision, especially when there is any degree of phimosis. The operation should be performed by a surgeon without administering an anaesthetic, as the brief pain attending the operation will have a salutary effect upon the mind, especially if it be connected with the idea of punishment, as it may well be in some cases. The soreness which continues for several weeks interrupts the practice, and if it had not previously become too firmly fixed, it may be forgotten and not resumed. If any attempt is made to watch the child, he should be so carefully surrounded by vigilance that he cannot possibly transgress without detection. If he is only partially watched, he soon learns to elude observation, and thus the effect is only to make him cunning in his vice.
>
> *In adults* or youth a different plan must be pursued. In these cases, moral considerations, and the inevitable consequences to health of body and mind, are the chief influences by which a reform is to be effected, if at all. These considerations may be urged with all possible eloquence and earnestness, but should not be exaggerated. The truth is terrible enough. If there are any special influences which may be brought to bear

upon a particular individual,—and there always will be something of this sort, owing to peculiarities of temperament or circumstances,—these should be promptly employed, and applied in such a manner as to secure for them their full bearing.

Through the courtesy of Dr. Archibald, Superintendent of the Iowa Asylum for Feeble-Minded Children we have become acquainted with a method of treatment of this disorder which is applicable in refractory cases, and we have employed it with entire satisfaction. It consists in the application of one or more silver sutures in such a way as to prevent erection. The prepuce, or foreskin, is drawn forward over the glans, and the needle to which the wire is attached is passed through from one side to the other. After drawing the wire through, the ends are twisted together, and cut off close. It is now impossible for an erection to occur, and the slight irritation thus produced acts as a most powerful means of overcoming the disposition to resort to the practice.

In females, the author has found the application of pure carbolic acid to the clitoris an excellent means of allaying the abnormal excitement, and preventing the recurrence of the practice in those whose willpower has become so weakened that the patient is unable to exercise entire self-control.

The worse cases among young women are those in which the disease has advanced so far that erotic thoughts are attended by the same voluptuous sensations which accompany the practice. The author has met many cases of this sort in young women, who acknowledged that the sexual orgasm was thus produced, often several times daily. The application of carbolic acid in the manner described is also useful in these cases in allaying the abnormal excitement, which is a frequent provocation of the practice of this form of mental masturbation.

Chicanery of the Self-Fulfilling Prophecy

Because of his medical status and his immense popular prestige, Kellogg was more responsible than any other person of his generation for popularizing the fallacious disease of masturbation. Here was a self-fulfilling prophecy if ever there was one. People with a history of masturbation paid to read a book in which they were diagnosed as suffering from a disease. Believing it, they turned to the profession that diagnosed them for a cure—paying again, of course! Kellogg made a fortune from the international industry that published his books to persuade readers that they or their children had the disease of masturbation.

The chicanery of this maneuver, no matter how serendipitous, is chicanery nonetheless. Elbert Hubbard (1856-1915), the American writer and so-called Sage of Roycroft who died in the sinking of the Lusitania, saw through it when he called Kellogg the "Battle Creek Dynamo," behind whom was "the Sanitarium and a great religious denomination, preaching a doctrine of fear and making invalids faster than Kellogg can cure them."[2] Hubbard might well have added that Kellogg himself did the preaching too.

Kellogg made more money from selling books on the disease of masturbation than he did from selling cures for it. His center was not known as a great center for treating the disease of masturbation. By not having hoards of masturbators clamoring to be admitted to the Sanitarium, Kellogg never did have to face up to the fact that he had no cure for it, whether in diet, exercise, punishment, or sermonizing.

The lesson to learn here is that everyone who enters a hospital ought to require that an authorized hospital officer sign a contract of agreement that the hospital will keep track of every patient's diagnosis, treatment, and outcome of treatment, in order to be able to produce proofs and percentages of whether, for each diagnosis, the correct treatment was given, and whether it brought about a cure or not. Today, a doctor must get a patient's signed agreement to participate in medical research. The other side of the coin is that, tomorrow, a patient should get the doctor's signed agreement that he will not fail to keep records of the outcome of the treatment he provides, and that he will use them in outcome research to test the efficacy of treatment.

The Circumcision Fallacy

By way of example, consider Kellogg's recommendation of circumcision as a remedy for masturbation in small boys. Unless he kept follow-up statistics, he had no proof. The only alternative would have been to compare the statistics of masturbation in Jewish and Gentile boys, for Gentile boys in those days were not routinely circumcised as newborns, but Jewish ones were. If Kellogg had bothered to collect these statistics, he would have known that boys who have been circumcised masturbate the same as do boys with their foreskin intact. Everybody knows that is the case; because most of today's plentiful crop of masturbators, Gentile as well as Jewish, did get circumcised as babies. The rate of newborn circumcision in the United States is between 70 and 90 percent and varies in different regions of the country.[3]

If Kellogg or someone else had kept statistics, it is quite possible that today's American boy babies would go home from the hospital with their foreskins intact. Neonatal circumcision crept into American delivery rooms in the 1870s and 1880s, not for religious reasons and not for reasons of health or hygiene, as is so commonly supposed, but because of the claim that, later in life, it would prevent irritation that would cause the boy to become a masturbator.

Though it is easy to arouse controversy as to the merit or nonmerit of circumcision, there is not a single valid health reason why it should be done routinely. It is not even a harmless procedure, for there are always some babies who suffer complications, including injury which in severe cases means complete loss of the penis, or infection that causes death.

Circumcision became fashionable in both England and America at about the same time, much less so in continental Europe. In England it ceased very abruptly soon after World War II, the reason being that the officials of the new national health-insurance system decided not to pay reimbursements for neonatal circumcision.

So it is that neonatal circumcision persists in America today chiefly because private medical insurance and public medical assistance pay for it, and it is a significant source of income for hospitals and doctors. It is the only unnecessary operation that is paid for, with no questions asked. In fact, it is very undiplomatic to ask questions about its necessity, for there are so many individuals and institutions that jump to the defense of this relic of history. They pay no attention to the 1975 policy statement of the American Academy of Pediatrics that there is "no medical indication for routine circumcision of the newborn"—a policy endorsed by other medical groups also.

Since circumcision proved not to be a cure-all for masturbation, the disease of masturbation continued its textbook life until World War I and beyond. Publishers of piety and greed cashed in on the antimasturbation crusade with books on what every young boy or girl, man or woman, ought to know. Then, slowly, the findings of science began to be incorporated into the message, and the sermonizing became less strident. Nonetheless, the old bugaboo of masturbation, the disease, with extraordinary resiliency lived on.

Masturbation Disease Dies Hard

Max Huhner (1873-1947) was a serious and scientifically minded author whose writing shows very clearly the intellectual struggle of a studious medical practitioner as he wavered between allegiance to old doctrines and new evidence.

The final, revised edition of his book *Sexual Disorders* came out in 1945 and was reprinted in 1946. It was an important book in its time, if only because, by its title, it recognized sexual disorders as a specialty.

Huhner, obedient to his forebears, first warned of the dangers of masturbation as "the most widespread of all sexual diseases, not even excepting gonorrhea" (p. 187). Then he rejected the absurdities of his forebears by warning against "quacks" who exaggerate and mistreat.

He got himself off the hook regarding females by not dealing with it as a serious disease: "as a rule masturbation has not nearly the same depressing or psychic effect on the female as it has on the male" (p. 233).

In the case of the male, he had another strategy to get himself off the hook: two types of masturbation. "I am certain," he wrote, "that if we were to take the histories of 100 of the greatest geniuses we would find in over 90% of them a history of masturbation." He addressed himself not to that type of masturbation, even though he castigated the new profession of psychoanalysis that attributed the bad effects of masturbation to exist only in the imagination of the doctor. His concern was with masturbation that "is a real disease, causing real discomforts, and is not an imaginary condition." His professional pride as a urologist was at stake here, for he was certain that he could diagnose the "real disease" by the congestion and hyperesthia it caused in the prostatic urethra. Masturbation and not normal coitus can cause this disease because it begins at an earlier age and is done more frequently. The cure required a series of treatments. With a full bladder, each began with prostatic massage with the index finger, covered with a finger cot, introduced into the anus. Next, the bladder was emptied. Then, with a syringe, a 1:3,000 silver-nitrate solution was instilled into the deep urethra. The patient was then cautioned to avoid tea, coffee, beer, all alcoholic drinks, also eggs and oysters.

The dietary caution was an old wives' tale of ancient vintage. The prostatic massage and the silver nitrate had the trappings of physiology and pharmacology, but in fact they had no other function than a ceremonial one. Except for a possible placebo effect, they led the doctor into the same realm of quackery that in others he found appalling.

Huhner gave a detailed "picture of the confirmed masturbator":

[He] is apt to be a physical coward, a man who will stand all sort of insult, who will run away rather than fight or stick up for his most obvious rights. All the spirit of manhood seems to be crushed out of him. He is very often praised for his gentleness, for his saintlike demeanor, his humility, etc., but if we carefully study the individual, if we dive into his thoughts and make a psychical study of them, we will find that these traits are not virtues. We will find that he feels his wrongs as keenly as another, that he makes plans of revenge in his mind which he would fain carry out, but which he has not the energy to undertake and is too much of a coward to attempt. He is good, not because of any virtue, but because he is too much of a coward to be bad.

After a while he comes to that stage where he masturbates, not because he likes it, but because he *has* to. He has that awful irritation in his deep urethra, and he simply must masturbate. The periods of previous excitement (pleasure) become less and less, as does also the amount of fluid ejaculated. Then there comes a time when he *cannot* masturbate. He has the irritation, he has the impulse to masturbate; but, no matter how he manipulates his penis or how he excites his brain, he can neither obtain an erection nor an ejaculation. He is indeed in a most wretched condition. But long before this stage is reached his nervous system has been severely affected . . ." [p. 214]

Huhner's masturbatory moralism interfered with his efficiency in treating sterility. "I have never advised procurement of a semen specimen by masturbation," he wrote, "although such procedure has been suggested" (p. 26). Instead he tried to obtain a specimen by prostatic massage, even though he had to inform the patient that this method might prove worthless. Today, he would be open to a malpractice charge for not advising the patient that masturbation would provide a better specimen.

In its effect on patients' lives, the consequence of malpractice might have been even more serious in the case of a married couple seeking to overcome pregnancy failure at home by having the wife inseminated in the clinic with the husband's semen. So as to avoid masturbation, Huhner endangered the chance of success by requiring the couple to have intercourse at home, and catch the semen in a "clean sterile jar." The delay in getting the semen first into the clinic and then injected up into the uterus may have defeated the whole purpose of the procedure. Moral squeamishness does not fit well with professional skill.

The Masturbation Peril Wanes Slowly

Moral squeamishness about masturbation did not officially disappear from American medicine until the American Medical Association published its *Human Sexuality* in 1972. "Masturbation is a normal part of adolescent sexual development and requires no medical management," declared the AMA Committee on Human Sexuality (p. 40). It is "practiced by men and women of all ages, often as a supplement to marital coitus, and women tend to masturbate more often as they grow older" (p. 60).

It was at around this same time that the Boy Scout Manual dropped its moralizing about the health hazards and evils of masturbation. Many youth leaders among the clergy, especially of Protestant denominations, unobtrusively did the same. The Papacy equivocated. Securely tied to the archconservatism of its Inquisitional past, its Sacred Congregation for the Doctrine of the Faith, under Paul VI, in 1975 issued the "Declaration on Certain Questions Concerning Sexuality." It preserved its moral condemnation of masturbation as "an intrinsically and seriously disordered act"; but followed medicine by not trying to claim that masturbation is injurious to health. Catholic youth still can be subjected to the psychological abuse of being made guilty for the sin of masturbation, but they are no longer threatened with being made sick by it.

As defined by the church, the intrinsic and serious disorder of the act of masturbation is none other than the sin of Onan. The seed is spilled upon the ground. Procreation is not possible. When done by a partner, masturbation is an alternative to sexual intercourse with contraception. Both have the same outcome. Both permit erotic passion and orgasm to exist for their own sake alone, and exclusively for pleasure. The church is not yet ready to accept that reversal of its ancient rules, except for allowing married people to practice the rhythm method of limiting family size.

It is not easy to comprehend how sane and rational men and women can defy logic and the evidence of experience everywhere apparent to them. On the issues of masturbation and antisexualism in general, they are able to do so on the basis of the principle that the abused becomes the abuser; and the brain-washed, the brain-washer. This principle is also known as identification with the aggressor.

In its sexual application, this principle means that when prohibition, prevention, and punishment of sexual expression begin early enough in life and are hammered into a child often enough and brutally enough, the brain-washing and abuse eventually take hold. The child eventually joins the enemy camp and grows up to apply sexual brain-washing and abusing, just as he once received it. Do what I say, is the maxim, not what I do. Self-righteous moralizing and discipline applies to others, not oneself. The self-righteous moralizer on Sunday is Monday's hypocrite, caught in the very sin he preached or prayed against.

Thus one need not be surprised at how slowly antisexualism is waning. The surprise is that it is actually waning at all. It does so in response to the accumulation of new factual evidence that contradicts antisexualism. The death knell of the old masturbation peril was sounded by germ theory, but it is taking a long time to be heard and assimilated.

Reference Notes

1. The section on treatment in *Plain Facts for Old and Young* occupies pp. 290-327. The long quotation is from pp. 294-296.

2. This quotation is from Carson (1957), p. 114.

3. Contemporary and historical information about circumcision is taken from Wallerstein (1980).

Persistence of Prudery

Germ Theory Attacks the Ignorant

Like a disciple of Janus, the two-faced God, John Harvey Kellogg saw medicine with two faces. One face was fixed to the image of health through diet, exercise, and abstinence. The other concentrated on the new breakthroughs of scientific medicine and the knowledge that they yielded.

The breakthrough that completely changed the course of medical practice and theory was the discovery and confirmation of germ theory in the late 1860s and early 1870s by Louis Pasteur (1822-1895) in France, and Robert Koch (1843-1910) in Germany.

If Kellogg had been a medical Einstein, he would have combined the views from his two faces into one united image, and he would have distinguished the cause of disease from its treatment. His error was that, in his system, food, exercise, and sex were both the cause and the treatment. Diseases caused by germs were an embarrassment to him if they could be treated with a germ-killing agent instead of by diet, exercise, and sexual restraint.

Germ theory, then, really made Kellogg's system outmoded before he left New York in 1875 to become superintendent of the Battle Creek Sanitarium in 1876. But germ theory was only a beginning. It would be followed eventually by hormone and metabolic theory, immunological theory, and molecular-genetic theory, each of which would leave less and less health territory that Kellogg and his professional descendants could lay claim to. Metabolic theory was so precise regarding the effects of trace minerals, vitamins, and other components of food or health, that it knocked Kellogg's diet theory into a cocked hat. That left him exercise and sex, which still remain relatively unaffected by the great theoretic breakthroughs of the present century. For this reason, Kellogg's brand of antisexualism has proved to have great length of life, and a long, lingering death. It still is not buried.

The Comstock Laws

It might have been decently dead and buried already had it not been for Anthony Comstock (1844-1915), who personally lobbied Congress and in 1873 had his extreme doctrine of antisexualism legislated into the law of the land.[1] The so-called Comstock laws continue to be the basis of legal antisexualism in the United States.

As a young man of twenty, Comstock spent a year as a soldier in the Civil War. He served in Florida, where his battles were with the Devil rather than the Confederate Army. Judging by the evidence of his diary, the Devil was his constant adversary:

> Today has been a rather sad day to my heart. O that I could overcome sin. O God how long must I be thus straying and sinning. O wilt thou keep me from sin. O make me pure.

> Again tempted and found wanting. Sin, sin. Oh how much peace and happiness is sacrificed on thy altar. Seemed as though Devil had full sway over me today, went right into temptation, and then, Oh, such love, Jesus snatched it away out of my reach. How good is he, how sinful am I. I am the chief of sinners, but I should be so miserable and wretched, were it not that God is merciful and I may be forgiven. Glory be to God in the highest.

> O I deplore my sinful weak nature so much. If I could but live without sin, I should be the happiest soul living: but Sin, that foe that is ever lurking, stealing happiness from me. What a day will it be when that roaring Lion shall be found & his wanderings cease, then will we have rest, the glorious rest free from sin. O hasten every welcome day, dawn on our souls.

> Today Satan has sorely tried me; yet by God's grace did not yield.

> This morning were severely tempted by Satan and after some time in my own weakness I failed.

Swearing, drinking, and chewing tobacco were three sins that he had three other Christian soldiers pledge themselves against. The sin of sex did not get mentioned explicitly. There was no chaplain for his unit, so he acted as a substitute in arranging and conducting prayer meetings and other devotions. Many of his fellow soldiers found him too self-righteous.

After completing military service in 1865, he had no place to call home, as his mother had died when he was ten years old and his father's second marriage was troubled. He tried his luck in New York, where he found a job as a clerk in a dry-goods store. By 1868 he had already begun to discover his true calling in life: He had two bookdealers arrested for selling erotic materials. At this same time the YMCA in New York had, through its Board of Directors, embarked on a campaign of clean living for young Christian men migrating to the city for work. They had supported a bill in Albany for the suppression of obscene literature. It was this bill that enabled Comstock to make his first arrests. By 1872 Comstock had become sponsored by the YMCA, which formed a Committee for the Suppression of Vice. In 1873 the Committee was supplanted by an independent Society for the Suppression of Vice. Anthony Comstock was its secretary. His police power was immense because of his status as Inspector for the Post Office, and because of the laws that Congress had passed on his behalf that same year. He was, in effect, the national censor.

As the fires of his personal inquisition grew increasingly intense, Comstock's diary entries ceased being confessions of his feuding with the Devil and became, instead, records of his vendetta against the Devil in others, and of his readiness to be a victim in the cause of righteousness. He exalted in his physical assaults on gambling halls, was pious about the ruin he brought on others, and callous about the suicides of those he entrapped. By law he was entitled to use the undercover methods of espionage in order to arrest and prosecute not only for obscenity but also for other vices, including gambling, prostitution, abortion, contraception, and newspaper advertisements of medical quackery. From his diaries it is clear, however, that his most venomous satisfaction came from suppressing advertisements and publications that had to do with what he defined as the vices of contraception, obscenity, and female nudity. Like Sylvester Graham, he blamed these vices for tempting young men into ever increasing depravity.

In his book *Frauds Exposed*, Comstock expounded his dogma regarding the danger of literature that he defined as obscene. By obscene he meant that it would suggest impure and libidinous thoughts to the young.

It is a deadly poison, cast into the fountain of moral purity. This business and intemperance are twins; but they are twin devils. Intemperance strikes down the flower of the land, openly and publicly. The bleared eye, the bloated face, and the reeling step, mark the drunkard's downfall. This cursed business of obscene literature works beneath the surface, and like a canker worm, secretly eats out the moral life and purity of our youth, and they droop and fade before their parents' eyes.

The effect of this cursed business on our youth and society, no pen can describe. It breeds lust. Lust defiles the body, debauches the imagination, corrupts the mind, deadens the will, destroys the memory, sears the conscience, hardens the heart, and damns the soul. It unnerves the arm, and steals away the elastic step. It robs the soul of manly virtues, and imprints upon the mind of the youth, visions that throughout life curse the man or woman. Like a panorama, the imagination seems to keep this hated thing before the mind, until it wears its way deeper and deeper, plunging the victim into practices that he loathes.

This traffic has made rakes and libertines in society—skeletons in many a household. The family is polluted, home desecrated, and each generation born into the world is more and more cursed by the inherited weakness, the harvest of this seed-sowing of the Evil one.

Comstock himself had little schooling and was not well read. He had a special loathing of free-thinking intellectuals and their ideas on sex and love. Some of them he persecuted with multiple arrests and imprisonments. One victim was Ezra Heywood of Princeton, Massachusetts, whom he had convicted for having sent through the mail a pamphlet of his own writing on love and marriage, *Cupid's Yokes,* and Russell Trall's medical text, *Sexual Physiology* (see Chapter 10).

With age, Comstock became not more mellow, but more cantankerous. He directed his attacks to "classical traps" in literature, fine arts, and drama. In 1887, from the Herman Knoedler Gallery in New York he seized 117 photographs of masterpieces of living French artists. In 1905, he attempted to suppress the New York production of Bernard Shaw's *Mrs. Warren's Profession.* Shaw retaliated by coining the word *comstockery.* In 1906 Comstock hit the New York Art Students' League, whose young bookkeeper, Miss Robinson, was arrested for distributing the League's catalogue. It contained reproductions of nude female life-class drawings.

In 1871 Comstock had married a Presbyterian preacher's daughter ten years his senior. She brought to the household her younger sister, who became a chronic invalid and permanent resident. There was only one child, a daughter, who died at the age of six months. Comstock soon thereafter rescued from poverty and adopted a newborn girl whose mother had died in childbirth. She did not turn out well, having been developmentally disabled from an undisclosed cause—of which child-abuse is a possibility.

After he married, Comstock made some tender references to "Wifey" in his diary, but marriage did not mitigate his war on sex. His domestic life was more drudgery than joy, and he ruled his women with the same fierce and messianic authority that he expended on society.

Comstock's Legacy

Kellogg applauded Comstock for suppressing the traffic of the "secret agencies . . . . and emissaries of evil men and their Satanic master . . . by arresting the publishers and destroying their goods." In *Plain Facts*, he quoted what Comstock had written in a published report:

> I have succeeded in unearthing this hydra-headed monster in part, as you will see by the following statement, which, in many respects, might be truthfully increased in quantity. These I have seized and destroyed:— Obscene photographs, stereoscopic and other pictures, more than one hundred and eighty-two thousand; obscene books and pamphlets, more than five tons; obscene letter-press in sheets, more than two tons; sheets of impure songs, catalogues, handbills, etc., more than twenty-one thousand; obscene miroscopic watch and knife charms, and finger-rings, more than five thousand; obscene negative plates for printing photographs and stereoscopic views, about six hundred and twenty-five; obscene-woodcut engravings, obscene lithographic stones destroyed, three hundred and fifty; stereotype plates for printing obscene books, more than five tons; obscene transparent playing-cards, nearly six thousand; obscene and immoral rubber articles, over thirty thousand; lead molds for manufacturing rubber goods, twelve sets, or more than seven hundred pounds; newspapers seized, about four thousand six hundred; letters from all parts of the country ordering these goods, about fifteen thousand; names of dealers in account-books seized, about six thousand; lists of names in the hands of dealers, that are sold as merchandise to forward circulars or catalogues to, independent of letters and account-books seized, more than seven thousand.
>
> These abominations are disseminated by these men by first obtaining the names and addresses of scholars and students in our schools and colleges, and then forwarding circulars. They secure thousands of names in this way, either by sending for catalogues of schools, seminaries, and colleges, under a pretense of sending a child to school; or else by sending out a circular purporting to be getting up a directory of all the scholars and students in schools and colleges in the United States; or of taking the census of all the unmarried people, and offering to pay five cents per name for lists so sent. I need not say that the money is seldom or never sent, but I do say that these names, together with those that come in reply to advertisements, are sold to other parties; so that when a man desires to engage in this nefarious business, he has only to purchase a list of these names, and then your child, be it son or daughter, is liable to have thrust into its hands, all unknown to you, one of these devilish catalogues.
>
> Since the destruction of the stereotype plates of old books, secret circulars have been discovered of a notice to dealers that twelve new

books are in course of preparation, and will soon be ready for delivery.
[p. 181-182]

The Comstock laws of 1873 are to sex what the consitutional amendment of 1919 was to alcohol, and what today's laws are to street drugs—prohibition. The lesson from alcohol is that prohibition creates an untaxable black-market monopoly for the gangster syndicate of the underworld. Paying no taxes, the syndicate becomes astronomically wealthy. Operating outside the law, it becomes a law unto itself and obliterates competition. Thus it becomes ever more wealthy and powerful. In effect, it establishes an economy within the economy, a law within the law, and an underground government within the government of the nation.

Zealots and crusaders are so dazzled by their own self-righteousness that they never put two and two together and see in advance what will be all the undesirable and underground effects of their crusade. Comstock would have been the last to admit that his laws were, in fact, the charter that created, outside the law, the underworld of pornography and illicit sex.

In the world of everyday affairs, the Comstock laws were a challenge to the ingeniousness of Americans to find ways of circumventing them while still technically obeying their injunctions. They did so with a vengeance. They created a national obsession, especially in advertising, with imagery that, by allusion and innuendo, was erotically suggestive. It is legal because it omits the genital organs and sexual intercourse and is not explicit about the passion and pleasure of orgasm. It is also not explicit about contraception. The American obsession with sex is not an obsession with chastity and abstinence, as both Kellogg and Comstock prescribed. It is an obsession with only those erotic thoughts and imaginations that the law does not expressly forbid. It is an obsession with sex above the belt. Sex below the belt is cut off, and cut out, except by implication and what the viewers' and readers' prurience may, or may not, supply. As a nation, our sexual obsession is with prurience, thanks to Anthony Comstock.

Woman's Emancipation

Comstock's laws were very effective in retarding the emancipation of the sexes to have equal status, which, historically, meant first the emancipation of women. They made it illegal for women to have access to information or techniques that would enable them to regulate the frequency and number of their own pregnancies. For Comstock, contraception was a form of pornography. It belonged to the devil. In order to establish the right of Brooklyn's wives of poverty to use birth control and not to be overburdened with childbearing and infant mortality, Margaret Sanger (1883-1966) had to defy the federal Comstock inspectors. She was a small wisp of a woman who graduated from being a public health nurse to a world leader of family planning. In defense of her cause, she and three women associates had to subject themselves to being arrested and, protesting, dragged away by a team of hunky New York policemen. The battle was won finally, less by protest than by latex condoms and the vending machines that sold them not as contraceptives but as hygienic devices for protection against disease (Chapter 1). The Comstock agents could not arrest either distributors or buyers for purchasing disease protection.

Resistance to women's emancipation was a gut reaction of the apostles of prudery who preached modesty and chastity as the natural nobility of womanhood and a restraint on the lust of men. These apostles in many instances were medical men who, like Kellogg, camouflaged their moral prejudices under the guise of medical fact. One of them was William Acton (1813-1875) a British surgeon who became an authority on venereal disease, prostitution, chastity, masturbation, and copulation of the honey bee. His most influential book went through six editions after it first appeared in 1857. The sixth was in 1875, the year he died. It was titled: *The Functions and Disorders of the Reproductive Organs in Youth, in Adult Age, and in Advanced Life.*

Kellogg admired Acton. In *Plain Facts*, he several times quoted him as confirming and agreeing with his own conception, as in Acton's following declaration on sexuality in women:

> I have taken pains to obtain and compare abundant evidence on this subject, and the result of my inquiries I may briefly epitomize as follows: I should say that the majority of women, happily for them [and for society, says the 5th edition] are not very much troubled with sexual feeling of any kind. What men are habitually, women are only exceptionally. I admit, of course, the existence of sexual excitement, terminating even in nymphomania, a form of insanity that those accustomed to visit lunatic asylums must be fully conversant with; but, with these sad exceptions, there can be no doubt that sexual feeling in the female is, in the majority of cases, in abeyance, and that it requires positive and considerable excitement to be roused at all; and even if roused, which in many instances it never can be, is very moderate compared with that of the male.

Many men, and particularly young men, form their ideas of women's feelings from what they notice early in life among loose, or at least low and vulgar women. There is always a certain number of females who, though not ostensibly prostitutes, make a kind of trade of a pretty face. They are fond of admiration; they like to attract the attention of those immediately around them. Any susceptible boy is easily led to believe, whether he is altogether overcome by the siren or not, that she, and hence all women, must have at least as strong passions as himself. Such women, however, give a very false idea of the condition of sexual feeling in general. Association with the loose women of London streets, in casinos and other immoral haunts, who, if they have not sexual feeling, counterfeit it so well that the novice does not suspect but that it is genuine, all seem to corroborate such an impression.

Married men, medical men, or married women themselves, would, if appealed to, tell a different tale, and vindicate female nature from the vile aspersions cast on it by the abandoned conduct and ungoverned lust of a few of its worst examples. There are many females who never feel any excitement whatever. Others, again, immediately after each period, do become, to a limited degree, capable of experiencing it; but this capacity is only temporary, and will cease entirely until the next menstrual period. The best mothers, wives, and managers of households know little or nothing of sexual indulgences. Love of home, of children, of domestic duties, are the only passions they feel. As a general rule, a modest woman seldom desires any sexual gratification for herself. She submits to her husband, but only to please him; and but for the desire of maternity, would far rather be relieved from his attention. [pp. 473-474].

Acton could, perhaps, have been very content with a species in which nature had designed that the female, like the queen bee, needed to be fertilized only once in a lifetime. Other writers were more realistic about women and their sexuality as it is. One of them, whose approach to female sexuality was positive, in the tradition of Trall, was Denslow Lewis (1856-1913), professor of gynecology in the Chicago Polyclinic and a respected senior gynecologist in the Illinois State Medical Society.

Scandal at the AMA

In the year 1899, a scandal rocked the meeting of the American Medical Association, held that year in Columbus, Ohio.[2] Lewis read a paper on "The Gynecologic Consideration of the Sexual Act." He covered the importance of the subject; the description of the sexual act; the education of girls and young women; the rights of women; and the nature of sexual responses in women. Under the latter, he dealt with absence of sensation; repugnance; aneroticism; anatomic interference with sexual relations; and the effect of hysterectomy on gratification.

His straightforward style and observational accuracy was as up to date in 1899 as anything that might be written by a clinical sexologist today:

> On the part of the female the increased secretion of mucus and the relaxation of the vulva and vagina have been a preparation for the reception of the penis. There is normally a participation in the pleasurable sensation and a reciprocity in the movement, which occasions increased and repeated contact. There is alternate contraction and relaxation of the vagina and a variable movement of the pelvis. There is a spasmodic expulsion of mucus, simulating an orgasm, which occurs several times in some women during the act, with a variable and sometimes progressive increase in the voluptuous sensations experienced. In some women such a pseudoorgasm takes place at least once, usually at the time of ejaculation on the part of the male. It has been claimed that at such times there is a forcible contraction of the sphincter vaginae around the base of the penis.
>
> Following the act there is normally a feeling of pleasurable lassitude, during which erection subsides and the spasmodic contractions of the vagina cease. . . .
>
> The physiology and philosophy of sexual erethism in the female require no detailed description. . . . Suffice it to say that the clitoris, introitus vaginae, and portio vaginalis are the chief factors in its production. These parts vary, in different individuals, in relative excitability. Moreover, they are not the only factors. The nipples, the tongue, the lips, the neck, indeed almost the entire body may be judiciously utilized to maintain and increase *libido sexualis*. It must be remembered that in women the desire for courtship often exceeds the desire for the sexual act. The preliminaries are therefore with her of chief importance, and should receive proper consideration in every instance. The secretion from the glands of Bartholin and the relaxation of the vulva and vagina are the normal indications for intromission, which should be accomplished without pain. This is always possible by the exercise of due caution and kind consideration, which is no more than a wife has a right to demand.
>
> As regards the movements which by repeated contact produce and intensify the voluptuous sensation experienced, there is much variation in different women. In certain instances, the extreme degree of pleasure is experienced when the penis is in direct contact with the clitoris or introitus vaginae. In these cases deep penetration will be avoided. By judicious maneuvering, titillation of the most sensitive regions by the glans penis will be practiced, and the endeavor will be made to cause repeated orgasms on the part of the woman, very much to her satisfaction. In other cases there is a variable degree of vaginismus. When

this is the case it is the part of wisdom for the man to be passive. . . .

Women differ very greatly in relative susceptibility to external influences as a means of influencing *libido sexualis*. In some instances a caress or a clasp of the hand is sufficient to induce mucus secretion and an orgasm. The woman turns pale, her lips quiver, her eyes dilate, she almost faints at the anticipation. During the act she experiences frequent orgasms, accompanied sometimes by convulsive seizures almost epileptiform in character. The orgasms vary in intensity. There is not always a progressive increase. More often a violent orgasm will be succeeded by others of less intensity. There is great variation even in the same woman at different times, dependent on the degree of excitability and the influence to impressions.[3]

Eventually, Lewis published his paper as a small monograph (1900).[4] It was refused for publication in the *Journal of the American Medical Association*. The editor, George H. Simmons, was opposed to "this class of literature." A member of his publication committee appealed to the Comstock laws, saying that the AMA trustees would be open to a charge of sending obscene matter through the mail. The famous lawyer Clarence Darrow did not agree.

A leader of the opposition was a professor of gynecology at The Johns Hopkins University School of Medicine, Howard A. Kelly (1858-1943). He was one of the four famous founding professors of the Hopkins Medical School. He was a devout fundamentalist in religious faith, a Sunday School teacher, profoundly prudish, and deeply antisexual. His response to his colleague's paper was as follows:

With all due respect to Dr. Lewis, I am strongly opposed to dwelling on these elementary physiologic facts in a public audience. I am very sorry he has read the paper. I think we can sum up these matters very safely and be guided by our common sense and experience. The husband should show due respect to the wife and the wife to the husband in the consideration of this subject, and I do not believe in the current teaching of the day, i.e., talking freely about these things to children. The child always follows the immediate impulse, and I do not believe in going into details further than necessary in the elementary instruction which the child receives from teachers in botany and the elements of zoology, because I should be very sorry if in this country these matters became as freely talked about as they have been on the other side of the water. I do not believe pleasure in the sexual act has any particular bearing on the happiness of life; that is the lowest possible view of happiness in married life, and I shall never forget the utter disgust which I felt once when a professional friend of mine in Philadelphia told me that he had repaired the perineum of a mistress for the sake of increasing sexual gratification of her paramour. I do hope we shall not have to go into details in discussing this subject; it is not necessary. Its discussion is attended with more or less filth and we bismirch ourselves by discussing it in public.

A Boston gynecologist, B. Sherwood Dunn, came to Lewis's defense:

> All that I have heard I endorse and commend, and I am free to say that I believe that if the majority of our essayists had his courage the result would be beneficial to the profession and to the public at large. There is not a gynecologist in this room, who has been ten years in this specialty, who has not had women consult him, telling him that they did not have the slightest conception or knowledge of the act of menstruation when they were children. . . . Neither is there a gentleman who has been a long time in practice, that has not met women who have told him that when they got married they did not have the slightest conception as to the sexual act, what it pertained to, of what it consisted. I consider that state of affairs a disgrace to the motherhood of America. This is due to a great extent to the false modesty that pertains to our American civilization, which descends to a maudlin degree of sentimentality when it excludes a discussion of the physiologic process which is the foundation of the propagation of the race. . . . I think the time has arrived when false modesty should be relegated to its proper sphere in the human household, and we should approach these questions, which are vital to our well-being and the propagation of the race, with some sort of common sense.

Lewis had the floor for the closing statement:

> I am aware that I have only a minute or two in which to reply to the remarks of Dr. Kelly, so I will simply suggest that there is something more to gynecology than suspensions of the uterus and catheterization of the ureters. I contend that we, as physicians, and especially as gynecologists, have a duty to perform toward society, which is not fully performed by the use of the knife or application of a tampon. I contend that gynecologists above all others should take a stand in the community and exert an influence for the public good. In no way can they do this better than by impressing the truth on the public. The age of consent in certain states is nine years; that means a child can be offered a box of candy, can be seduced, can become a mother, and the man goes free. . . . I have seen many pregnant young girls in the Cook County Hospital, Chicago, and in other institutions with which I am connected, and I have talked with them. Often I find that they permitted sexual intercourse without knowing what it was. Unquestionably children should be taught, not necessarily in a brutal way, regarding sexual intercourse and reproduction. I think, as I stated in my paper, that while their modesty

may be shocked their virtue will be saved. As regards the question of marriage, it is nice to take a high and lofty view; but if some of the gentlemen will study the philosophy of the subject, they will reach the conclusion that the sexual act is the basis of love, otherwise there is only friendship. The affection which draws one man toward a particular woman is a desire for intercourse, or as Schopenhauer says, it is the genius of the genus, seeking to assert itself.

Lewis decided to appeal the rejection of his paper at the annual meeting of the Association in 1900. His appeal was rejected by the Executive Committee, and the policy of prudery became the official policy of American medicine.

Lewis was not burned at the stake, as in an earlier era he might have been. Nor was he required to recant and destroy his manuscript, unpublished. His example and his protest were not in vain. They gave heart to Margaret Sanger and the birth-control activists. They created a precedent for an intrepid few who have already become legends in the history of American twentieth-century sexological medicine. Some, like Alfred Kinsey (1894-1956), mounted their assaults on medical and social prudery as biologists. Others worked from within the medical profession: Robert Latou Dickinson (1861-1950); Harry Benjamin (b. 1885); and William H. Masters (b. 1915) along with his wife, Virginia E. Johnson (b. 1925).

Prudery Defines Womanhood

Despite challenge, the official policy of antisexual prudery had extraordinary staying power. It became imbedded in the clerical doctrine of many fundamentalist religious denominations, including the Seventh-day Adventist, where it had put down its tap root early in its growth. It persisted in dozens of religious and medical manuals of sexual advice to the young and adolescent, and in marriage manuals for the newly wed, where it lurks still. It distorts all public education texts for juveniles on sex education and family life, for they scrupulously avoid the topics of the love affair, sexual intercourse, sexual orgasm, and birth control.

In medicine itself, the antisexual heritage of prudery twisted whole sections of sexual medicine texts into manuals of moral judgment and malpractice that masqueraded as nonjudgmental statements of fact. Max Huhner (see chapter 13) got trapped in this dilemma. He swung on the pendulum of whether to respect the prudery and moralism of his forebears, or reject it in favor of his own scientific observations. In consequence, he fell into the trap of retracting in one place what he said in another.

Reference Notes

1. The sourcebook for information on Comstock is by Broun and Leech (1927). Quotations are taken from Chapter 2, pp. 26, 55-56; and Chapter 6, pp. 80-81.

2. Marc H. Hollender, M.D., wrote of this historic scandal in the *American Journal of Obstetrics and Gynecology*, September 1970. It is to his article that the present recounting is indebted. See also Denslow Lewis (1900; reprinted 1970).

3. Lewis's radical defense of women's sexuality was compatible with a moralistic understructure of traditional male chauvinism, typical of his era. Women's sexuality was not only for themselves alone, but to please their husbands. Lewis (1900) was a self-righteous eradicator of "pernicious" lesbian practices:

> There are women for whom the sexual act is not only devoid of pleasure but positively repugnant. In certain instances these women have been accustomed to find gratification in abnormal practices from their earliest girlhood. It is, I fear, not generally known to what an extent these practices exist among young girls. They would look with shame on any familiarity with a boy. They are circumspect in their behavior and modest in their demeanor. The thought of ever allowing a boy to kiss them would not be entertained. They have been warned perhaps against indiscretion, and their regard for conventionality, their natural refinement of character protects them against all semblance of impropriety. They think no harm can come from any form of intimacy with one of their own sex. With the awakening of sexual appetite there too often develops an objectivation of affection toward a congenial girl friend. No warning has ever been given against the dangers of such an intimacy. The parents look with approval on the growing friendship between their daughter and the daughter of worthy neighbors. They are thankful, perhaps, that their daughter shows no inclination to associate with boys. The young girls, thus thrown together, manifest an increasing affection by the usual tokens. They kiss each other fondly on every occasion. They embrace each other with mutual satisfaction. It is most natural, in the interchange of visits, for them to sleep together. They learn the pleasure of direct contact, and in the course of their fondling they resort to cunnilinguistic practices.
>
> I do not wish to be an alarmist, but I can positively assert the existence of these pernicious practices to an extent that is not imagined by most physicians, simply because they have given the subject no thought. The poor, hard-working girl is not addicted to this vice. The struggle for life exhausts her capabilities. The girl brought up in luxury develops a sexual hyperesthesia which is fostered by the pleasures of modern society. She indulges in these irregular and detrimental practices, perhaps for years, and when she assumes the responsibilities of the wife the normal sexual act fails to satisfy her.
>
> In the treatment of such a condition I have often found an overdue hyperemia of the external genitals, which has been relieved by the application of a cocain solution and the exhibition of saline cathartics. Often the

glans clitoridis will be especially irritable. On two occasions in my experience it was adherent. When liberated it was possible, by the means indicated, to control the hyperesthesia. In one case the clitoris was hypertrophied and excessively sensitive. As a last resort I felt justified in performing an amputation, and the ultimate result in this case was gratifying. Systematic treatment is usually indicated. The patient is apt to be anemic and debilitated, and the tension of the nervous system is often extreme. In certain instances large doses of the bromids are indicated, sometimes combined with cannabis indica. At other times calomel and salines are given for a time and followed by pyrophosphate of iron. It is sometimes my practice to give strychnia by hypodermic injection, in connection with the remedies mentioned. The result in fifteen of the eighteen patients thus treated by me was satisfactory. The intense reflex excitability subsided. By moral suasion and by intelligent understanding of the duties of the marital relationship the patients became in time proper wives. Thirteen of these became mothers. Of the three unsuccessful ones, two of the patients never experienced any gratification during the sexual act, but they both became mothers and their family life has been undisturbed. In one instance the patient, a marked neurotic, finally became insane and is now in an asylum.

4. Lewis's paper was also included in: "*Section on Obstetrics and Diseases of Women*: Transactions of the Section at the Fiftieth Annual Meeting of the American Medical Association, Held at Columbus, Ohio, June 6 to 9, 1899." Chicago: American Medical Association Press, 1900. In 1983, the *Journal of the American Medical Association*, in response to the urging of Marc H. Hollender, lifted its censorship of Lewis's paper, and published it: *JAMA*, 250:222-227.

CHAPTER
15

Fragile: Handle with Care

Protection Imposed

Max Huhner belonged to the generation that modernized female prudishness by renaming it "being protected and cared for." Independent people resent being protected and cared for. What they want is their freedom. Women would have to fight for their emancipation. Before the women's movement got under way in the mid-nineteen hundreds, however, a woman was supposed to be satisfied with being under the protection of a man. If he loved her and married her, then sexual intercourse changed from being immoral and dirty. It became sacred and beautiful, even if not enjoyable.

Though Huhner begrudged women the right of birth control, in his *Diagnosis and Treatment of Sexual Disorders in the Male and Female, Including Sterility and Impotence* he conscientiously described the methods of contraception. But he also warned against "the harm that is often done to both male and female by the use of certain methods of contraception [including] a later sterility" (p. vi).

Having warned against the consequences of masturbation in married women, he then allowed that some "women easily fall prey to masturbation to complete the orgasm" that their husbands failed to bring to fulfillment. On this account he gave practical advice to husbands:

> The husband is to be made aware of the fact that the wife has a well-marked sexual sense and desire, and her desire and passion should be taken into consideration in his marital duties. He should be informed that sexual intercourse is just as important to her as to him, and the lack of it is just as injurious to her as to him. He should then be informed that it is just as necessary for his wife to "come"—that is, to have complete orgasm—as it is for him; and that to simply excite his wife either by withdrawal or too soon removal of his penis, and to leave her moaning with an excited but uncompleted passion, is sure to lead to trouble. [pp. 237-238]

Though he emancipated woman to the extent of allowing her right to orgasm, he left her traditional dependency on her husband unchanged: orgasm was a gift from her husband. Lest even this was going too far with emancipation, however, he backed off, as adults so often do, protecting traditionalism by imposing it on youth. Female puberty was treated as an ailment requiring protective care:

> Parents and teachers should see to it that the developing child of preadolescent and adolescent age should have plenty of outdoor recreation, which means that it should not be too much burdened with extra studies. The normal school work has been properly arranged not to be too burdensome, but when to this is added extra work such as foreign language study, music lessons and the like, the result may prove a hardship. Every child is a rule unto itself, and the amount of work must be intelligently arranged for each child. I cannot go into detail but must merely indicate general principles.
>
> It is just before and during puberty, however, that intelligent care must be exercised. The child should be thoroughly but tactfully instructed what is to take place, what the meaning of the various changes are, so as not to become alarmed at the onset of the periods. Care should be taken not to overburden the child at this time with either mental or physical work. Constipation long previously should have been overcome by proper diet. Preventive measures regarding colds should have become automatic and the child otherwise should be as physically at ease as possible before the advent of such periods. Of course, long before this, the child should have had all questions regarding sex frankly and tactfully explained; but I do not believe in going to the other extreme and in removing all traces of modesty from children and girls. We must recognize that even today there is such a thing as feminine modesty and it is an attribute which normal men admire and which constitutes one of the greatest sexual attractions of men toward women. Of late there has been too much sex talk among both sexes, which partly accounts for the great sexual laxity among the unmarried females of today. The removal of the double standard does not seem to have meant that men strove to reach the high state of sexual morality which was common in the girl of yesterday, but that men should remain as they were, while modern girls should degrade themselves to the vices common to men, in order to assert their equality.
>
> All decent associations with the opposite sex may be permitted and even encouraged, but the girl must be taught to resent the first indication of indecency or "freshness" on the part of the male, and should estimate the character of her male friends by their behavior in this regard. The extreme of such behavior as "petting parties" reacts deleteriously to the sexual health of both the male and female; but aside from this, there is the great danger that both parties are playing with fire and may mis-

judge their sexual power of resistence until it is too late. It is best and therefore easy for the modest girl to stop at the first indication of too much familiarity. The male, if not encouraged, as a rule, will take the hint and realize that this particular girl is not one with whom to become "fresh."

"Too early stimulation of the sexual feeling is not sex development," he wrote. Then, inventing a fact to suit his argument, he added: "in those countries like Arabia, for instance, where the girl marries at the age of 11, she is sterile at 22. Alcoholic drinks in particular should be avoided as much as possible."

> In addition to these general suggestions, the girl's endocrine system should be investigated if necessary. If the girl does not start her menstrual life at the time which is normal for her particular race and country, it is not wise to wait in order to see what may develop, but we ought to forestall (if possible) the non-development of the sexual apparatus. By this I do not mean a pelvic examination, but the possibility of a hypothyroidism or other endocrine disturbance must be considered and investigated. We must also think of the possibility of homosexualism. If necessary the child should be relieved of all mental work, and an outdoor life instituted, with good nourishing food. [pp. 93-95]

Psychoanalytic Victorianism

Huhner's hand-me-down Victorianism was not the only one of its kind, nor was it the last. In the present century, Victorianism became Freudianized, and with it the sexual psychology of women. The psychoanalytic remnants of antisexualism as applied to women appeared in *Obstetrics and Gynecology* by Willson, Beecham, and Carrington through its fourth edition (1971). These authors used the professional jargon of psychoanalysis in full. They compared feminine narcissism, masochism, and passivity with masculine narcissism, aggression, and activity. The woman is not as active or aggressive as the male, they claimed, because of her constitution and lesser muscular development. Her sexual organ is receptive and cannot be easily used actively or aggressively. As a young girl, the female has oedipal feelings toward her father. Her assumption of feminine traits makes her desire for and attraction toward him compatible with loving and pleasing her mother. The parents and the culture both encourage the girl in her feminine ways. She grows up to love differently than men do. As quoted in Money (1980, pp. 163-165) the authors wrote:

> The woman falls in love with the idea of being loved, whereas the man loves an object for the pleasure it will give. The woman receives gratifi-

cation from the idea of being loved and bases an increased sense of her own value on her image of the person who loves her. She says, I am valuable, important, etc. because he loves me. This type of narcissism finds expression in many aspects of a woman's life, the most obvious being her interest in clothes, personal appearance, and beauty. Such interest is normal and entirely feminine if its main object is to have someone admire and love her. It is subverted when it becomes an end in itself. Every phase of a woman's life is influenced by narcissism. To an adolescent and young woman it gives impetus to her efforts to attract a man. As a wife it allows her to be gratified by the success and achievements of her husband. In pregnancy and labor it expands her conception of herself in that she is going to reproduce and give her husband a gift of a child.

The authors regarded ordinary feminine masochism as not being neurotic. In a woman's life, they said, the idea of suffering is an essential part,

since every woman has to face the fear of childbirth and the fear of pain that is attached to this. Pain is not an integral part of the male's concept of his role. He can fantasy a life without physical pain that does not produce a conflict in his sexual identity. The woman cannot do this. Every aspect of a woman's life is colored by her ability to accept the masochism that is part of her feminine role. As a young girl being courted she must *allow* herself to be won by the man she chooses. In the role of a wife she often must submit her own needs to build up the personality and strivings of her husband and family. Sexually there is always an element of rape in that the male organ penetrates. As a mother she sacrifices her own needs to those of her children. Finally, she must accept her children's marriage and separation from her.

[Feminine passivity allows a young woman] to put great efforts into making herself attractive, so that the male will pursue her while she seemingly waits. As a wife she must show interest in the home and in the well-being of its occupants. She must accept the idea that she is given things by her husband and even by her children, rather than assuming an active and aggressive role in attaining these things for herself. Sexually she must be passive and receptive to the male.

A balance between narcissism, masochism, and passivity is the mark of maturity. Too much feminine narcissism without masochism and passivity produces a self-centered woman interested only in attaining love and admiration from those around her. There is no element of giving. Too much feminine masochism without the protective narcissism produces a woman who sacrifices herself without idea of rewards. The overly passive woman is continually waiting to receive without any willingness to give of herself in a masochistic or narcissistic manner. No formula is given whereby narcissism, masochism, and passivity can be kept in balance, as it is asserted they must be; and there is no formula for the proper control of opposing masculine elements of the personality. Implicitly, the burden of responsibility rests with the individual as a matter of choice and willingness to conform to the criteria set forth.

What actually happens is that the cultural stereotype embodied in this writing becomes imposed on a girl form infancy onward by those who themselves are the agents of its transmission, whether or not they are obstetricians and gynecologists. Developmentally, the girl either assimilates or disassimilates the stereotype, in much the same way as she either assimilates or disassimilates the foreign accent of her parents, should they happen to be immigrants who speak English with an accent. If the stereotype has been assimilated by her sisters and brothers, by other family members, and above all by her peer group, then its impact is pervasive and intrusively irresistible. She assimilates it until it takes on the appearance not of second nature, but of first nature. That is to say, it is mistakenly labeled as hereditary, constitutional, or biological in origin.

The Madonna and the Whore, the Provider and the Playboy

The strategists who Victorianized the sexual relationship between men and women were almost exclusively men. Women were not consulted about having their own sexuality idealized into sexlessness. Their men were notoriously diligent in sentimentalizing the sexual purity of their mothers, sisters, and daughters. They admonished all boys and young men to do the same and to respect all womanhood 'as they would their own mothers and sisters. The not so hidden implication in this admonition is that respect for a lover or wife makes sexual intercourse with her comparable to incest and therefore is to be avoided.

Of course one may argue that the Victorians didn't really mean what they said and that they trusted their listeners or readers to make an allowance for sentimental exaggeration. The trouble with this argument is that those who from infancy are brain-washed by the forces of exaggerated and sentimentalized antisexualism may become unable to make allowances. They accept what they have been exposed to as the gospel of reality.

For woman, the reality of the Victorian gospel of antisexualism is that she bears the two faces of Eve. One face is of the virginal innocence of Adam's helpmeet. The other is of the naive servant of the serpent in the Garden of Eden, lacking will power to resist taking the apple-bite of

Adam's downfall. She is the saint and the sinner. She is the madonna and the whore.[1]

For man, the reality of the Victorian gospel of antisexualism is that he also is both saint and sinner. He wears the two faces of Adam. One face is of Adam the patriarch and provider, made in the image of God. The other is of Adam the playboy, powerless to resist eating the apple of his own downfall with voluptuous Eve.

If men and women were either pure saints or pure sinners, and if like would always attract like, then madonnas would meet with providers and lead sexually inert lives. Conversely, whores would meet with playboys and lead sexually abandoned lives.

In most, if not all people, the split between saint and sinner is not all or none. Saint and sinner coexist as contradictions within themselves. The saint dwells chiefly above the belt in the realm of sensuous love. The sinner dwells chiefly below the belt in the realm of carnal lust.

Love is lyrical and romantic. It whispers, kisses, caresses, cuddles, and hugs. It is the stuff of sonnets, stanzas, and song, celebrated by troubadours both ancient and modern. Without let or hindrance, it may show its face in public, in print, on stage, on television, and in movies (but no kissing, please, in movies shown in India and the orient!).

Lust is epic and passionate. It is noisy, sweaty, fleshy, baudy, and frolicky. It is the stuff of limericks, jokes, dirty books, and locker-room ballads. If it dares to show its face in public, in the media, or for entertainment, it is branded as obscene or pornographic, and the publishers or exhibitors are subject to prosecution.

The Failure of Lust

The chasm between love and lust is deep and treacherous. Most boys and girls, in growing up, are overtly prepared predominantly for saintly love. Their preparation for sinful lust is covert. The crossing from love to lust confronts them with a tricky conflict. Though lust is of the flesh, and sinful, it must be reserved exclusively for the one they love. Few achieve a reconciliation of this conflict as they grow up. The majority have to get along as best they can with a compromise. It is not a compromise that they design for themselves, but one that designs itself in response to the various contradictions that they encounter in relationship to sex and eroticism.

A common compromise is one in which love wins out over lust. The trouble begins when it comes time to take off the belt. That is when lust is defeated. The man may discover that he cannot get an erection, or that he gets one and comes too soon. The woman may discover that she cannot get lubricated, or that her vaginal muscles clamp up and won't release.

Failure to reach the peak of orgasm may happen to either men or women, as may pain or other alteration or loss of feeling in the sex organs. Either the man or the woman may lose interest in having sexual intercourse and give up completely, perhaps not bothering even with preliminary hugging and kissing so as to avoid the danger of what it might lead to. Giving up, however, is less common than trying and failing to be able to carry through.

The formula shared by each different type of these failures of lust below the belt is that the saint who engages in actual sexual intercourse becomes a sinner—and also drags the partner down into sin. He who fucks the madonna, turns her into a whore! And the provider can similarly be degraded into a playboy.

Among couples who come to a sex-therapy clinic, the prevalence of the madonna/whore or saint/sinner phenomenon is astonishingly high. It wears a proverbial coat of many colors and designs, and so has many disguises. A classic example is that in which the period of romance and courtship was intensely positive for both partners. They engage in much above-the-belt activity and some heavy petting of the genitals to the point of climax, but no genital union itself. They don't actually say that they are saving the dirty part of sex until after they are legally married. Their own explanation is that they are applying their own moral standards by postponing actual penovaginal penetration.

Once they are legally married, they gradually reach the discovery that they can't have ordinary sexual intercourse. He blames himself for ejaculating too soon and for not being able to arouse her to have much active desire or enthusiasm for his penis. She goes along with his self-blame and keeps both of them blinded to the fact that she has a paralyzing fear of having anything actually penetrate into the cavity of her vagina. For her that would be as degrading as being a whore.

Therefore, it is not possible for her to help him out by exercising her birthright, which is to be the one who quims him—that is, takes the initiative, and sometimes lets him be the sensuous recipient of her active erotic endeavors.[2] Conversely, he cannot do his share by being the one who swives her—that is, allows her to be the sensuous recipient of his erotic ministrations.

Eventually they do succeed, despite their handicap, in getting the tip of the penis to release enough sperms into the opening of the vagina to result in conception. They are able to stay together as a family because they become dropouts from sexual intercourse and make do with a companionship in which she takes on the role of madonna, and he of provider.

It is not always, of course, that both partners become dropouts together. There are dropout relationships that are one-sided. If only the wife is anerotic, then she exploits her husband as an equivalent of stud service. He is sexually irrelevant except for her next season for pregnancy and motherhood. If only the husband is anerotic, his wife becomes erotically abandoned. Her erotic longings are unfulfilled. Sexual intercourse is for him a laborious intrusion, and an interruption of his other preoccupations. Like a migratory bird, he always misses the flight to the spring breeding grounds.

In a lopsided relationship, the sexually inert or apathetic partner may become the victim of the active partner's retaliation. It may be insidious, covert retaliation, and a kind of mental torture; or it may be overt abuse and coercive violence—or a complex of both. The abused victim may settle into the role of being the henpecked husband or the martyred wife. Or retaliation may erupt into destructive feuding and jealousy. The revenge of lovesickness in its most virulent form is suicide or murder.

The saint-and-sinner formula of the failure of lust derives from the history of antisexualism. The story of how this formula gets translated into the sexology of the body and into the physiology of the failure or insufficiency of the genital organs to function correctly has not yet been discovered. When it is discovered, it will be necessary then to go one step further and show the relationship of this kind of failure or insufficiency to other kinds with different causes. It will also be necessary to discover how, in the brain, the governance of malfunction of the genital organs is related to sexual fantasy. There is often more than meets the eye when the sexual organs fail to perform in sexual intercourse. The hidden something meets not the eye, but the mind's eye. It is a private erotic fantasy star-years away, mentally, from what is actually happening, in the room, on the bed, with the partner.

Reference Notes

1. The madonna/whore tradition has by no means become defunct. In an essay on the sexuality of males in William Buckley's four epic novels, Jack Friedman (1982) quotes *The Official Preppy Handbook* (Birnbach, 1980): "In the chapter titled *Prep Sex—A Contradiction in Terms*, we read that most Prep men suffer from the virgin/whore complex, and they only want to have sex with 'bad' women. . . . Prep men will not marry these women; they will marry other Preppies."

2. See John Money, "To Quim and to Swive: Linguistic and Coital Parity, Male and Female" (1982).

Degeneracy Theory Lingers On

The Vice of Concupiscence

The Victorian antisexualists followed their predecessors, Tissot and Graham, in taking for granted that the concupiscent vice was the vice of heterosexual lust. Heterosexual lust with paid or promiscuous women was the social vice. The secret vice was heterosexual lust in the imagery of a private masturbation fantasy. Whether social or secret, the vice of concupiscence led to debility and disease not simply because it depleted the vital fluids but even more because it depleted the vital energy of the nervous system and the moral energy of the mind. Depletion of energy was far more important to Victorian sexual theorists than was the detailed erotic content of the mental imagery of lust.

The Victorian theorists did, in fact, prudishly steer away from explicit erotic imagery. Even their laws, still extant in some jurisdictions, did not require them to be explicit. When pressing charges against a sex offender, it was sufficient to define the offense as the abominable or unspeakable crime against nature. If the unspeakable crime was further defined, it was with a term such as *sodomy*, which meant anything from oral sodomy to anal sodomy, bestiality, or homosexual acts between males.

The same moral prudery that required imprecision in the courts of law spilled over into the Victorian sex manuals. They were modestly reticent on the subject of homosexuality. It was mentioned, if at all, in terms of older boys or men teaching younger ones the sin of masturbation. Nursemaids also might commit the same sin, or worse still, might teach young boys to have intercourse with them.

Reticent prudery imposed on Victorian sex manuals a high degree of imprecision and avoidance of any activity or imagery classified as pornographic or obscene. Mention of oral sex, even between husband and wife, was evaded. The content of material confiscated under the Comstock laws was in general defined as lewd, the details being not otherwise specified. Likewise, the content of the wet dreams of nocturnal pollution was not specified other than as lascivious or voluptuous. Their very explicit imagery was an embarrassment to the Victorian ideal of modesty, which also kept lights out in the bedroom and the body covered while having sexual intercourse—not to mention pantaloons on the piano legs.

Victorian sexual theorists did not need to know the detailed erotic content of the mental imagery of lust. Their theory was complete without it. It could, indeed, explain how lust became increasingly depraved. Progressive depletion of energy led to progressive degeneracy as a result of concupiscence, regardless of the content of the concupiscent longing. So claimed the theory. Then, as degeneracy progressed, so also did the depravity of concupiscent longing. Depravity fed upon depravity until eventually no sin was too horrible for the jaded victim of concupiscence to engage in. Ultimately he would transform himself into a sex fiend. A fiend, in the dictionary definition, is a demon or even Satan himself. Here is a living reminder that demon-possession theory still survives. Its survival is evident still today in media headlines of sex fiends and monsters and in stories of sex crimes in which depravity is depicted as feeding upon itself in an ever downward spiral of degeneracy and fiendishness—witness contemporary headlines about child molesters.

Police and attorneys working for the criminal justice system fall into the same error, and so do many judges. Under the adversary system of the law, psychiatrists and other physicians without special expertise in sexual medicine can easily be found as expert witnesses who testify to the truth of degeneracy.

It is no longer the fashion to blame degeneracy and depravity on the concupiscence of masturbation. Concupiscence, however, is still the culprit. The depravity that it causes is now blamed not on the imagery and longings of masturbation fantasies, but on the imagery and fantasies of pornographic books, magazines, movies, and videotapes, and the longings they create.

In early December 1975, newspapers in Ottawa and elsewhere reported in lurid detail the story of a studious and religious eighteen-year-old Canadian youth who acted out his personal erotic fantasy, a particularly morbid one. One morning, instead of going to school, he brought a girl classmate from the bus stop back to his own apartment. It had a private entrance and was in the basement of his parents' house. He had for years occupied it alone. His mother heard the sound of a scuffle below, but did not investigate. He forced the girl into sexual intercourse, and strangled her. Then, with a gun, he went to school, shooting indiscriminately into his religion class, killing one student and wounding others. Then he shot and killed himself. His diaries contained the prophetic scenario of the drama of this, his first and only attempt at sexual intercourse, and his anguished prayers that a higher power would intervene before it was too late. It had repeatedly been his masturbation fantasy, supplemented visually with *Playboy* centerfolds. They were found open, in his apartment. The police blamed the nude pinup pictures of the centerfolds as the cause of his degeneracy into sexual murder and suicide. Reporters obtained the opinions of "experts" who agreed but who were not required to explain why *Playboy* does not turn all teen-aged readers into lust murderers and suicides.

Erotosexual Rehearsal Play

The sexual doctrine of Victorianism was inconsistent with respect to what it had to say about the erotic and sexual development of children. This inconsistency has persisted into the present. One Victorian version of childhood is that it is a period of sublime sexual innocence and remains that way until shattered by the onset of puberty and the "turmoil" of adolescence. The other version is that childhood is the period when the intrinsic wickedness of having been conceived in iniquity and born in original sin has to be diligently curbed and kept in check, so that the weeds of wickedness do not wither the rosebuds of righteousness.

According to the doctrine of sexual innocence, children had to be protected from the ravages of those who, regardless of age, were already depraved. The innocent could be easily led into the quagmires of depravity. The broad path of destruction was easier to travel than the narrow path of righteousness.

William Acton, an architect of Victorianism in England in the 1850s, held to the doctrine of sexual innocence in childhood. He wrote:

> Previously to the attainment of puberty, the normal condition of a healthy child is one of entire freedom from sexual impressions. All its vital energy is employed in constructing the growing frame, in storing up external impressions, and in educating the brain to receive them. During a well-regulated childhood, and in the case of ordinary temperaments, there is no temptation to infringe this primary law of nature. . . . Thus it happens that with most healthy and well brought up children no sensual idea or feeling has ever entered their heads, even in the way of speculation. I believe that such children's curiosity is seldom excited on these subjects except as the result of suggestion by persons older than themselves. [Acton, 1875, pp. 1-2]

According to the doctrine of original sin, the enticements and destructive glitter of the broad path were alone sufficient to lead to depravity, even without a guide. Parents needed, therefore, to watch out for beginning signs of depravity and eradicate them.

There is no significant difference between the doctrines of original sin and original innocence in their application to child-rearing practices. From the Victorian era until the present, both doctrines have been used to justify restraint, deprivation, humiliation, and corporal punishment of children for showing any signs of eroticism and sexuality involving the genital anatomy, alone or with a playmate.

Persecution of children for manifesting normal erotic and sexual development applies even to their talk about such matters. The very words of sex and eroticism are forbidden as dirty. In consequence, explicit terms must be either avoided or replaced with infantilisms and evasions in the presence of adults.

In the world in which we live today, no child may grow up without becoming acquainted with the taboo on talking about sex. No matter how unrestrictive the conversation may be at home, or among age-mates, every child discovers sooner or later that certain everyday sexual words are absolutely forbidden in school, at church, on television, and elsewhere. Thus it becomes a part of every child's heritage that sexual explicitness is classified as dirty and naughty. By contrast, sexual evasiveness is classified as clean and pure. Herein lies a child's acculturation into the antithesis between the sexual sinner and the sexual saint. One way or another, this antithesis of irreconcilable opposites will affect every child's sex life in adulthood.

The impact of the antithesis between dirty, sinful sex, on the one hand, and pure, saintly sex, on the other, is very pervasive in society. At home, as well as in school or church, it dictates a policy of neglect and abuse of children's developing sexuality and eroticism. No matter how high-minded we may be regarding all other aspects of infantile health and child development, we are Draculas of institutionalized neglect and legalized abuse when face to face with healthy erotosexual development. Child abuse is our socially sanctioned way of dealing with the normal heterosexual rehearsal play and interests of childhood. Child neglect is the official way in which the majority of adults deal with uncensored sexual knowledge. Childhood learning about the realities of sexual intercourse and erotic passion as legitimate human experiences is subverted. The birds-and-bees curriculum covers, at best, eggs, sperms, and menstrual periods.

There is no balance sheet showing the price we pay for the deprivation of sexual rehearsal play and sexual learning that our Victorian forebears imposed on their children, and which many parents continue to impose on today's children. The cost can only be guessed at. The best guess is made on the basis of studies on humankind's closest primate relatives, the monkeys and the apes. The young of these species engage in sexual rehearsal play, mounting and presenting, just as human children do.[1] If they are deprived of their sexual rehearsal play, by being reared in isolation cages, as they were in experiments done at the University of Wisconsin, rhesus monkey children grow up to be sexually abnormal. They are forever unable to breed and reproduce their species.

By comparison, if the young are allowed as little as a half-hour of play together each day, they engage in some sexual presenting and mounting play. They are clumsy and slow and do not get the hang of it until around the age of eighteen months to two years, which means they are retarded by a year or more. Even then, two out of three fail completely and forever; and those who do not fail have a low birth rate as adults.

If when the baby monkeys are allowed to play, they are restricted to having playmates only of their own sex, then when they grow up most of them stay socially with a sexual partner of their own sex. They cannot relate well with a partner of the opposite sex.

Lovemaps

The most conclusive evidence concerning the importance of sexual rehearsal play in human childhood comes from the study of tribal people whose ancient tribal ways have not been over-Westernized.[2] In some cases, the tribal tradition of child-rearing does not require that their children be punished when they engage in sexual rehearsal play, which they do from time to time, though without being obtrusive about it. Because anthropologists themselves have typically been too prudishly Victorian to have recorded sexual rehearsal play in children, there is not as much evidence as one would like. However, from the evidence available, the conclusion is that heterosexual rehearsal play in childhood lays the foundation for uncomplicated heterosexuality in adulthood.

Children get their native language by practicing it. Similarly, they get a native lovemap by practicing their sexual rehearsal play. When their play is not interfered with, the basic geography of the lovemap develops typically as heterosexual. At puberty and thereafter, when the lovemap is heterosexual, the erotic fantasies, daydreams, and nightdreams are heterosexual. So also is the fantasy of the ideal love affair and the ideal lover.

The features and requirements of the ideal lover may be fairly generalized and nonspecific, or they may be very detailed and personalized, so that only relatively few people in everyday life will qualify as perfectly matching the specifications of the lovemap. For example, the lovemap may specify that the ideal lover be a stand-in for a childhood sweetheart, or a popular hero or heroine, idolized in the early years.

It goes without saying that, in the human species as in any other species, the majority of individuals in each generation have an inbuilt determinant to have young ones, and so to replace themselves with a new generation of successors. This inbuilt determinant is phyletically programed. That is to say, it exists simply because an individual is a member of the species. Like a cluster of wild mushrooms that can push through the paving of an asphalt court, it cannot easily be sealed over. However, it can encounter abuses that interfere with its normal expression. In childhood, for example, it may be unable to express itself in normal heterosexual rehearsal play. One source of such interference is the abuse of too much prohibition, prevention, and punishment. In that case the standard heterosexual lovemap does not develop properly in the brain.

In consequence, the lovemap may become defaced in such a way that parts are missing, thus impairing in adulthood the functioning of the sex organs in genital intercourse. This is the hypophilic solution. By contrast, the hyperphilic solution is one in which the lovemap defies defacement, so that the sex organs, in adulthood, are used with exaggerated defiance, frequency, and compulsiveness, and/or with great multiplicity of partners, in pairs or in groups.

There is a third solution, one in which the lovemap is not completely defaced but redesigned with detours that include either new elements or relocations of original ones. In some, if not all, instances, the new elements or relocations may derive from a history of atypical sexual rehearsal play and/or erotosexual experience in childhood. Or they may derive from some other childhood encounter or series of encounters in which the sexual organs became stimulated—as, for instance, in receiving an enema, or a whipping. Whatever the reason, overt or covert, the continued existence of the lovemap depends on its becoming compromised and distorted, perhaps to the extent of being circuitous and changed almost beyond recognition.

A lovemap carries the program of a person's erotic fantasies and their corresponding practices. Distortions, therefore, get carried over into fantasies and practices. The foregoing case of erotic murder/suicide is an example of what can happen when a lovemap is programed to end in disaster and self-destruction. The penalty written into the boy's lovemap was that forbidden lust must be followed by the supreme sacrifice, death.

This case illustrates the basic formula of both a distorted lovemap and also the paraphilia for which it is responsible. Two terms of the formula, love and lust, are irreconcilable, and the solution is to find a third term, which in the present instance is sacrifice, with which to reconcile them.

Love is undefiled and saintly. Lust is defiling and sinful. The sinful act of lust, therefore, defiles those who participate in it. It turns the saint into a sinner—the madonna into a whore, and the provider into a playboy.

By sacrificing himself and his partner, the boy carried out a paraphilic act of atonement for the degenerate sin of carnal lust. For good measure, he sacrificed also a member of his religion class. Because the class he shot into was a religion class, it served as a reminder of the paraphilia's connections with religious doctrine on sexual sin.

Reference Notes

1. The information on rhesus monkeys was supplied by Dr. David Goldfoot and is taken from J. Money, *Love and Love Sickness*. See also Goldfoot, 1977, 1983; Goldfoot and Wallen, 1978; Goldfoot et al., 1984.

2. Sexual rehearsal play and gender dimorphic behavior in five ethnic traditions are summarized in Chapter 7 of *Man and Woman, Boy and Girl: The Differentiation and Dimorphism of Gender Identity from Conception to Maturity* (Money and Ehrhardt, 1972). The contrast between a sex-positive (Polynesian) tradition and a sex-negative (rural Irish) tradition is found in Chapters 5 and 1, respectively, of Marshall and Suggs (1971). See also Malinowski (1929).

The Paraphilic Cost
of Degeneracy Theory

Paraphilias: Distorted Lovemap Animations

The erotic fantasies and their practices or animations that are programed in distorted lovemaps are popularly known as kinky or bizarre.[1] In law and the criminal justice system, they are known as perverted, and perverted practices are known as perversions. In science and medicine, perversions are today known as paraphilias.[2] Paraphilia means love, *philia*, which is beyond the usual, *para*. There are about thirty different paraphilias, the exact count depending on whether overlapping ones are separated or not. (See Table 1.[3]) Each paraphilia has its own lovemap.

A paraphilic lovemap may not unfold itself fully at puberty, although it commonly does. Instead, the complete extent of its imagery may remain in hiding for some years, until eventually it reveals itself from beginning to end as a complete fantasy. It may first appear as a wet dream or as a masturbation fantasy. Or it may be a copulation fantasy, without which the penis will not erect (or the vagina lubricate), and the orgasm will not occur. The fantasy may be played or replayed silently in the imagination, or enacted as a paraphilic practice.

The lovemaps of the paraphilias can be understood in terms of sex strategies. Each strategy, in its own roundabout way, is a cerificate of permission to enter what would otherwise be the inaccessible city of lust and ecstasy. The price of the certificate is that the saint is sold into sin. The six strategies comprise, by type, the sacrificial paraphilias, the predatory paraphilias, the mercantile paraphilias, the fetish paraphilias, the eligibility paraphilias, and the allurement paraphilias.

In individual cases, a paraphilia of one type may share characteristics of another type. It is rare, however, for a person to have more than one paraphilia, or to change from one to another. A lovemap, once it has formed, is rather uniquely personalized. It tends to be remarkably stable throughout life—quite the opposite of what degeneracy theory would lead one to believe.

According to the evidence available today, paraphilias occur more often and in more varieties in boys and men than they do in girls and women. This inequality may derive from the fact that nature has designed males more than females to be dependent on their eyes for erotic turn on, and females to be more dependent than males on skin feelings. Lovemaps get into the brain mostly through the eyes, which is in contrast with language, which gets in through the ears.

More boys than girls have difficulty in getting their native language, and in learning to read it. It appears that they also have more difficulty in getting their lovemaps. It is easier for misprints to occur. In some boys it may be easier than in others. Their brains may be geared in such a way that they are more vulnerable to misprint errors. Vulnerable or not, the brain does not program a misprint into its lovemap without instructions coming into it from the eyes and ears and the other senses. These instructions come in during the critical map-making years of early childhood. These are the years when sexual degeneracy theory, outmoded but still socially influential, lurks in a child's life like a polluted smog in biological warfare and sabotages the lovemap instructions that the brain receives. Consequently, the lovemap program gets misprinted, and the misprinting may turn out to be a paraphilia.

The same paraphilic misprintings may occur regardless of whether the partner relationship will prove to be, over the long term, homosexual or heterosexual or bisexual. The programing of the pathways of the sexual brain that governs the erotic matching of the partnership is another story, most of the details of which remain to be discovered—including the details that might relate to the covert residual influence of degeneracy theory.

Some of the paraphilias are playful and harmless. Some are an unwelcome nuisance to a partner who does not reciprocate their fantasy content. Some are dangerous and destructive, notwithstanding a consenting partner.[4] Some of those that are legally classified as sex offenses are violently dangerous, and some, like exhibitionism, are harmless offenses against modesty.

The Sacrificial Paraphilias

The sacrificial paraphilias are those in which one or both of the partners must atone for the wicked and degenerate act of defiling the saint with ecstatic lust by undergoing an act of penance or sacrifice. The penalty ranges from humiliation and hurt to a blood sacrifice and death. Self-sacrifice is masochism; partner-sacrifice is sadism. Either may be consenting or enforced.

TABLE 1

Paraphilias

Acrotomophilia (amputee partner)
Apotemnophilia (self-amputee)
Asphyxiophilia (self-strangulation)
Autagonistophilia (on stage)
Autassassinophilia (own murder staged)
Autonepiophilia (diaperism)
Coprophilia (feces)
Ephebophilia (youth)
Erotophonophilia (lust murder)
Fetishism
Frotteurism (rub against stranger)
Gerontophilia (elder)
Hyphephilia (fabrics)
Infantophilia (infants)
Kleptophilia (stealing)
Klismaphilia (enema)
Masochism
Mysophilia (filth)

Narratophilia (erotic talk)
Necrophilia (corpse)
Olfactophilia (smell)
Pedophilia (child)
Pictophilia (pictures)
Peiodeiktophilia (penile exhibitionism)
Rapism or Biastophilia (violent assault)
Sadism
Scoptophilia (watching coitus)
Somnophilia (sleeper)
Stigmatophilia (piercing; tattoo)
Symphorophilia (disaster)
Telephone scatophilia (lewdness)
Troilism (couple + one)
Urophilia or undinism (urine)
Voyeurism or Peeping-Tomism
Zoophilia (animal)

Masochistic death may be autoerotic (masturbatory) suicide, or the finale of a self-staged murder of oneself enacted in collaboration with a sadistic partner. Sadistic death, in all probability, is rarely invited. More likely, it is violent and imposed without forewarning. The victim may be either spouse, companion, or stranger. There may be many victims. Multiple lust murder is the most gruesome of the paraphilias, and the one that provokes the most public outrage and the most severe criminal punishment.

The repertory of sadomasochistic sacrifice varies in degree of harmfulness and playfulness. At one extreme are the acts of a merciless Dracula: horror, shock, assault, brutality, and torture. At the other extreme are the acts of a velvet dragon: games of humiliation, bondage, punishment, and discipline. At either extreme the participants may have been previously acquainted or not. They may participate together by mutual consent. There is one sadistic scenario, however, in which it must be an unsuspecting partner or stranger who is subjected to unprovoked outrage, suffering, and abuse.

The sadomasochistic sacrifice is not, of necessity, directed at the sex organs. Either the sadist or the masochist may find erotic arousal from other afflictions of the body, and of the mind. But there are some instances of direct mutilation of the sex organs, some of them by consent of the victim. The sex organs may be bound, beaten, squeezed, stretched, penetrated, pierced, or cut.

In some, if not all cases of erotic masochism, the first pain that a procedure produces fades and becomes transformed into sensuous ecstasy. In religious and penitential masochism, such as flagellation and being harnessed to flesh hooks, a similar transformation may also be experienced.

Sadomasochistic, hand-in-glove partner-matching is difficult to achieve, as it requires that the fantasies of the two people match reciprocally. There is an insufficiency of sadistic women to match up with the excess of men who, though brokers of immense political, business, or industrial power by day, are submissive masochists begging for erotic punishment and humiliation by night.

A special form of sacrificial paraphilia, for which a suitable name is symphorophilia (being erotically turned on by accidents or catastrophes), culminates in an arranged disaster, such as an automobile crash. Like a game of Russian roulette, it may end in death—alone or with the partner. However, flirting with disaster, rather than suicide and murder, is the trigger responsible for erotic arousal and excitement. Being the daredevil who will live to risk a love-death again is an essential part of this paraphilia.

As a photographic print is the positive made from its negative, so also the positive of self-crashing is arranging for a disaster to occur on the highway or elsewhere and then watching the carnage from a preselected observation post. Disasters other than on the highway may be arranged—catastrophic fires, for example. For those members of the general public who have a touch of sadomasochism in them, disaster as an unrehearsed event is often a large part of the appeal of entertainment stunts and sports, from the circus to stock-car racing, and their replay in media coverage. Public executions once served the same function, and their detailed media coverage still does so. Fantasy imagery for the sado-masochist is readily provided in daily television programs.

The Predatory Paraphilias

The predatory paraphilias are those in which the wicked and degenerate ecstasy of the sinful act of lust is so defiling that it can be indulged only if it is stolen, or taken from the saint by force. The person experiencing one of this group of paraphilias may have the fantasy of being either predator or prey. Though it is not known for sure, it is probably fairly rare for predator and prey to match up with one another, except by setting themselves up in mutually consenting play-acting. Thieving, by definition, is taking something without permission, and so is plundering and rapine.

The most notorious of the predatory paraphilias is biastophilic rapism, or raptophilia. The raptophilic lovemap prescribes that the partner, typically a stranger, should be unsuspecting of what is about to happen, and should be maximally terror-stricken and resistant, until the fantasy enactment has run its course.

Biastophilia may include breaking and entering, and stealing things as well as stealing sexual intercourse by force. The things stolen may be of value, or they may be more in the nature of tokens. In some cases, stealing alone takes place as a substitute for genital intercourse.

In the "sleeping-princess syndrome" (somnophilia) the sexual approach is a gentle and nonviolent stealing of caresses after breaking and entering, maybe involving cunnilingus, but not necessarily followed by penovaginal intercourse. Of course it is generally mistaken for rape.

Stealing as a paraphilia may also manifest itself as kidnaping or elopement. Though totally unprepared for the event, the victim may become devotedly bonded to the abductor in a way that totally bewilders those unacquainted with this paradoxical phenomenon (the so-called Stockholm syndrome[5]).

The Mercantile Paraphilias

In the mercantile paraphilias the wicked and degenerate ecstasy of the sinful act of lust is the social vice practiced only by whores and hustlers for pay. Saintly people do not defile themselves with lust. Therefore, if a saint does become sexual from time to time, the act is equated with taking on the role of a sinful whore or hustler, or of one of their customers. The mercantile paraphilia is not necessarily actual prostitution, for it may be the impersonation of prostitution with an orthodox partner in a conventional home life.

In some mercantile paraphilic fantasies, there are elaborate ruses and pretenses of prostitution. In troilism, for example, it is a third person, maybe a stranger, whose role is to create an illusion of prostitution. Thus a husband leaves a phone number and invitation in a public place for another man to have intercourse with hs wife. He watches, and while watching is enabled to get an erection. Then he achieves penetration and orgasm, which is not possible except when his wife plays the role of a whore.

In a related paraphilia, a man is able to have the same success if he talks to his partner as if she were a whore, and if she responds in character. A woman, by contrast, may have the fantasy that her husband is a casual pickup, or gigolo. The enactment of this fantasy may in either partner include paying, or having money demanded.

Another prostitution fantasy that has widespread male appeal is that of two women involved in wicked and degenerate lust together. Not only is the stimulus in duplicate, but the two Jezebels cry out for rescue from themselves, and he of course is the male who can do it.

The Fetish Paraphilias

The fetish paraphilias are those in which a compromise is made with the saintliness of chastity and abstinence not by trafficking with prostitution but by including in the sexual act a token that symbolizes the wickedness and degeneracy of the sinful act of ecstatic lust. The token symbolically permits the partner to remain as if saintly, pure, and undefiled. The token is a fetish, and it is the fetish that is the sinful agent of erotic and sexual excitement and arousal. For example, undergarments, especially brassieres and panties or garter belts and stockings, are a fetishistic turn-on for countless American males. In some cases they are stolen from laundry lines. Erotically, they may be more important than the woman who wears them. In the case of the transvestite male, they must be worn by the man himself before he can perform genitally. If his partner objects, then he must fantasy that he is wearing them in order to perform successfully.

Fetishistic inclusion objects are, with great frequency, sexy because of their texture (hyphephilias; the feely fetishes) or their smell. A rubber fetish combines feel and smell. It almost certainly has its origin traceable, at least in part, to the rubber training pants formerly popular for infants. Plastic will presumably take the place of rubber in the future. A diaper fetish has a similar early origin, presumably, and so does an enema fetish (klismaphilia).

Like the sexual act itself, many fetishes are related to the tabooed parts of the body, their smells, and their functions—crotch smells, for example, and soiled underclothing or articles of menstrual hygiene; and the products of elimination that are ingested and smeared in urophilia and coprophilia.

The Eligibility Paraphilias

The eligibility paraphilias are those in which self-abandonment to the wicked and degenerate ecstasy of the sinful act of lust can be achieved only if the partner qualifies as eligible by reason of being beyond the pale, that is, beyond the limits, privileges, and protection of being saintly and undefilable. By some criterion or other, the partner must qualify as an erotic pagan or heathen, not at all resembling the likes of one's own parents, who in the proverbial wisdom of many children would never do anything so dirty as genital intercourse. The criterion may quite literally be that of belonging to another religious faith.

Interfaith marriage, by itself alone, need not be a paraphilia, for one of the yardsticks by which a paraphilia is measured is that it is addictively repetitious and compulsive. This same yardstick applies to all of the eligibility paraphilias.

Instead of religious affiliation, the criterion of being an outsider may be that of racial or nationality type and color. The specifications of what the partner should look like may be extremely detailed—blue-eyed and blond, genitally large, facially lopsided with a crooked smile, or with a wash-board furrowed brow, and so on.

The entire physique may be involved, as when the specification requires that the partner be dwarfed or giant in height; fat or skinny in weight; disfigured, deformed, or crippled in appearance, and so on. The ultimate extreme of erotic eligibility distancing is in necrophilia: the partner must be dead.

Social or occupational status, rather than physique, may be the criterion that establishes an erotic eligibility distance between oneself and a partner. The occupational status that is probably the most prevalent as the basis of an eligibility paraphilia is that of paramour. A paramour relationship exists outside the institution of marriage and is legally defined as adultery or fornication. It may be long term or short term, living together or living apart. Only a thin line divides this type of relationship from a paid one with a courtesan or gigolo, especially if, in both instances, the relationship is a continuing one with one person. Marriage ruins such a relationshp, because it respectabilizes it and robs it of the ecstasy of lust, which is stigmatized as defiling, naughty, and illicit, as well as wicked and degenerate.

Rough and sweaty labor as compared with cultured and perfumed leisure is another example: occupational and social-class disparity serves to establish an erotic eligibility distance between the self and partner. Uniforms as insignia of occupation may play an important, almost fetishistic ancillary role.

Along with or in place of a uniform, body tattoos may be insignia of tough occupational status. For some people, the eroticizing of a tattoo is accompanied by erotic piercing (stigmatophilia) and the wearing of gold rings and rods in the nipples and genitals as well as in other parts of the body.

In some paraphilias alterations of the body go far beyond tattoo and piercing and involve mutilation and/or surgical amputation, amateur or professional, of the genitalia or limbs. In the paraphilia of acrotomophilia, erotic eligibility requires that the partner be an amputee, or a person born with a birth defect of missing limbs.[6] Erotic turn-on is to the stump. The counterpart is apotemnophilia, a paraphilic compulsion to get oneself amputated. In some cases the person stage-manages an injury, by means of a planned hunting accident, for example, so as to ensure a professional amputation in a hospital.

Surgical alteration applies in some instances not to the limbs but to the genital organs. In males only rarely is genital amputation not associated also with a more pervasive transposition of gender status, namely, the compulsion to be reassigned to live as a member of the other sex. In either sex, surgical and hormonal reassignment completes a male/female or female/male transposition of erotic eligibility. Some individuals are highly responsive to a sex-reassigned partner, more so than they are to a nonreassigned man or woman. In the same vein, among men there are some whose ideal fantasy is fulfilled by a lady with a penis, that is, a surgically unreassigned transexual who takes female hormones to feminize the body from male to female and who lives full time as a woman—a gynemimetic.

Age matching, like male/female matching, is a routine social norm of erotic eligibility. Discrepancies, when they exist, are yet another circumvention of the conventional norm. They effect a social distancing that serves to circumvent the wickedness-depravity conception of lust and to preserve its ecstasy. The age-discrepancy paraphilias are gerontophilia, ephebophilia, and pedophilia (which includes infantophilia).

In gerontophilia, a young adult is subjectively compelled always to have a partner old enough to be either a parent or, in some instances, a grandparent. In ephebophilia, an older person is subjectively compelled always to have a partner who is in the adolescent age range. In pedophilia, an adolescent or adult is subjectively compelled to have a partner who is pubertal or juvenile. The mathematician Charles L. Dodgson (1832-1898), better known as Lewis Carroll, author of *Alice's Adventures in Wonderland* and other books for juveniles, was a pedophilic lover of prepubertal girls.[7] Sir James Barrie (1860-1937), author of *Peter Pan*, was a pedophilic lover of prepubertal boys.[8]

The pedophile is a Peter Pan whose erotic age does not advance with birthday age. Likewise the age of the partner stays always in childhood, so that the relationship is a mixture of parent-child and lover-lover bonding. Often the adult pedophile has had, in childhood, a relationship with an older partner. A pedophile relationship wanes and breaks up when the younger partner gets to be adolescent. Similarly, an ephebophile relationship may wane and break up as adolescence advances into the maturity of young adulthood. Some divorces occur on this account, if one or both of the partners is an ephebophile. Erotically, they are unable to advance in age together, for the ephebophile is compulsively driven to have a new partner of nubile age.

A pedophile and ephebophile relationship within the family, even when there is no blood relationship, is a particularly disruptive double-bind. The sanctions of the incest taboo are so threatening and devastating that those involved are almost inevitably damned if they do and damned if they don't disclose the existence of the relationship and try to leave it.

All the foregoing specifications and provisos that dictate a degree of erotic distancing between the self and an eligible partner apply to human beings. In zoophilia, the distance that separates is the distance between species. Pets are for petting, and so are lovers. No one knows the prevalence of genital-genital contact between species, but it is not restricted to human-animal contacts. It may happen between other species also.[9] Among human beings, especially the erotically isolated, non-penetrating stimulation of the crotch by a pet may be a more prevalent comfort than is generally believed.

The Allurement Paraphilias

The allurement paraphilias are displacement paraphilias, whereas those in the foregoing five categories are inclusion paraphilias. The inclusion is some more or less extraneous quality, ritual, or artifact not typically a component of heterosexual mating practices. A displacement paraphilia is one that involves a segment of the preparatory phase of an erotic and sexual activity before genital intercourse begins. This is the phase of eye-talk and finger-talk, when the partners give signals or invitations to one another. They flirt, coquet, woo, or lure one another. It is sometimes known as the phase of courtship or, in animals, as the phase of the mating dance or display.

In a displacement paraphilia, some part of the preparatory or courtship phase pushes its way into center field, instead of remaining on the sidelines. It displaces the main event, which is genital intercourse, and steals the limelight. In this way, the wicked and degenerate ecstasy of the sinful act of lust is disconnected from the sacred act of genital union, and displaced onto a substitute act. The saint is thus redeemed from defilement. This strategy of disconnection is a rather sneaky one, for the build-up of ecstatic lust can be brought back to the marriage bed and used to power the sexual organs into a successful performance. Without this auxiliary power, they might fail. Exhibitionism is an example.

The paraphilia of exhibitionism has its origins in the primate courtship or allurement ritual of displaying the genitalia as an invitation to copulation. The paraphilic male exhibitionist is compulsively driven to display his penis (peiodeiktophilia) in erection so as to elicit from a stranger a startle response ranging from curiosity or surprise to alarm or panic. A neutral response, for example, telling him that a penis should be covered in public, will bring the episode to a docile end.

In some instances, it is possible to retrieve and authenticate information of early-childhood erotic pleasure associated with showing the penis in erection, and maybe of defiance in response to being chastised for doing so. In adulthood, the peak intensity of ecstatic feeling associated with exhibitionism, even without ejaculation, surpasses that of orgasm in genital intercourse. Punishment and imprisonment do not prevent recurrence. It is extremely rare for exhibitionism to include any activity other than display of the penis, even though many people fear that it will lead to an attempt at genital intercourse, perhaps by coercion.

The opposite of showing is looking, which in paraphilic terms means voyeurism or being a Peeping Tom. The voyeur learns from experience where he is likely to find lighted and uncurtained windows, and where, at night, he may glimpse a female occupant undressing. His erotic excitement is in the forbidden act of looking at her. It is rare that he will attempt to meet with or communicate with her. He may make noise that attracts attention to his loitering and gets him arrested. If a woman sees him through the window and continues to appear naked, he may exhibit his penis and masturbate, though it is not usual for one person to be both an exhibitionist and a voyeur.

The erotic distancing achieved in both exhibitionism and peeping is achieved also in explicitly erotic telephone-calling. The recipient may be a stranger, or a consenting listener. Professional consenting listeners, trained to take part in erotic telephone fantasies, charge for their play-acting role on the telephone.

The erotic telephone-caller has counterparts in those whose primary sexual turn-on is not genital sex with a partner but erotic narrations or readings. Similarly there are those who look at erotic burlesque shows, picture books, or movies, and those who take erotic pictures, videotapes, or movies of themselves (autagonistophilia). All of these entertainments occupy center stage instead of being preliminaries, when they are paraphilias. When shared with a partner, they augment arousal and genital performance. The contents of the entertainments do not necessarily match what happens with the partner. In one case, for example, a man's maximum turn-on was from sermons, from which he could ejaculate, without using his hands to stimulate his penis, in church.

Erotic distancing is achieved despite body contact in frotteurism. This is the paraphilia in which erotic arousal, and maybe orgasm also, are achieved anonymously by rubbing and pressing against a stranger in a crowded public place, like a subway car or bus. The stranger sometimes may reciprocate.

Reference Notes

1. Material in this chapter is taken from Money (1984), "Paraphilias: Phenomenology and Classification."

2. Definition: A paraphilia is an erotosexual condition of being recurrently responsive to, and obsessively dependent on, an unusual, personally or socially unacceptable stimulus, perceptual or in fantasy, in order to have a state of erotic arousal initiated or maintained, and in order to achieve or facilitate orgasm. For examples, see Table 1.

3. The classification of the paraphilias in Table 1 supersedes those of Money 1977; 1980. The following new terms in Table 1 were formed from Greek roots in collaboration with Diskin Clay, professor of Greek, Johns Hopkins University: acrotomophilia; apotemnophilia; autagonistophilia; autonepiophilia; erotophonophilia; peiodeiktophilia; biastophilia; stigmatophilia; and symphorophilia.

4. The criterion of where to draw the dividing line has long been contentious and difficult for society and the law with respect to both personal erotosexual practices and their portrayal in published pornography. For more detail on this issue see Money (1979), *Sexual Dictatorship, Dissidence and Democracy*. For an applied example in couple counseling, see Money, 1981; and in child abuse, Money and Werlwas, 1982.

5. The term *Stockholm syndrome* originated with the case of a female Swedish hostage in a bank robbery. She became so attached to one of her abductors that she maintained the attachment while he was in prison and broke off her engagement to her former lover.

6. Acrotomophilia was first named by Money, Jobaris, and Furth (1977), along with its counterpart, apotemnophilia. A group of people who have an erotic fascination with amputation have named their fascination *amelotasis* (etymology: a = without; melos = limbs; tasis = desiring). See Natress, 1978; Dixon and Dixon, 1983.

7. Dodgson wrote *Alice's Adventures in Wonderland* to entertain one of his juvenile friends. He lavished much care on daguerreotype nude studies of girlhood and experimented with techniques of coloring them. He destroyed most of them before his death, but four copies, given to the mothers of the subjects, have survived (Cohen, 1979).

8. Barrie became an as-if member of the family of Arthur and Sylvia Llewelyn Davies and an intimate of their five sons, George, Jack, Peter, Michael, and Nico. The wooded, shallow lake at his summer place became the scene of a game of Boy Castaways that Barrie devised for the older boys in the summer of 1901. By 1906, this game had metamorphosed into the play *Peter Pan*. Barrie himself was the prototype of the boy who never grew up (Birkin, 1979).

9. Pairbonding and attempted mating between different species is relatively rare and is related to atypical experiences of cross-species contact earlier in life. See Maple (1977).

CHAPTER
18

Degeneracy and
Social Contagion Theory

Tragedy into Triumph

Neither the fantasies nor the actions of a paraphiliac are socially contagious. They are not preferences borrowed from movies, books, or other
people. They are not voluntary choices. They cannot be controlled by
will-power. Punishment does not prevent them, and persecution does not
eradicate them, but feeds them and strengthens them. They are an
addiction, or the equivalent of an addiction, and they are defiantly
autonomous and persistent. They are theatrical and showy. Their vanity
leads the paraphiliac to self-incrimination.

The person afflicted with a paraphilia is like a survivor of a concentration camp. He (or she) repeatedly goes public to disclose the story of
how he turned the tragedy of persecution into the triumph of survival.
The tragedy that deprived him of heterosexual normality was the neglect
and/or abuse of the heterosexual rehearsal play and development that are
normal and healthy in early life. Instead, a paraphilic substitute took their
place. The triumph that counterbalanced the tragedy was the paraphilic
formula whereby lust was saved from total wreckage or extinction. It was
transferred to a substitute source of arousal—one that seemed at the time
less prevented and less censored. It was a hollow triumph, alas, for
paraphilic sexuality commonly carries with it a cost that is paid later in
life in the currency of more personal suffering and tragedy.

Knowing the developmental history of a paraphilia is not the same as
knowing the whole explanation of its cause. There is no final certainty as
to how one particular paraphilic fantasy instead of another gets personalized, though it seems to be related at least in part to a personalized
experience of early genital arousal. For example, it is often possible to pin
down an early history of too much fussing with enemas in the infancy of
those who as adults have klismaphilia—an obsession with getting an
enema as a subtitute for genital intercourse.

Apart from the issue of the personalization of a particular paraphilia,

149

there is the larger question of why there should be as many paraphilias as there are and no more. The brain may be species-limited as to how many paraphilias it can invent. That is to say, there may be a limit to how many types of behavior not specific to the reproductive act can become attached to erotic arousal.[1]

Once a paraphilia gets lodged in the brain, it is like an addiction that firmly resists dislodging. It is additionally like an addiction in that it needs a new "fix," or repetition, every so often. In between fixes, an outsider would not even suspect its existence. But, when it is in action, then it may put the person who has it into what resembles a spell, or a trancelike state; he or she is almost like a robot doing things that he or she normally would not do. As aforementioned, in the case of an exhibitionist flashing his penis to a stranger, if the woman, instead of being startled or scared, would tell him that this was no place to have his penis showing and that it should be in his pants, then the spell would be broken, and the compulsion to exhibit would cease for the time being—according to the actual testimony of a patient.

Paraphilias are found more often, and in greater variety, in men than in women. Many paraphilic men are able to have several ejaculations, as many as ten a day, compulsively. Usually they must either carry out, or replay in imagination, while masturbating or having genital intercourse, the personalized scenario of the paraphilic fantasy.

Paraphilic fantasies and behavior, as aforesaid, are not caused by social contagion. A person who does not have klismaphilia can look at five, fifty, or five hundred enema movies of someone getting erotically and genitally turned on by getting an enema, and never be able to get turned on that way himself or herself. Klismaphilic movies are a turn-on only for people who have klismaphilia. For other people they are a curiosity, though to see more than one is uninteresting and a chore.

Scandal and Pornography

Curiosity about information that is forbidden or withheld is the basis of gossip. Revelation of the forbidden, or of as much of it as can be dared, is scandal. In the media and in advertising, scandal is a major industry. Sexual revelations are the mainstay of the scandal industry. Political revelations are a runner up, but they do not make headlines as sensational as sexual revelations do.

Some sexual revelations are about the sex lives of actual people that leak out in court cases and gossip columns and hit the headlines. But they are a minority compared with those that, though true to life, are fabricated especially for the entertainment media. Some are heavily censored, some lightly, and some are erotically explicit and uncensored. The more explicit the depiction of erotic and sexual activities, naked and below the belt, the greater the likelihood that the story, picture book, movie, or soap opera will be branded as pornographic and obscene.[2]

Pornography, in its Greek derivation, means the writing of or about harlots. *Obscenity* means language or acts that are offensive to chastity or modesty. Material that is pornographic and obscene is, therefore, material that deals with whores instead of madonnas, and with lust instead of love. Instead of being modest and chaste, as a madonna-wife ought to be with her provider-husband, pornography is explicit about lust. It depicts openly and without shame the sorts of things that might be expected of a whore and a playboy—lust for its own sake, instead of exclusively as a pregnancy duty.

Lust for its own sake is the same as the venerable sin of passion, long condemned by the church. It is the same as what Sylvester Graham and the Victorians condemned as concupiscence, the vice of thoughts and imaginations that stir the penis to erect and the vagina to lubricate. Concupiscence, then, is what makes pornography a vice.

Graham and the Victorians blamed concupiscence as a cause of degeneracy, and Comstock ensured that pornography was classified as a prime source of concupiscence. They blamed infirmities of the body on degeneracy. Today's Victorians, unable to ignore germ theory, must limit degeneracy to moral degeneracy. They oversimplify the definition of moral degeneracy to include anything from the fall of ancient Rome to unwed pregnancy. Their argument is circular. Pornography is blamed as a social contagion that causes moral degeneracy, which causes the social contagion to spread, which causes an increase in pornography, which causes an increase in moral degeneracy, and so on.

The Market for Pornography

Those who fall into the trap of this circular reasoning offer as proof of their argument the allegation that commercial pornography is getting more and more degenerate. They are wrong, and their error is historical. The recent history of pornography is that it has been expanding from explicitly sexual stories and postcards to encompass new and cheaper techniques of color-printed picture books and color movies and videotapes. With each technical advance, the industry saturates first the regular heterosexual and homosexual markets and then enters the more esoteric specialty market of the paraphilias.

Pornography that depicts homosexuality has only a cursory, curiosity appeal on the heterosexual market, and vice versa. The steady customers of specialized paraphilic pornography are those who themselves have the particular paraphilia. For others it has only one-shot curiosity appeal. Most of the paraphilias have so small a population that there is no commercial pornography portraying them.

The explicit depiction of erotic subject-matter could just as well be labeled erotography as pornography. Pornography is pejorative and automatically condemns the material as bad. Erotography is a neutral term. If erotic pictures or stories appeal to you, they are those that more or less correspond to your own lovemap. They may have an almost automatic power to turn you on erotically when you first encounter them. Then, very rapidly, they lose that automatic power and take their place as an erotic stimulus in your life only if your system is erotically ready to be stimulated. They do not enslave you, and they do not take you on a downhill slide from depravity to depravity. All that they do is increase the enjoyment of your next sexual experience, which will be of the same type as you normally have, with or without a partner, and with or without a change of partner. The timing of the experience may or may not be sooner than would otherwise have been the case. The variety of things that you discover you can enjoy doing erotically may or may not be enlarged on the basis of what you read or see; and you may or may not become a more expert lover.

A sexually somewhat reticent young man once told me that he became a more expert lover after seeing the famous pornographic movie *Deep Throat*. He was a radio engineer in Antarctica at the time and had been on a search mission for a party overtaken by a blizzard. His own party had arrived at an American base camp where, exhausted, they had to rest up. The movie was part of the Americans' leisure-time entertainment. It was being shown under the auspices of the American government. Back in New York City, the same movie had been seized by the same goverment on an obscenity charge. I was an expert witness at the trial. The case was lost in New York, but *Deep Throat* kept circulating in Antarctica, nonetheless, and in many other places as well.

Porno movies that are primarily heterosexual and not outlandishly paraphilic are often used to defuse sexual tension when men are segregated together for long periods of time without the company of women. They are used on a submarine, for example. Soon, no doubt, they will be shown to astronauts on space voyages.

Definition of Pornography

The old definition of pornography was in terms of concupiscence, that is, whether it aroused the genitals or not. That definition assumed that concupiscent arousal was always bad. Even if husband and wife turned each other on erotically, that would be pornographic, or the next best thing to it!

No prosecutor could win an argument along those lines before a jury in a pornography trial today. Most men and women serving on a jury believe that explicit stories, movies, or pictures of plain heterosexual activity are not pornographic, even though they might vote to restrict their circulation. Therefore, jurors struggle to find the dividing line between erotically normal and pornographic pictures (almost all trials are nowadays not about reading material but pictures and movies).

That means that the definition of pornography becomes shifted from plain sex (heterosexual) to so-called kinky sex (paraphilic). But that shift doesn't help, because kinky sex doesn't appeal to plain-sex people. Instead or arousing them, it leaves them cold. It certainly doesn't degenerate them.

Pornographic degeneracy theory simply doesn't hold up in the court room. It lost its power with the discovery of germ theory. In all the rest of medicine, degeneracy theory has been tossed out the window. It lingers on only in sexual medicine. Though its name be changed from degeneracy to depravity, it effectively makes judges, juries, and attorneys for the prosecution and defense alike masquerade as fools, because degeneracy theory is just plain wrong.

One of the justices of the United States Supreme Court, Justice Potter Stewart, said a few years ago that he might not be able to give an intelligible definition of pornography but that "I know it when I see it."[3] That is the criterion that most people use. What it amounts to is that you rate explicit sexual material as pornographic if you feel like a sneaky Pete, reading or looking at material for which, earlier in your life, had you been caught at it, you would have been doomed to punishment. There is no absolute definition of pornography and no absolute criterion to use in the courtroom.

The U.S. Supreme Court struggled with this problem in the *Miller* case of 1973,[4] but to no avail. Still unchanged, the criteria that the Court specified are three, the first being "whether the average person, applying contemporary community standards, would find that the work, taken as a whole, appeals to the prurient interest." There are three reasons this criterion fails. The average person is nobody, for nobody can be average in height, weight, religion, education, income, age, family size, attitude toward pornography, and everything else there is in which to be average. Community standards can be bad and wrong, as they were under Hitler, when the community tolerated the Holocaust of the concentration camps. *Prurient*, of which the literal meaning is "itching," is used to signify erotic arousal; but erotic arousal is not pornographic when the stimulus is a picture of one's lawful sexual partner, either fully clothed or completely nude.

The second Supreme Court criterion is "whether the work depicts or describes, in a patently offensive way, sexual conduct specifically defined by the applicable state law." This criterion fails because it passes the buck back to the laws of the individual states, the majority of which are desperately in need of being updated, witness Maryland's law that makes oral sex between married people a crime. Possession of a picture of one's own baby nude at the pool or in the bathtub is a potential federal crime, for any nude portrait of a person under the age of eighteeen can be prosecuted as pedophilic pornography. To show it is, per se, a crime.

The third Supreme Court criterion is "whether the work, taken as a whole, lacks serious literary, artistic, political, or scientific value." This criterion fails because there is no way of measuring when a value is serious and when it is not. Pornography always has serious scientific value for a scientist doing research on the effects of pornography, for example, or using it in a program for treating sex offenders.

Just about every lawmaker, judge, attorney, or arresting officer responsible for pornography laws and prosecutions had some experience with pornography while growing up or, if not then, certainly in the course of the proceedings of a pornography trial. Such persons never argue that they have been transformed into moral degenerates by what they have seen, heard, or read—and of course they haven't. Nor have the members of the jury. They know that pornography, no matter how much its explicitness may offend them, does not degenerate or deprave them as adults. So they do not argue that they should be their brothers' keepers, protecting other adult men and women (wives perhaps excepted) from pornography. Children, they say, always with the self-righteous pride of being moral on behalf of the young, are the ones who need to be protected, for they are suggestible and easily led astray.

Social Contagion Theory and Sexual Learning

The social contagion theory applied to erotic and sexual learning in childhood is wrong. It assumes that children are like paper towels that indiscriminately soak up anything wet that touches them. On the contrary, children do have discrimination. They do not come home from Sunday school and crucify their neighbors and their dolls. They learn the explicit details of how to do it, but they also are given the moral lesson of the Crucifixion, and they apply it. By contrast, on television they learn all the details of a wild-west shoot-out and the moral lesson that the bad guy always gets killed. Provided with toy guns, they apply that lesson too, and play games of killing one another.

Children grow up in a world in which pornography and explicit sex exist. No matter how much they are supposedly protected from it, they have their own agents who capture the classified documents and bring them and other sexual information back into the secret world of childhood. They may incorporate this information into their sexual rehearsal play and their erotic fantasies. But they have, more often than not, no other moral guidance than that born of the inexperience of their own-aged crowd.

Adults typically restrict not only pornography but all sexual learning. They restrict knowledge that they make available to their own children and to those of others in the community. The great debate that currently goes on about whether sex information should be in the home, church, or school is really a debate about excluding it from school so that it can be omitted altogether, in the home and in the church also.

When it is not omitted, sex education is usually about eggs, sperms, and menstrual periods, with genital intercourse glossed over. Some high school courses include birth control, pregnancy, and sexually transmitted diseases. Orgasm, positions of intercourse, and sexual delight are avoided, if not specifically excluded. Unrestricted knowledge regarding erotic imagery in all its varieties and fantasies, and its importance to love, attraction, and pairbonding, as well as to sexual enjoyment, is withheld.

When the adult world withholds explicit erotic knowledge from juveniles and adolescents, it applies to them the last vestiges of degeneracy theory. Its official policy is that they will be victimized by explicit sex and pornography and become degenerate and depraved by putting it indiscriminately into practice.

The reverse, in fact, is true. Children are victimized by lack of education on explicit sex and pornography. They are deprived not only of the actual knowledge but also of the opportunity to learn the moral principles that apply to explicit sex and pornography in their own lives.

Lacking political rights, children and teenagers have no recourse to the insult and injustice of being the victims of the last vestiges of degeneracy theory. There are only two reactions available to them. One is to succumb to defeat. The other is to become defiant and to resist defeat. Neither reaction brings with it a sense of well-being, nor of family and social harmony. The upshot, in today's world, is that teen-age, in the media and among professionals, is measured in degrees of turmoil and treated as if it were a disease. Teenaged pregnancy is despised as one of its chief symptoms. Though reluctant to admit it, America really does think contemptuously of teenaged sex as degenerate and withholds its moral and economic respect from teenaged parents.

The average age of first use of birth control in teen-age is in fact going down. However, it is about two years behind the average age of first genital intercourse, which does, therefore, mean the risk of pregnancy.[5] By their own admission, some early teenagers consciously set out to be young parents. Many others become pregnant not by plan but because it is easier for them to risk pregnancy than to obtain effective contraception without being chastised as morally degenerate for using it. That is an example of the moral contagion of degeneracy theory biting the hand of the society that feeds it!

Reference Notes

1. There are two parts to the question of how a particular person develops a particular paraphilia. One part requires a personalized biographical answer in terms of that person's unique psychobiological history. The other part requires a more general phylogenetic answer in terms of the range of nonsexual behavioral programs that the human brain is capable of coupling with the erotically sexual. This latter issue is addressed in *Paraphilia: Phyletic Origins of Erotosexual Dysfunction* (Money, 1981).

2. Answers to the questions about pornography that have been put to the test of experiment are reviewed in Money and Athanasiou (1973).

3. Quoted in the 1971 *Technical Report* (vol. 2, p. 15) of the Commission on Obscenity and Pornography.

4. *Miller vs. California.* 413 U.S. 15 (1973).

5. The most extensive contemporary demographic research into teenaged sexuality and reproduction is that of John F. Kantner, Melvin Zelnik, and associates of the Johns Hopkins School of Hygiene and Public Health. See Zelnik, Kantner, and Ford (1981). Personal fears and considerations that govern the first use of contraception by females in teen-age are reported in Zabin and Clark (1981).

CHAPTER
19

Legacy of Degeneracy Theory in Sexual and Social Health

Sexual Change and Backlash

Degeneracy theory, like the eavesdropping of espionage, has effectively censored the truthful and public transmission of erotic and sexual knowledge. This censorship applies not only to children and teenagers but also to the very professionals, doctors, and pastors who have been allegedly the experts and the counselors in cases of need. In its Victorian heyday, degeneracy was all that medical students knew about human sexuality, apart from midwifery and diseases and surgery of the genital tract. There was little change until the intellectual earthquakes of dissent hit society in the anti-Vietnam and Hippie movements of the 1960s and 1970s.

One spin-off of that movement was an impetus toward increased honesty of sexual knowledge everywhere, medicine included. Beginning with Indiana, under the shadow of the Kinsey Institute for Sex Research, medical schools began to teach courses in sexual medicine. The illustrations were explicit slides and movies that were still classified under the law as pornographic. The method was adapted from the SAR (sexual attitude restructuring, or reassessment) pioneered by the National Sex Forum, now part of the Institute for the Advanced Study of Human Sexuality, in San Francisco.

The usefulness of sexual medicine courses was that they prepared students to diagnose sexual and erotic afflictions correctly. If they were not prepared to treat them themselves, they knew when to refer their patients to a specialist. Following the example of Masters and Johnson (1970) a new specialty of sex therapy grew up, practiced partly by physicians and partly by paramedical specialists, for the treatment of impotence, so-called frigidity, and other problems of the marital (or cohabitational) bed. Eventually, this form of therapy became extended to the rehabilitation of the physically handicapped and injured and those whose genital function was adversely affected by other diseases.

At The Johns Hopkins Hospital, new subspecialties developed for the combined surgical, hormonal, and sexological treatment of birth defects of the sex organs (Money, 1968), sex reassignment in transexualism (Benjamin, 1966; Green and Money, 1969), and combined hormonal and counseling therapy of sex offenders (Money, 1970).

The challenge of revolutionary change in human affairs is a threat to those whose conservative lives are ordered by conformity to the status quo. Change is, therefore, commonly followed by a backlash. The backlash in sexual medicine began to be felt by the late 1970s, and it is still increasingly endorsed by those who hold the reins and the funds of power. Progressively, sexual medicine courses have been dropped from some medical schools and curtailed in others. Degeneracy theory has been given a reprieve.

Pediatric Sexology

Even before the backlash began, pediatric sexology was a major casualty of degeneracy theory. Sexual and erotic development is the only branch of child development that is excluded from textbooks on child development. We poke and probe into every other aspect of child health, measuring and analyzing and using million-dollar machines. We scan what happens inside the skull, in the brain. But sexual development is subject to a scary taboo that even a Nobel Prize winner, through fear of being stigmatized, found excuses to avoid breaking rather than lend his prestige to fund raising.

There is no textbook of pediatrics that has a chapter or section on children's sexual and erotic health and its developmental disorders. Textbooks of child psychiatry have the same omission, even though they may include a section on the psychoanalytic theory of the stages of psychosexual development and the oedipus complex.

What the textbooks exclude, so also do the children's hospitals. There is no hospital in the country that has a special clinic for the sexological disorders of childhood. There are clinics for virtually every aspect of child health except sexual and erotic health. The absence of such a clinic can have a major adverse effect on the development of many patients, such as in the case of a girl with premature onset of puberty at the age of five. The pediatrician in charge of her case may send her to a gynecologist for a vaginal examination. The examination requires her to do what at home she has been forbidden to do—to show her sexual organs to an audience of strangers, and to have a man poke his finger into her vagina, and into her anus for a rectal examination. For her, the experience may be the equivalent of sexual abuse and rape, but if she objects she is scolded, humiliated, or punished. She reacts with panic and develops a phobia of doctors and hospitals, as a result of which she is beaten when she disobediently runs away rather than go to the hospital for her next appointment.

No one explains to her why she needs to go to the clinic, except that she is "growing too fast." Her mother refuses to let anyone talk to her to give the beginnings of sex education, because she is convinced it will be morally harmful to a child her age and might teach her depraved things that she ought not to know. Moreover, the endocrinologist holds out the promise of a new and experimental hormonal treatment with an LHRH analog that will retard the progress of her pubertal development, provided she gets an injection every three days for as long as two years, or more.

The end result of a scenario like this one is that fifteen years later the girl freezes up every time she tries to have intercourse. She has a phobia of vaginal penetration. She and her husband want a baby, but she can't have intercourse and can't cope with the prospect of more gynecological examinations, nor of delivery. She has no pregnancy. Her only prospect of parenthood is by adoption.

Though there is no guarantee that a specialty of pediatric sexology will solve all the sexological complications of childhood, the very fact that pediatric sexology clinics exist would soon allow the public to agree that it is respectable to use them and to utilize the services they offer.

Clinics are the places where clinical research is done. There certainly would, therefore, be a lot more research done on which to base better decisions concerning childhood sexual and erotic health if pediatric sexology clinics existed across the nation. Today it is a virtual certainty that any research-grant application for funds to do research on either normal or abnormal sexual and erotic development in childhood would be dropped like a hot potato. It is not permitted even to ask questions of teenagers, to say nothing of juveniles, about their sexual thoughts and dreams. Moreover, it was not permitted, in a recent study at the National Institutes of Health, to ask such questions, even though the children were being treated with the new LHRH analog to stop the changes of a too early puberty, including the mental changes of erotic thoughts and dreams. The scientists involved were afraid of being branded as degenerate, and of losing their jobs—and their fear was realistic! Similar evasiveness is known to apply in sexual child-abuse treatment programs.

The Bastard Science of Victimology

Scientists are not alone in avoiding the sexual stigmatization of degeneracy theory's legacy. The bureaucrats and councilors of research funding are equally sensitive. In Washington, the office of the assistant secretary of educational research and achievement now vetoes the funding of research if the application has sex or women in the title. It is virtually impossible for explicit sex-research to find financial support anywhere. Animal research is easier to get funded than human research; and organic or reproductive human research is easier than anything that has to do with love or lust, the mental and erotic aspects of sex.

Love research is officially ridiculed, even by senators and congressmen.[1] Lust research is put in the same class as obscenity. Its grant applications are doomed even before they are mailed, because they deal with sexual pleasure—that same sexual pleasure and passion that degeneracy theory declared to be the abomination of concupiscence. Only antisexualism is funded. There are grants for the prevention and punishment of sex—to prevent birth control and abortion, to deny gay rights, to punish sex offenders, to eradicate pornography, and so on.

Antisexual funding is not for research, but rather for the implementation of policy. In a partial attempt to gild the lily, the bastard science of victimology was recently invented. Victimology is not a research science, however, but a subsidized treatment policy. Whether the treatment is efficacious or not has not yet been proved. In at least some cases, it does more harm than good.

Without a vast amount of more research into the cause of the sex-offending paraphilias, it will not be possible to have a true science of sexual victimology. A true science searches for cause and effect, without which prevention is not possible. Without prevention, there will continue to be more victims. With more victims, there will be a self-perpetuating bureaucracy of victimologists requiring public money for their salaries. Such an outcome is guaranteed under the legacy of degeneracy theory, if it continues unchanged.

The bleakness of this picture is not mitigated by the historical fact that a treatment for sex offenders has been under investigation since 1966.[2] However, from 1966 until 1984, direct governmental research funding for this program has been zero.

The treatment combines medication with counseling therapy. The medication is a hormone, medroxyprogesterone acetate, of a progestinic type normally found in the body as a precursor of testosterone but, in the male, in small quantity. Its effect, while being taken, is to provide a man with "a vacation from his sex drive." That gives him a period of months, or longer as need be, in which, with the help of counseling therapy, to reorder the pattern of his sexual life and the broader pattern of his life in general into which his sexual life fits.

The reordering is speedier, and probably more lasting, if the regular sexual partner enrolls also in a program of couple therapy.

It is a costly program, though not as costly as the $30,000 a year (more than an average family's income) that taxpayers in many states pay to keep a person in prison. Times may be changing; but, as of the present, degeneracy theory still is the word of the law. It decrees that most sex offenders go to prison, not to a hospital for treatment and remission of the illness.

Equal Rights

Victimology and antisexualism, like the wooden horse of Troy, rode right into the center of the women's movement in the 1970s and helped to defeat the Equal Rights Amendment. The naive designers of this self-defeating bit of sabotage could not have done it more cleverly had they been the enemy itself. They were, in fact, not the enemy, but a group of unwitting self-saboteurs from within the ranks of women's rights.

Their error was that they played footsie with their natural enemy, the antisexualism of degeneracy theory. They fell into this error by equating violent rape with husband coercion; and by portraying themselves as victimized and denigrated as sex objects not only in violent pornography but also in all male-made pornography. Like angry mothers who destroy their fourteen-year-old sons' copies of *Playboy* and its centerfolds, they defined all explicit erotica as pornographic and degrading exploitation of women. No one taught them the difference between, on the one hand, paraphilic or kinky pornography and, on the other, healthy or normophilic pornography. Healthy pornography benefits the sexual well-being of couples together in love. It does not deprive women of their civil rights.

Intent on love alone, feminist militants lost sight of the fact that healthy lust, too, is part of their own erotic birthright and not only that of males. They projected an antisexual image of themselves. It was the image not of sexless Victorianism for themselves only, but for their men also. They became harpies bent on dismantling the masculine erotic birthright of their hen-pecked husbands, sons, or boyfriends. Their sexually ideal men became a species of live-in escort service. They pursued their attack on pornography with the same zealotry with which they pursued their attack on legal and economic inequality. It was a zeal that paid no heed to the probability that males and females respond differently to the visual erotic image. They despised men by reacting to their masculine turn-on to women as degenerate, and in doing so they subverted their own cause.

The leaders of the lesbian rights movement fell into the same trap. With their sisters of the women's rights movement, they skated on the thin ice of equating all of men's visual erotic turn-on with rape, sadism, or the degradation of women as sex objects. They were also on the thin ice of indecisiveness regarding political unity with their male counterparts in the gay rights movement.

This failure of unity aided and abetted the traditionalist defenders of degeneracy theory in their abhorrence of women's rights and their even greater abhorrence of homosexual rights. For them, sexual rights of any variety were defined as the very core of moral degeneracy in society.

Black rights also came under traditionalist fire, with a barely disguised accusation of black sexual degeneracy. That meant the degeneracy of a word that is seldom uttered—*miscegenation,* or interracial breeding. The labeling of miscegenation as degenerate is a stereotype of false labeling left over from the age of slavery. It is a stereotype of black men as rapists and of black youth as irresponsible teenaged parents.

The historical truth is that, under slavery, teenaged girls were either required or coerced to breed.[3] They had no legal right of marriage or parenthood. They were obliged to have their children reared by yard slaves—the elderly and infirm—who were supported by handouts from the plantation manager. Customs die slowly. Today, with the handout replaced by the welfare check, this three-generation system still shapes the lives of millions. Its failure is the degeneracy not of a moral failure but of an economic one—poverty.

Under slavery, black women could be legally forced to be sexual partners of white males belonging to the plantation. Their offspring were slaves. By contrast, white females who had a black partner could not be the white mother of a black slave. Therefore, all black males who had a white female as a partner were automatically found guilty of rape and were lynched or executed. The black male in interracial sex was branded as degenerate, and the white woman was disgraced. But the white male in interracial sex was a virile macho, covertly applauded by his male comrades, provided he disqualified himself as lover and repudiated himself as father of his colored offspring.

Miscegenation is the legacy of degeneracy theory that surreptitiously shapes all the issues of black rights today. It is the politely unmentionable issue that lurks behind every fight over school integration. It is the abhorrence and fear that black and white teenagers who become lovers will marry and have an interracial family.

The Revolving Door

Confronted with sexualism and eroticism in its citizens and in its children, society has barely begun to deal with the self-righteousness of its outmoded faith in degeneracy theory. Scratch the surface of the self-righteous, and you'll expose the sinner beneath—thus speaketh proverbial wisdom. Its accuracy is headlined, from time to time, in the exposure of public figures who are antisexual crusaders by daylight and paraphilic offenders by night.

In recent years there were two such exposures of moral crusaders of the antisexual New Right. By day, one was a television evangelist, and the other a congressional leader.[4] By night they were ephebophiliacs, bisexual and homosexual, respectively. Some call it hypocrisy, and some call it the two faces of Dr. Jekyll and Mr. Hyde. The two faces may know each other, but they are not on speaking terms. Thus Mr. Hyde does not have to account for his after-dark degeneracy to Dr. Jekyll, his daytime self. Conversely, Dr. Jekyll does not have to justify his daytime condemnation of Mr. Hyde, his nighttime self, as a sexual degenerate. Dr. Jekyll condemns as degenerates all Mr. Hydes he knows of, not only the Mr. Hyde that is the other half of himself.

This is the way that the antisexualism of degeneracy theory and the practice of sexualism that it condemns can coexist, side by side, as do the negative and positive poles of an electrical wiring or a flashlight battery, in one and the same person. It is also the way that the same coexistence of contradictory sexualism keeps alive in society.

Condemnations carried out by the self-righteous in the name of degeneracy theory backfire and have a contradictory effect in society. They clear the way for the return of exactly the same alleged manifestations of degeneracy they were supposed to eradicate. Just like the burn of a brush fire, they clear the way for new growth.

Families and communities get caught in degeneracy theory as in a revolving door. Those who were in some way or another molded by it impose it on the generation of their children, who, in turn, are likewise molded by it. When this new generation reaches teen-age, some of them emerge, as regeneration may emerge from a burn, scarred and misshapen. Their fate is to be the new generation of the erotically and sexually crippled and disabled.

Some will be destined to be paraphiliacs and sex offenders. Some will become police officers and crusaders against vice and degeneracy, condemning in others what they are acquainted with in themselves. Some will become defiant and illegal leaders of the underworld of vice and degeneracy. Some, skirting the edge of the law, will amass vast fortunes exploiting sex in the advertising, media, and entertainment industries. Pulling the lion's tail, they go as far as they dare in selling eroticism and sexuality, defying degeneracy theory to the uttermost limits of the law. They avoid prosecution as degenerates. They demonstrate to society its addictive fascination with the eroticism that, in its own self-righteousness, it also condemns as degenerate.

Confronted with the evidence of its fascination, society intensifies its self-righteousness against what it condemns. In the name of morality and of law and order, it redoubles the sanctions against degeneracy and imposes these sanctions on yet a new generation of children.

The more intensified the sanctions against degeneracy, the greater the guarantee of an ever-enlarging crop of offenders, generation by generation. Expanding its influence exponentially, degeneracy theory preys upon an increasing proportion of the community. until it holds hostage the society that embraces it.

The principle is the same as when human policy assists in the contagious perpetuation of any epidemic. In cholera, for example, or typhoid fever, infectious organisms contaminate food or drinking water, which, in turn, infect more victims whose excretions contaminate still more food and water, and so on. Unless some public-health intervention stops the revolving door of ever-increasing contamination, hundreds of thousands die as the epidemic spreads.

Spread of the malnutrition of poverty is similar. Poverty and malnutrition are passed on from one generation to the next, which, in turn, is too malnourished and poor to transcend either its poverty or malnutrition, and so are its children, and their children, indefinitely.

The revolving-door phenomenon applied to degeneracy theory in its antimasturbation heyday. Sanctions against masturbation created a generation of sexual cripples who, enslaved to their suffering, intensified antimasturbation sanctions against their children, who became sexual cripples who intensified . . . and so on. The revolving of this door was eventually brought to a halt by the advent of germ theory. This new theory showed that masturbation-degeneracy theory was not the cause of the diseases attributed to it.

Despite this evidence, doctors gave up masturbation-degeneracy theory only slowly and reluctantly. Today, over a hundred years later, many nonprofessional people still hold to it. Its victims still file into sex therapy clinics and offices. It was to meet their needs, in fact, that sex therapy came into being as a profession.

Degeneracy and Dictatorship

In scientific history, it was a coincidence or serendipity that germ theory appeared when it did to put an end to masturbation-degeneracy theory. Even though both theories were theories about the causes of diseases, no one had been expressly looking for an alternative, least of all the doctors who believed in it. Left unchallenged, masturbation-degeneracy theory would have gone on, increasing the proportion of its victims in each generation, blowing up bigger and bigger until, like a balloon, it burst.

The death of masturbation-degeneracy theory did not spell the end of all degeneracy theory. Erotic fantasy as the cause of social ills and individual afflictions has had a long life. It was the basis of demon-possession theory in the age of the Inquisiton, when people were put to death for confessing under torture that they had had night fantasies of cohabiting with Satan. Next it became the basis of degeneracy theory, the actual loss of semen in masturbation being less degenerative than the accompanying erotic fantasy of masturbation or the wet dream. Today erotic fantasy is being accused of causing moral and spiritual depravity, when merchandised as entertainment (otherwise known as pornography or obscenity) or taught in the sex education of juveniles.

This modern version of erotic degeneracy can conveniently be called depravity theory. Depravity theory blames sex education as the cause of adolescent pregnancy, unwed motherhood, abortion, breakdown of the family, homosexuality, and sundry aspects of teenage delinquency in general. With respect to pornography, depravity theory blames it as the cause of rape, sexual exploitation of women, sexual child abuse, sex crimes in general, and the moral decay and godlessness of the nation.

The balloon of depravity theory is still being inflated, larger and ever larger. There is no prophecy as to what will either stop its inflation or cause it to burst.

The present period of history is one in which the forces of depravity theory are dedicated to accelerating their momentum. They have mounted crusades against, in particular, abortion, sex education, homosexuality, and pornography. They meet with a politically organized opposition, except in the crusade on pornography.

Pornography has always unmasked the Jekyll and Hyde in even the man who purchases or uses it, for he does not admit in public what he reads or looks at in private, or watches at the all-male stag party. Therefore, he makes no public objection to the tactics of the antisexual crusaders who condemn him and would even put him in prison. He might wisely learn a lesson from the Hitler era.

In 1933, at the outset of his career as dictator, Hitler destroyed the

Institute for Sexology in Berlin, of which Magnus Hirschfeld was director. The library and all the research documents were burned in the street. The story was headlined in German newspapers.[5] There were three telltale accusations in the fine print. They charged that all sexologists were pornographers, homosexuals, and Jews. Hitler knew that decent people would condone his eradication of pornography and homosexuality, even if it did mean that he had used this ruse to get their acquiescence to the eradication of Jews.

For those who follow pornography trials, there is ample evidence that the proponents of depravity theory in the United States today, in and out of government, use secret-police methods and very large sums of money in their crusade against pornography. They also elicit widespread public acquiescence. For legislators it would be political suicide to defend democratic freedom, or even academic freedom, when the issue is so highly charged as, say, "kiddie porn"—showing child or adolescent actors in erotic movies or picture books.

However, acquiescence itself may also be, in the long run, suicidal. Degeneracy theory has a bad track-record, from the Inquisition to the present, when it comes to secret-police tactics, disregard for human rights, and suppression of democratic freedom. The leopard does not change its spots. Depravity theory, the latest version of degeneracy theory, without blinking an eyelid quite happily retraces Hitler's route of secret-police brutality and dictatorship.

It could be that graham crackers, corn flakes, and four-letter words have a great deal to say not only about our past but also about our future, and whether our children and grandchildren will live in a political democracy or a dictatorship. Degeneracy theory not only affects the sexual health of the individual person. It impinges on the political health of the body politic as well.

Reference Notes

1. The most publicized of the ridiculers is Senator William Proxmire, with his infamous Golden Fleece Awards.

2. Antiandrogenic hormonal therapy for sex-offending behavior was begun in 1965 at the Institute for Sex Research, Hamburg, West Germany, under Hans Giese. The hormone used in Europe, cyproterone acetate, has not yet been released by the Food and Drug Administration for use in the U.S. Therefore, a closely related hormone, medroxyprogesterone acetate, is used instead. The first U.S. patient was treated in 1966 by Money, Migeon, and Rivarola (Money, 1968; 1970; 1980).

3. There is a description of the Amerafrican system of pairbonding as a legacy of slavery in Money (1977; 1980). This system coexists in the U.S. with the system,

Mediterranean in origin, of the virgin bride and the double standard and with the betrothal system of erotic equality, which is of ancient north European origin and which still survives intact above the Arctic Circle and in Iceland.

4. The case of Reverend Billy James Hargis was reported in *Time*, February 16, 1976, p. 52. The case of Congressman Robert E. Bauman was reported widely in newspapers, for example, in "Special Report: The Two Worlds of Robert Bauman," *Sunday News American*, Baltimore, October 26, 1980.

5. The history of early twentieth-century European sexology, including the destruction of Hirschfeld's institute, is recorded in Haeberle (1983).

CHAPTER
20

Historical Synopsis

Sexosophy and Sexology

From Tissot in the eighteenth century to Kellogg in the nineteenth and twentieth centuries, there existed a loosely knit fraternity of medical intellectuals for whom a strict doctrine of antisexualism and the practice of abstinence or continence were integral to their doctrine of health and disease. This was a general doctrine, applicable to general practice. It was not a specialty doctrine applicable to a specialty of sexual medicine. There was no such specialty in existence.

Nor was there a specialty of sexual science, or sexology, to which these theoreticians might turn for empirical and experimental verification of their concepts and hypotheses. The very term *hypothesis* was foreign to them, for they wrote with the certainty of doctrinal truth revealed. Strictly speaking, their doctrine belongs not under the rubric of science, and not under sexology, the science of sex. Instead, it belongs under another rubric, one which I named *sexosophy*.[1]

Sexosophy is to sexology as alchemy is to chemistry, or astrology to astronomy. Sexosophy is the philosophy of sex. It comprises moral values and principles of sex, and the rules and regulations of sexual conduct prescribed according to custom, law, religion, or any other authority with power to impose sanctions on behavior.

Vital Spirits: Semen versus Hormone

The sexosophy of antisexualism that became synonymous with Victorianism, and is still today extensively adhered to, had very ancient origins in what may be called proverbial sexosophy. Equating the conservation of semen with the conservation of strength is an ancient bit of proverbial sexosophy. The term for semen in Sanskrit is *sukra dhatu*, which translates as "white matter." In addition to matter, *dhatu* may also translate as

169

"relic," or "metal," which allows the possibility that the white matter is also sacred and precious.

Logically, it would have been odd if farmers in the dawn of civilization, once they had discovered and adopted the practice of castrating the male animals of their herds, did not comprehend that early loss of the testicles prevented sexual maturation of the body and made the behavior more tame. To be tame might be equated with being less strong, rather than less violent.

It would be an easy next step to recognize that castrated animals produce no semen, and then to reach the wrong conclusion that human beings who lose too much semen would weaken themselves and become more like eunuchs who had been castrated as boys. This belief has an ancient history and is geographically widespread. Today, in Asia and parts of Africa, for example, it is a common belief among men who complain of a problem in the sexual functioning of the penis. In Europe and America, it is part of the folklore of sports medicine that competitors should abstain from having sex before a big event.

The error in the folklore that loss of semen is equivalent to becoming weak and unmanly, like a castrate, is easy to explain historically. It stems from the centuries when absolutely nothing was known about hormones. Until about a hundred years ago, it was not known that, when the testicles are cut out, the body loses the testosterone, also known as the male sex hormone that they secrete invisibly into the bloodstream. The ancients knew that without testicles an animal is sterile and also unable to ejaculate semen. But they did not know that almost all of the fluid of the semen is produced in the prostate gland, and that only the sperms are made in the testicles. Thus, it was easy to arrive at the wrong conclusion that, because castration causes loss of semen, semen itself must be the vital fluid that should be conserved in order to be virile, strong, and healthy.

This wrong conclusion could have been exploded on the basis of commonsense observation alone, by totting up a few simple statistics to compare the working power and strength of men who saved their semen with that of those who didn't. Statistics, however, is a twentieth century way of solving problems. Our forefathers did not think that way. They looked to the prestige and authority of their predecessors for answers to problems.

Their wrong conclusion could have been proved wrong had anyone had the wisdom and insight to understand the significance of some of the first experiments involving what in the seventeen hundreds were called vital spirits, fluids, or humors and are now called hormones. No such luck! John Hunter (1728-1793) himself did not spell out, in full, the implications of his experiments. Using chickens, he transplanted the testicle of a rooster chick into the abdominal cavity of a hen chick, and discovered that, if the transplant took root, then the hen chicken would take on some of the bodily and behavioral characteristics of a rooster.[2]

The existence of sex hormones was not proved until the end of the eighteen hundreds. It was as recently as the 1920s that they were extracted in pure chemical form; and the 1930s when they were synthesized and marketed for use in treatment.

Without absolute proof about the existence of sex hormones, wrong ideas about the power of semen persisted and became virtual science-fiction. One wrong idea was that the body purifies semen from only the most precious vital spirits in the blood. Another error was that semen is made from neurine robbed from nerve tissue. Another error even went so far as to warn boys against masturbation because it drained away brain fluids down the spinal cord.

It was always necessary to gloss over girls and women in formulating theories based on the dire effects of the loss of semen. Since women couldn't lose semen, their ills and afflictions had to be based on menstruation and the wandering of the womb (hysteria).

Sexually Transmitted Disease

When Tissot medicalized the masturbation-degeneracy theory of the anonymous author of *Onania,* he was quite explicit in acknowledging his debt to his forebears, even as far back as Hippocrates, with respect to the doctrine of semen loss.

It is quite possible that Tissot also recognized, as explicitly as the medical concepts of the day permitted, that medicine needed an explanation for what nowadays we would call the epidemiology of sexually transmitted diseases. The only terminology for these diseases available to Tissot was the social vice, which for him was part of the same plague as the solitary vice of masturbation. Both were caused by sexual excess. Sexual excess meant excessive loss of semen, and excessive concupiscence. Each influenced the other, and together they debilitated and degenerated their victim.

Tissot, and later his followers, did not clearly distinguish between semen and any other fluids, except urine, that passed through the penis. The opaque, yellowish pus of gonorrhea and the clear glairy exudates of other infections or "strains" were regarded as evidence that sexual excess led to the various symptoms of the disease known as spermatorrhea. In women, the corresponding disease was leucorrhea. Syphilis was not recognized as a separate disease, but there was apparently some recognition of the degeneracies it could induce, long term; and of those that could be transmitted to the offspring of a sexually degenerate mother, that is, a syphilitic prostitute.

The logic, or rather the illogic, of all this diagnostic chaos was the idea that loss of too much semen, especially in the solitary vice, could produce all the symptoms and diseases of the social vice. Thus did masturbation become blameworthy as the cause of all infectious genital and urinary discharges in both sexes. Since syphilis was not distinguished from the infections that produced discharges, masturbation was also held accountable for its advanced-stage degenerative symptoms and for the sins of the fathers (and mothers) being visited on the offspring in the form of birth defects.

Erotic Imagery: Concupiscence

Tissot borrowed from the anonymous author of *Onania* in formulating his sexosophy of degeneracy caused by loss of semen in solitary and social vice. Neither author made reference to the sexosophy of demon possession or to the idea that onanistic theory filled the gap left by the demise of demon-possession theory. Both theories were all-purpose, general-utility sexosophical explanations of a wide range of social and individual afflictions.

Demon-possession sexosophy, unlike onanistic sexosophy, had been equally applicable to both sexes. Historically, accusations of witchcraft were leveled more often at women than men. Women's nocturnal copulations with demonic incubi and succubi were considered more dangerous to men than were their counterpart in men to women. Yet, it was, of course, adolescent boys and men, not girls and women, who had actual wet dreams culminating in orgasm and discharge of semen. Both sexes, however, could be accused of lascivious dreams in which, by witchcraft, they copulated with a servant of Satan. It was the erotic content of the dream that constituted the crime for which a witch, male or female, was burned at the stake.

The idea that erotic imagery in thoughts, fantasies, and dreams is the crime, or at least the sin, was taken up by the crusaders against onanism. For them it solved the problem of why loss of semen in solitary vice should be more dangerous and degenerative than in social vice. In either case, abstinence and the conservation of semen was also a sign of the conservation of moral purity. Indeed, moral purity became equated with abstinence or, at least, continence. Above all, moral purity meant renunciation of concupiscence, the sin of sexual desire in imagination, thoughts, fantasies and dreams. Masturbatory loss of semen was particularly condemned because it was associated with masturbation fantasies of explicit concupiscence and lust. Wet dreams also were condemned as evidence, spilling over into sleep, of concupiscence and lust undisciplined while awake.

Wet dreams and semen loss left women unaccounted for in degeneracy theory. Concupiscence and lust saved the day and allowed degeneracy theory to apply to females as well as males. To achieve moral purity, women also were required to relinquish concupiscence and the wickedness of erotic imagination and desire.

According to the doctrine of the Inquisition, women were so sinfully incapable of resisting concupiscence, including the imagination of copulating with Satan or his demons, that the redemption of their immortal souls required the sacrifice of their mortal bodies by burning them alive.

The price that women had to pay to be rescued from the fires of the Inquisition was the renunciation of all claim to concupiscent sexuality and eroticism and the assimilation of an antithetical new doctrine of woman's preternatural moral purity, erotic apathy, and sexual inertia. This new doctrine reached its zenith by the mid-nineteenth century. It declared that women copulated not out of lust but in order to be relieved of their husbands' attentions and to fulfill the obligations of maternity.

Concupiscence was the sinful imagination or mental portrayal of lust and copulation, regardless of whether men or women were the sinners. From being the sin of demon possession, it became historically recycled as the sin of masturbation possession. It would be recycled yet a second time, after masturbation had become morally decriminalized in the present century. Its new name is the crime of pornography possession. Its condemnation and persecution are militant, politically tyrannous, still very much in vogue as well as assiduously antimasculine.

From demons to masturbation to pornography, the representation of eroticism and lust in mental imagery and fantasy has continued to be condemned and accused as the cause of degeneracy and depravity, both personal and social. Depravity and degeneracy, in turn, are accused of being the cause of the afflictions of both the individual person and the society. The reasoning is circular. Circular reasoning disobeys the rules of sexology as science. It is perpetuated as the rhetoric of negative sexosophy.

The Way of Change

The gradual decline of the European Inquisition by the end of the sixteen hundreds, and in Spanish America somewhat later, has received scanty historical explanation. It is, like the Nazi Holocaust, a chapter in human behavior that is traumatically accusatory and inconsistent with most peoples' religious ideals and allegiances. To think of it is also a reminder that society still endorses penal abuse and the death sentence.

The same forces that terminated the Inquisition terminated also the scientific acceptability of demon-possession as an explanation of social and personal ills. The modern renaissance of science in the sixteen hundreds undoubtedly helped to discredit demon possession as a causal explanation of anything.

With the theory of demon possession discredited, and degeneracy theory taking its place, antisexualism held the field for the best part of two centuries. Degeneracy theory fell into disrepute and was replaced by modern biomedical theory regarding the causation of illness, beginning with germ theory in the 1870s. At around the same time, the discovery of contraception dealt another mortal blow, since it discredited the argument that marital continence, if not abstinence, was morally necessary to spare a wife from the hazards of too many pregnancies. A third blow was delivered around the middle of the present century, when the discovery of antibiotics pioneered the way, still to be completed, to the cure and public-health control of the diseases of the social vice, the sexually transmitted diseases (STD), of which the newest threat is AIDS.

New technology, whether discovered, invented, or borrowed from one's cultural neighbors, is a sure-fire way of bringing change into a nation or community and into the customs and behavior of its people. Major population shifts, increases or losses will do the same.

In addition to the scientific discoveries that brought discredit to masturbation-degeneracy theory, there was also an age shift in population when, in the 1960s and 1970s, the children of the postwar baby boom reached adolescence and young adulthood.

Today the remnant of degeneracy theory, otherwise known as depravity theory, is quietly being discredited by new video technology. The new technology allows more and more people to see erotic and pornographic material, privately at home, and to discover that they do not become depraved from it. It is not yet possible, however, to prophesy whether this new technology will doom degeneracy theory to extinction. It is still upheld by those who have rescued it by redefining it as moral degeneracy theory. Militant, fervent, and fanatical, they are today's crusaders of antisexualism, the twentieth-century descendants of Victorianism.

Gradual change, like a drifting current, often leads to an unforeseen destination. Guided change toward a definite destination is legislated. Americans currently are living through the experience of guided change toward use of the metric system.

There are three steps in legislated guided change. First there is public debate and a formal decision to make the change. Then follows a period of technological preparation and public education. Finally, change goes into effect, by law, at the proverbial stroke of midnight. Next morning, the disobedient are subject to prosecution or arrest! As a life-and-death matter, it had to be that way in Sweden when the change was made from left- to right-hand drive on the highways.

When the time comes to put degeneracy theory and its antisexualism to rest once and for all, guided change may well be the successful way to do it. Then, at the stroke of midnight, the truth of sexual democracy will have been realized, and our democratic freedoms will be complete.

Reference Notes

1. The term *sexosophy* was published first in *Love and Love Sickness* (Money, 1980), and set forth at length in the opening lecture of the 5th World Congress of Sexology, June 1981 (Money, 1982).

2. More details of John Hunter's experiments are given in *Love and Love Sickness* (Money, 1980); and more about the discovery of hormones and hormone theory in Money (1983).

Theory of Sex, Love, and Health Without Degeneracy

Sexology of Proception, Acception, Conception

Smoke from the incineration of hundreds of thousands of live Europeans, tortured and brain-washed by the Inquisition until they falsely confessed to copulation with the devil or his demons while asleep and dreaming, still pollutes human sexuality and eroticism at the end of the twentieth century. Sexology as the science of human sexuality still barely exists.

In all of Europe or America, or any other continent, there is in the 1980s still no university or medical school that has a complete and autonomous department of sexology. Only very few have a subdepartment, institute, or clinical division of sexology in which to systematize, expand, and apply sexological knowledge. With no written history of sexology, and no textbook, there has been inadequate continuity of knowledge about human sexuality. For example, the four phases of human sexual response analyzed by Masters and Johnson (1966) originally had been delineated by Albert Moll in *The Sexual Life of the Child* (1912). Masters and Johnson named them the excitement, plateau, orgasmic, and resolution phases. Moll's terms (p. 26) are: "an ascending limb, the equable voluptuous sensation, the acme, and the rapid decline" on a curve of "voluptuousness."

These four phases of response fit into the acceptive stage of sexual participation, which is preceded by the proceptive stage and followed sometimes by the conceptive stage of pregnancy and parenthood. Scientifically, these three stages have been developed in reverse order. The conceptive stage, defined as reproductive biology, is nowadays scientifically respectable: fertility, sterility, conception, gestation, and birth, especially with reference to endocrinology, genetics, and neuroscience. The respectability of reproductive biology is often used as a cover for acceptive-stage research. For example, research into the contemporary progressive lowering of the age of onset of sexual intercourse in adolescence, as a phenomenon of the birth-control era, is often funded under the name of population dynamics and teenage fertility rate, not of sexual acceptivity and genital intercourse.

Kinsey was the first scientist of acceptivity.[1] He made physiologic measurements and movies of couples actually copulating, but he did not live to publish these findings. The political climate was against him. It remained for Masters and Johnson to take the political bull by the horns and publish their experimental data on the genital physiology of coitus. Their great achievement was like that of Vesalius before them. Vesalius defied the church and dissected the human cadaver to establish anatomy scientifically. Masters and Johnson defied ecclesiastical and civil prudery and the sexual climate of their time and made human sexual acceptivity scientific, and they were not tried or imprisoned on a charge of scientific obscenity.

The proceptive stage of human sexuality was first named and delineated in 1976 by Frank Beach with reference to animal sexology.[2] It is the stage of initiation and readiness, of attracting and being attracted, of arousing and being aroused, of approaching and being approached, and of soliciting and being solicited. Proception is the least understood and the least scientifically studied of the three stages of human sexuality. Proceptive research is likely to be branded obscene and pornographic and to go unfunded, for proception is not only sexual but erotosexual. Sex pertains to one's status as male or female, or possibly as hermaphroditic, as judged by genital anatomy and reproductive capability. Eroticism pertains to the entirety of one's personal experience (whether alone, paired, or in a group) and manifest expression of genital activation and function, especially with reference to mental imagery, either perceived or fictive. When imagery is perceived, the stimulus is present. When it is fictive, the stimulus is recalled and elaborated in fantasy.

Pairbonding, Limerence, Loveblots, and Lovemaps

The erotosexual imagery of proception is closely related to the phenomenon of pairbonding. In human beings, the most dramatic manifestation of pairbonding is falling in love or being love-smitten. Because in English there is no noun with which to refer to this experience, Dorothy Tennov (1980) coined the term *limerence*. As a human experience, limerence is an entity as specific as the grief of bereavement or the charismatic ecstasy of religious conversion. Limerence may be the culmination of an acquaintanceship, or it may begin suddenly as love at first sight.

Using the analogy of a Rorschach inkblot, one may ascribe to a lover the status of a loveblot. That is to say, the lover is a stimulus onto whom the limerent partner projects the idealized image of the perfect lover and love affair. This idealized image, writ large, is a lovemap. It carries with it all the expectancies and anticipations of how the idealized lover should respond. Thus the burden is on the beloved to respond by living up to these expectancies and fulfilling all the anticipations.

Unlike an inkblot, a loveblot is animate and responsive. Thus each partner of a pair may be a loveblot to the other. Each may perfectly reciprocate the lovemap of the other in a perfectly balanced two-way relationship. Then love is perfect and the two lovers undergo an experience of euphoria that is often characterized as floating on air.

When a mutually limerent couple are well matched, the ecstasy of their being together and the agony of even brief separation matures from extreme and passionate intensity to a more tranquil and sustained attachment. In the natural history of a young-adult love-affair, this maturation coincides with the amount of time required for the two-way bonding of the lovers to become the three-way bonding of first parenthood.

Good lovemap matching does not necessarily imply that the imagery and expectancy of each partner conform to conventional stereotypes. Thus, in a jurisdiction that forbids interracial marriage, it is perfectly possible that a member of each race respectively fantasies an interracial partner. The same may apply to partnerships between religious faiths, as when, for example, a Jewish girl has a fantasy of having as a lover a disciplinary master who is the blue-eyed, blond Aryan son of a concentration camp official—and does in fact meet up with such a person. Another example is that of a matching between an amputee and an acrotomophilic partner. An acrotomophiliac is a lover who is incapable of responding and performing erotically and sexually except with an amputee.

It is easy for an acrotomophiliac to recognize an amputee as the kind of person who satisfies his image of the ideal lover prerequisite to his erotic arousal and genital performance. In other cases, recognition is not so easy, and potential partners may need to assemble in special places, for example, a bar, in order to locate one another. Or they may display symbols in order to facilitate recognition, such as hanging a keychain on either the left or right of the belt to signify sadism and masochism, respectively. In some cases it may be that the two partners read subliminal signs of a rather nonspecific nature, such as readiness to be acquiescent versus assertive.

To illustrate, it is relatively common for a male transvestite to fall in love with a woman who marries him prior to knowing about his transvestism. Then, after she learns that his cross-dressing is an erotic ritual essential to his obtaining an erection and orgasm, as his wife she concedes, until eventually she colludes and assists him with his wardrobe and make-up. She does not opt out of the marriage. This woman had no expectancy of becoming the wife of a transvestite and did not knowingly pairbond with one. But she may have inchoately recognized ahead of time that her boyfriend's masculinity was in some way not stereotypic but atypical, and that its atypicality would, by her acceptance of the demands that it would impose on her, actually give her a leverage of power over him.

When a collusional relationship of the foregoing type becomes successful, then a paradox arises should one partner happen, by whatever means, to undergo a change. For example, the husband might change so that his erotic performance would no longer be dependent on the enactment or fantasying of his transvestite ritual. The paradox is that the wife, unable to accommodate to the changed sexual health in her husband, herself becomes sick, or else breaks up the relationship. Herein lies an explanation of why sexual therapy so often must be couple therapy.

Developmental Limerence

As a child grows, the rehearsal play of late infancy and early childhood includes the first developmental manifestations of limerent attachment and pairbonding. These manifestations are mostly play rehearsals with only a short history. There are, however, recorded instances of juvenile love-affairs that persist through puberty and beyond to become adolescent love-affairs culminating possibly in long-lasting marriages. It is not easy for a juvenile attachment to have such an outcome, for limerence in young people in our society as compared, say with Melanesian societies, is either indulged as cute or scorned and disparaged as infatuation or puppy love. If it includes rehearsal-play involving the genitals and erotic body contact, then the reaction of adults typically is negative and punitive.

The age at which limerent pairbonding is first socially sanctioned varies across cultures. Typically it is postpubertal, with a range from early postpuberty to mature adulthood in the middle to late twenties. In all cultures, the age of sanctioned pairbonding and marriage is integrally related to the economic system, the means of production, and the distribution of wealth.

There is no upper age-limit at which the phenomenon of limerence may occur. It may interrupt a marriage in which the relationship has become perfunctory, leading to separation and divorce, not only once, but multiplicatively. There are some people for whom a sequence of intensely limerent affairs is a compulsion that they cannot resist, regardless of the financial and career sacrifices involved. The converse is limerent celibacy, the condition in which a person is unable to experience limerence toward anyone.

In the elderly, after the death of one partner, if the survivor is the woman, the potentiality of limerence may be thwarted by the unavailability of a partner, for the life expectancy of females exceeds that of males, on the average, by five years or more. There is also a cultural tradition of ridiculing elderly lovers. Their adult children may intervene in order to protect their own inheritance.

There is no automatic guarantee that limerence will elicit a reciprocal response. In fact, it is even possible that the partner may be unattainable—an entertainment star, for example, known only through concert, filmed, or recorded performances. In teen-age, it may be an unremarkable and transient feature of erotosexual development to have such a secret and one-sided love-affair with a film star or singer. It does happen, however, that such one-sided limerence may be, in effect, autistic and perpetual. At the opposite extreme is the Don Juan's inability ever to establish limerence. Each affair is casual and transient. In today's state of knowledge, there is no adequate explanation of these two extremes in terms of sexological psychology and neuroscience.

Completely one-sided limerence is relatively rare as compared with lopsided limerence in which one partner is more intensely in love than is the other. In a lopsided love affair, each partner is a loveblot who falls short of matching the lovemap that projects onto him or her as the idealized lover. Love is blind, it is said proverbially. But, in fact, love is not blind—it overlooks and bides its time. The shortcomings of the partner become items on a hidden agenda of things to be rectified and improved. Each lover is a Pygmalion, a man or woman whose lovemap dictates that the partner will be reshaped into his or her idiosyncratic erotosexual mold.

In some instances, the reshaping is successful, for being in love is not an attribute but a developmental process. Either one partner or both may have the potential of being able to grow into an accommodation with the other, becoming more and more closely a mirror image of the other's lovemap.

Lovesickness and Jealousy

It is when this mirror image fails to develop that a desperate attack of lovesickness may afflict the limerently love-smitten partner who waits in vain for his or her love to be requited. In lovesickness, a wide range of processes of bodily function is affected: heart rate, blood pressure, breathing rate, perspiration, salivation, digestion, sleeplessness, dreaming, concentration, attention, and apprehension bordering on panic.

Lovesickness does not respond to reason. It is self-defeating insofar as it readily manifests itself as tyrannical jealousy and ruthless possessiveness of the partner. Any suspected threat to the establishment of pair-bonding with this partner evokes irrational intervention, which, in an exaggerated degree, may lead to murder or suicide, or both. The victim may be the partner him/herself or any actual or suspected rival. Bystanders may also be included. In some cases, the victim has no involvement but is a powerful public-figure whose assassination is symbolic of the power of the one responsible for the assassin's lovesickness.

Another outcome of jealousy and possessiveness is that neither partner is able to make the concessions that bring about a reconciliation, nor do they separate. Instead, they live together as adversaries, waging a war of unfulfilled expectancies. Their rate of erotosexual exchange is metaphorically far less than fifty cents to the dollar. Some people live together reciprocating aggression and passive resistance for a long time. For others the day of disillusionment finally dawns and the partnership falls asunder, often with acrimonious bitterness and violent retribution. If there are children, they are used as ammunition in the feuding, or at best are victims of the crossfire.

A Partnership Gone Wrong: Illustration

It is in the very nature of unfulfilled loveblot expectancies that their complexity is not self-apparent. The partners concerned cannot explain to themselves or anyone else what has gone wrong. The case of a young man with a history of anorchia illustrates this point. During childhood, his annual medical checkup made him well aware of having no testicles and of the prognosis of hormonal replacement therapy and sterility in adulthood. He underwent cosmetic surgery for the implantation of prosthetic testes and appeared singularly untraumatized by either his diagnosis or prognosis. He was far more concerned with the discrepancy between his own ambition to pursue music and become a popular recording star and his parents' very conventional ambition for him in business. He attributed his indifference to dating and sexual life to the demands of his musical studies and regular band performances and not to inhibition secondary to having no testicles. Limerence hit rather suddenly in his mid-twenties. The girl was known to him by name when he sat next to her one night at a concert after his own performance was completed. Six months passed before they met again. Thereafter, they were together regularly several times a week and very soon began their sex life together. He completely cleared the hurdle of revealing his anorchic status. Both rated their erotic sexual relationship highly. They decided not to delay in getting married. They both began working for the same employer, commuting seventy miles each way daily. At the same time, he kept the same nightly schedule of musical engagements, so that several nights a week he arrived home to his wife as late as 4 A.M. Their sex life became negligible, not only through lack of time, but also because of the antagonism that began developing between them as each imposed a different set of expectancies on the other.

Their source of unanimity lay in their having fallen in love, though with him more heavily smitten than she. Their lack of unanimity was revealed in what they said when they talked separately. He believed that both of them were sure that they would not want to raise a family. She was sure that she wanted children and preferred donor insemination to adoption, provided her husband agreed. He had an ambition of being able to earn a living as a musician and of taking his wife with him, when on the road, as a business manager. She was convinced that the best thing her husband had done regarding his band was to disband it. He did so after he became sick with an ulcer while trying to maintain his marriage and two jobs, a salaried one by day and the band by night. The wife was uncompromising in her verdict that her husband's ambition to reconstitute his band would be at the cost of losing her. He could not have both. Her justification was that their sex life had been better after he quit the band. She was sure that the main reason he had needed to see a psychiatrist was because of worry over debts and not the loss of his band.

A key to the dilemma of this marriage is that the wife's expectancies were endorsed by both families and, ambivalently, by her husband himself, insofar as he had never successfully freed himself of the negative view that his parents had had of his musical ambition. He was caught in a Catch-22 position of having to sacrifice either his wife or his music. Without his wife, he might again revert to being erotosexually inert and incomplete as a man. Permanently without his music, he might become erotosexually apathetic and incompetent with his wife, as part of the price of having had his ambition destroyed. The wife, of course, was equally a victim of the same dilemma with respect to her own future erotosexual life.

Genital Warfare: Hypophilia

When sexual partners fail to fulfill the ideal image and expectancy that each originally projected onto the other, then they are likely to become opponents in an adversary relationship in which the chief weapons are the sex organs. Passive resistance and retreat predominate over active assault in genital warfare. The war may manifest itself at the proceptive stage as sexual apathy or aversion in place of being either aroused and desired or arousing and desiring. Aversion may be so intense that it applies to any form of body contact, even a kiss of greeting or farewell, to say nothing of sleeping in the proximity of the same bed.

In the absence of profound erotosexual apathy or aversion, conflict between two people in their expectancies of one another may manifest itself erotosexually as failure or partial failure of the genitalia to function optimally.[3] The malfunctions thus manifest represent some degree of hypofunction or hypophilia. There are parallel hypophilias in men and women. (See Table 1.)

TABLE 1

Hypophilias, Male and Female
(Partial or Complete)

Male	Female
coital aninsertia	coital aninsertia
penile anesthesia	vulval anesthesia
anorgasmia	anorgasmia
erectile impotence	vaginal dryness
premature ejaculation	vaginismus
coital pain	dyspareunia

Hypophilic participation at the acceptive phase may be a carryover of apathy or aversion from the proceptive stage. Alternatively, it may also apply to the acceptive stage only and may be limited to specific aspects of erotosexual participation. For some men and women, for example, participation in oral sex either as performer or recipient is an impossibility. If one partner is intensely dependent on the odors (pheromones), flavors, and sensations of oral sex for erotosexual arousal, and if the other has an intense aversion to it, compromise may prove unattainable and the partnership may prove unviable.

A similar incompatibility with respect to the use of either the penis or the vagina in penovaginal insertion renders a relationship even more unviable, legally as well as personally. This is the condition of coital aninsertia. It may manifest itself as neglect or denial of one's own penis or vagina, as though it did not exist—a characteristic of, for example, some unoperated transexuals. More commonly, coital aninsertia may manifest itself as a phobic anxiety or panic at having one's vagina penetrated, or one's penis inserted into a vagina.

Insertion phobia is not a problem in those cases in which the chief hyposexual symptom is genital anesthesia or numbness. The penis or vagina performs its insertorial function but is deficient in inducing erotosexual feeling. If an orgasm is achieved, it too lacks the feeling of climax as judged by prior experience. It is possible that the achievement of orgasm will also be excessively delayed or will fail completely (anorgasmia).

Anorgasmia may manifest itself without genital anesthesia, in which case it represents simply a failure to have a sexual climax. In men it includes failure to ejaculate. Failure to climax may be interpreted subjectively as positive or negative. It is positive if the build-up of erotosexual sensation fades and ceases without a climax, thus creating a pause in readiness for resumption later. It is negative if the build-up of erotosexual sensation neither fades nor is released abruptly in orgasm, thus creating an awareness of frustration. Anorgasmia may be specific to the stimulus input. Thus a man or a woman may be able to climax from masturbation, but not from stimulation with a partner; or when with a certain partner but not another; or with a partner of one sex but not the other. Women more often than men may be less able to climax from penovaginal thrusting than from some other form of stimulation. For some women, oral stimulation of the vulva is orgasmically superior. For others pressure stimulation of the clitoris, the clitoral hood, and the labia minora is superior. For some men, oral stimulation of the scrotum may be orgasmically superior. In either sex, augmentation of stimulus input from the nipples or other part of the body may increase the possibility of orgasm. There is a high degree of idiosyncrasy as to the location of the most intense extragenital orgasmic sensitivity, ranging from the lips to the anus, and from pressure spots on the joints and the torso, to the fingers and toes. Some of these locations are not simultaneously accessible when there are only two people together. For some people, the stimulation of these extragenital locations may need to be so strong that to another person it would be noxiously painful.

Anorgasmia may be not a primary hypophilic phenomenon, but one that is secondary to failure, in the male, of the penis to become erect or stay erect and, in the female, of the vagina to lubricate or stay lubricated.

Vaginal dryness is not given as much attention in sexological texts as is penile impotence, which has long been known as the bane of men.

The antithesis of impotence and anorgasmia in men is premature ejaculation, corresponding to vaginismus in women. In both sexes, the muscles of the genitals contract too soon. In men, the ejaculate typically is lost at the moment the penis comes in contact with the warmth of the vulva or very rapidly after its insertion into the warm vagina, thus curtailing the sensations of thrusting for both partners. Premature ejaculation rarely occurs when the same penis is being masturbated or being fellated. Hence the stop-start method of therapy and the so-called squeeze technique, in which the partner is instructed to stimulate the penis manually and to stop just short of its ejaculation, possibly with a squeeze or pinch to discourage ejaculation. In women, vaginismus represents premature onset of the female postorgasmic refractory period. It is produced by constriction of the perivaginal (pubococcygeal) musculature together with drying of the vagina, thus effectively excluding the penis.

In women, the antithesis of genital anesthesia is dyspareunia, which means, etymologically, badly mated, and in current medical usage, difficult or painful coitus, regardless of cause. The same term is seldom applied to men, but they too may experience coital pain. Both sexes may also experience postcoital pain, either in the external genitals or the pelvic cavity. In rare instances, there occurs also a postcoital migraine headache.

Differential Etiology

In all of the hypophilias—and in the hyperphilias and paraphilias (see below)—the differential diagnosis and prognosis, as well as the method of treatment, require consideration of the factors listed in Table 2. A hypophilia is not a syndrome with a unique etiological origin. Rather it is a syndrome, or possibly a symptom, that, like fever, has different causal origins. Irrespective of its ultimate causal origin or agent, every hypophilia ultimately requires for its expression a pathological change in the way in which pathways of the nervous system, which are still poorly understood, service the genital organs. There are three subsidiary pathways by which this change expresses itself: by directly altering the regulation of the blood supply to the genitalia; by altering the release of hormones that affect genital function; and by altering the release of other tissue chemicals, like prostaglandins, that affect genital function.

Alterations that affect the neurogenital system or any of its three subsidiary pathways may themselves be engendered by birth defects; toxic substances, including drugs, medications, or other chemicals; infections;

neoplastic growths; mechanical and traumatic anatomic damage either surgical or nonsurgical; and changes in brain chemistries that today defy explanation and that may themselves be engendered by external stimuli, like olfactory and other stimuli from the developmental past or present. Changes in brain chemistries notorious for inducing hypophilic apathy or inertia are those responsible for the syndrome of severe depression. This syndrome involves an upset of multiple body chemistries and vital functions, including sleeping and eating as well as erotosexual function.

TABLE 2

Factors in the Etiology of Erotic/Genital Dysfunction

Birth defect
Hormonal, brain
Hormonal, target organ
Toxic, prescribed substance
Toxic, nonprescribed substance
Infectious
Neoplastic
Traumatic, surgical
Traumatic, nonsurgical
Vascular
Neurologic, peripheral
Neuropsychogenic

Those hypophilias that have developmental origins and that are classified as psychogenic may, in keeping with their classification as hypofunctions, be defined and analyzed in terms of a blockage or inhibition of some aspect of genital and erotosexual responsivity.. The variables responsible for this inhibition cannot yet be spelled out in terms of all the chemical messengers and brain pathways involved. Hence the classification *psychogenic* signifies that a hypofunction cannot be attributed to any so-called organic cause, like local infection, inflammation, or injury, that brings about a blockage or inhibition of function.

Erotosexual hypofunctions of the type classified as psychogenic have developmental origins in infancy and childhood. The most likely hypothesis is that these hypofunctions are a residual of a deficiency of juvenile sexual rehearsal play of the kind that is typical of normal primate development (Chapter 16). In other primates, notably rhesus monkeys, it has been demonstrated that prolonged deprivation of sexual rehearsal play with age mates in infancy results in permanent hyposexualism in adulthood. It may be so complete that affected animals, male or female, fail completely to reproduce their own species.

Among human beings, the heritage of sexual taboo in our society means that infants and juveniles are not simply deprived of sexual rehearsal play but subjected to threat, prohibition, and punishment if they show any signs of it. Then functional inhibition or blockage may ensue, and it may spill over to include the brain's memory of how the sex organs function. The resultant failure constitutes a hypophilia, either complete or partial.

Hyperphilia

Negation of sexual rehearsal play may bring about not hypophilia but a retaliatory defiance and rebellion manifested as hyperphilia. The hyperphilias are often joked about flippantly, perhaps with a touch of misguided envy. Their classification lacks professional unanimity exept for nymphomania and satyriasis (Don Juanism). A feature of these conditions is reiterative multiplicity of partners without durable pairbonding. Reiterative partner multiplicity may be a feature of swinging or group-sex parties. Reiterative multiplicity may occur also as a feature of autoeroticism. It may also take the form of compulsive cruising or polyiterophilia, the multirepetition of an erotosexual practice with many partners as an essential prerequisite to one's own orgasm.

There is no absolute frequency criterion as to what constitutes erotosexual hyperfunction. High frequency creates a problem if it usurps too much time or if two partners are grossly mismatched, as when one partner might initiate coitus eight times daily, and the other three times weekly.

Paraphilia

Negation of sexual rehearsal play may issue in neither hypophilic deficiency nor hyperphilic excess, but in paraphilic circumventions of conventional heterosexuality. A paraphilia exists both in imagery as a fantasy and in practice as a ritual. A paraphilia is defined as an erotosexual condition of being responsive to and dependent on an unusual and personally or socially unacceptable stimulus, in actuality or in fantasy, in order to become and remain erotosexually aroused. For example, rubber fetishism is a paraphilia. The rubber fetishist is erotosexually dependent on the smell, texture, and ritual of wearing rubber clothing. If he is not wearing it, then his imagination must supply it in fantasy, complete with the erotic ritual that accompanies its usage. The origin of a rubber fetish often can be traced to infancy and the wearing of rubber training pants. The origin of the content of the accompanying fantasy may also be traced to early experience—such as when one is fed with a baby's milk bottle and then diapered in order to obtain an erection.

Though a paraphiliac's fantasy, like his signature, has its own idiosyncrasy and embellishment, the varieties of paraphilia are limited. (See Chapter 17, Table 1.) All the different varieties are known from their occurrence in men and it is not yet known whether they all occur also in women. According to police and clinic statistics, they are more prevalent in men than in women, and greatly so. The best hypothesis by which to explain this sex difference is that the male brain is developmentally programed, beginning with the hormones of prenatal life, to differentiate a greater dependence on, and lower threshold for, visual imagery to initiate erotosexual arousal than is the female brain. The female is more dependent on touch. The difference is not absolute, but relative. The content of what constitutes the visual imagery of erotosexual arousal is not preordained at birth. Like the content of one's native language, the content of one's erotosexual arousal imagery becomes programed into the brain early in life. Thereafter it has remarkable persistence and continuity and is resistant to change.

Even the threat or the actual sentence of many years in prison as a punishment for having socially unsanctioned paraphilia—exhibitionism, for example—does not eradicate it.

The majority of paraphilias are paraphilias of inclusion. That is to say, they are erotosexual fantasies or actual rituals that include something over and beyond that conventionally associated with heterosexual arousal and copulatory participation. The apotemnophiliac must include an image of the stump of one of his amputated limbs, and the acrotomophiliac, the stump of an amputee partner. The zoophiliac must include the image of an animal partner. And so on.

Other paraphilias are paraphilias of displacement. In these, the erotosexual fantasy or ritual gets fixated on a component part of a more conventional sexual encounter. Thus, displaying one's sex organs and looking at those of one's partner become exaggerated in exhibitionism and voyeurism, respectively. The male exhibitionist is dependent on the surprised, shocked, or terrified response of a stranger to whom he exhibits his penis either in actuality or recalled imagery. If the stranger does not respond in the prescribed way, then she is erotosexually unsatisfactory to the exhibitionist. If she does so respond, then he may masturbate to orgasm immediately or later; or, returning to his regular partner, he may relive the exhibitionistic experience in imagery and thereby manage to maintain an erection and reach orgasm.

Partners in Paraphilia

Because paraphilic imagery and ritual are idiosyncratic even to the point of being bizarre, it is often not only difficult but well nigh impossible for a paraphiliac to find a perfectly reciprocating long-term partner. Thus it is a contradiction in terms for an exhibitionist to find a long-term relationship with a partner who, by definition, must be a stranger whose erotosexual fantasy is to be shocked or terrified by being exhibited to.

Paraphilia does not, per se, exclude the possibility of pairbondedness. A sadist and a masochist, for example, may enter into a mutually consenting relationship and become pairbonded.

Noxious Paraphilias: Antiandrogen

Such a relationship raises the problem of the dividing line between playfulness and noxious harmfulness in paraphilia. Paraphilic playfulness is a matter of personal aesthetics, not morality or legality. It does not justify the enforced intervention of the law, as noxious harmfulness may do. Some of the paraphilias, like rapism and lust murderism, are so noxious to others that they are socially not tolerated under any circumstances, including the bizarre circumstance in which a masochist stage-manages his own murder by a consenting sadist. These are the paraphilias for which a new form of combined hormonal (antiandrogenic) and counseling treatment has been developed (Chapter 20). In Europe, cyproterone acetate is the hormone used, and in America, medroxyprogesterone acetate. The same treatment can be used for noninjurious paraphilias if the affected person finds his paraphilia noxious to himself. There is some very preliminary evidence that the combined form of treatment is effective for women paraphiliacs also.

Sex Therapy

A paraphilia does not preclude the possibility of a conventional marriage. Many paraphiliacs do, in fact, from puberty onward, anticipate that having a marital sex-life will eradicate the paraphilic fantasy and ritual. What is far more likely to happen is that performance at the acceptive stage, even though covertly reinforced by the imagery of the paraphilic fantasy, becomes increasingly difficult and hypophilically inadequate. Hence the saying that behind every hypophilia may lurk a paraphilia. The same may also be said of hyperphilia. Without knowledge of the hidden paraphilic imagery, attempted sex-therapy for the acceptive dysfunction will be ineffectual. It is not possible to ignore imagery in the practice of sex therapy.

There are two approaches to sex therapy. One deals with images and ideas, and with the meaning and significance of a couple's behavior one to another. This is the ideogogic approach. The other is the somesthetic approach, the approach of touching, caressing, and the sensate focus culminating in penovaginal insertion. Neither approach can substitute for the other. The priority of one over the other varies from patient to patient. For most patients in sex therapy, both approaches need to be employed.

Fantasy that carries over too persistently from the proceptive stage disrupts the acceptive stage of erotosexual performance. The acceptive stage is one in which fantasy imagery ordinarily gives way to perceptual imagery, that is to say, to awareness of the bodily erotosexual sensations of the here and now, as the build-up to orgasm progresses.

Fantasy of the proceptive stage is individually variable and not, of course, necessarily paraphilic. When fantasy imagery is not of the actual partner, the most typical replacement is imagery of a substitute partner of different age, sex, ethnicity, or appearance.

Gender Transposition

Replacement of an opposite-sex partner in heterosexual coitus with a same-sex partner in fantasy occurs in people who themselves have some degree of bisexuality. The homosexual/heterosexual ratio in bisexuality may be 50/50, but also any other proportion such as 20/80, or 70/30, et cetera.

Bisexuality and homosexuality are classified among the gender transpositions (Table 3) and not among the paraphilias, primarily because they are consistent with falling in love and pairbonding, whereas the paraphilias, by and large, are not. Homosexuality is more accurately named homophilia, for its distinguishing criterion is not sex but love. The homosexual who has no bisexual potential is capable of falling in love with only a member of the same sex, just as, correspondingly, a heterosexual can fall in love with only a member of the other sex. The equipotential bisexual is capable of falling in love with either a man or a woman.

Table 3 shows that transvestism and transexualism are also classified as gender transpositions. Transvestism qualifies also as a paraphilia in those instances in which contragender clothes are a fetish, the wearing of which is imperative to erotosexual arousal and performance to orgasm.

TABLE 3

Transpositions of Gender Identity/Role

	Total	Partial	Arbitrary
Chronic	transexualism	gynemimesis andromimesis homosexualism	androgeny of sex-coded work, education, legal status
Episodic	transvestism	bisexualism	androgeny of sex-coded play, body-language, grooming, ornament

Episodic transvestism may metamorphose in middle adulthood into full-time transexualism, complete with hormonal and surgical sex reassignment. Transexualism is otherwise a gender transposition that remains constant from early childhood, even though it may manifest itself only privately until adolescence. There is a *forme fruste* of transexualism in which hormonal, but not genital-surgical, reassignment is sought. In gonadal males, this condition is gynemimesis, and in the vernacular the person is known as a drag queen (Money and Lamacz, 1984). The corresponding conditon in the gonadal female is andromimesis, for which there is no exact vernacular term. Andromimesis may include surgical breast reduction, and gynemimesis may include removal of facial and body hair by electrolysis.

The least profound of the gender transpositions pertain not to erotosexual status at all, but to behavior that is arbitrarily coded as being suited to either the male or female role. These gender-coded roles, and the components of identity that match them, apply to education, work, legal status, play, manners, demeanor, grooming, and cosmetics. They apply also to body language, vocal intonation, and, to a more limited extent vocabulary selection and idiomatic expression.

Arbitrary, Adjunctive, Derivative, and Irreducible Sex-Difference of Role and Identity

Transposition of arbitrarily coded male and female roles (and their representations in identity) means that they become shared by both sexes, or androgynous. Androgynous sharing or equality of these roles does not, per se, imply a bisexual erotosexual identity, though many people react as vehemently to androgyny and women's equal rights with men as though they implied a sharing of erotosexual identity as well. Other people more readily recognize that arbitrarily coded male and female roles are, like one's native language and accent, the product of social assimilation and training, and that they have no eternal verity dictated by the sex organs and their reproductive biology, even though they do enter the brain as part of one's personal identity.

In addition to arbitrarily coded male and female roles, there are those that are sex adjunctive, sex derivative, and sex irreducible.

The irreducible male and female roles (and correlative components of their identities) are, in the final analysis, that men impregnate and women menstruate, gestate, and lactate. The procreative organs and their erotosexual function are governed hormonally, especially by the sex steroids, androgen, estrogen, and progesterone. These same hormones govern, to some extent, the development of sex-derivative roles such as urinary posture, and roles secondary to skeletal size, brute strength, and body-hair distribution. In a tertiary way these same hormones influence sex-adjunctive roles, though less today than in the age before labor-saving devices and prepared baby foods. In an earlier era, for example, men roamed more widely in hunting, fighting, and doing heavy work than did women, who were constrained by pregnancies and suckling babies. Traditionally, women's role included more food preparation.

Hormones, Thresholds, Dimorphism

The steroid hormones from the gonads exert their sexually dimorphic influence not only at puberty and thereafter, but also prenatally. In fetal life, the amount of androgen present in the fetal bloodstream is of crucial importance in governing the anatomical formation of the sex organs as male instead of female, and also in governing thresholds in the brain. Later in development, these thresholds will either release or hold back the brain's regulation of certain types of behavior that, though they are sex-shared, are threshold-dimorphic. That is to say, they are more readily or more frequently displayed as manifestations of the gender identity/role

(G-I/ R) of one sex than the other (Table 4).

In laboratory animals it has been well demonstrated that manipulation of the amount or ratio of sex hormones in the developing brain before or immediately after birth is able to reset the thresholds for behavior that qualifies as sex-shared/threshold dimorphic. The behavior so affected includes aspects of mating, such as frequency of mounting and thrusting versus presenting and being mounted, that are capable of being manifested, though in differing degrees, by each sex.

TABLE 4

Nine Parameters of Sex-Shared/Threshold-Dimorphic Behavior

General kinesis—activity and the expenditure of energy, especially in outdoor, athletic, and team-sport activities

Competitive rivalry and assertiveness for higher rank in the dominance hierarchy of childhood

Roaming and territory or boundary mapping or marking

Defense against intruders and predators

Guarding and defense of the young

Nesting or homemaking

Parental care of the young, including doll play

Sexual mounting and thrusting versus spreading and containing

Erotic dependence on visual stimulus versus tactual stimulus arousal

Though it is not possible to impose animal experiments on human beings, there are unplanned clinical syndromes that indicate that prenatal sex hormones influence not only animal brains but human brains also. The extent of this influence cannot be measured with available methods. Thus it is impossible to specify the extent to which prenatal hormones may or may not predispose a baby's brain to function later in either a heterosexual or homosexual or bisexual G-I/R. What can be specified hormonally on the basis of the present state of knowledge about human sexuality and eroticism is that hormones do influence the sexual brain both prenatally and following puberty; that the brain influences sex-hormone secretion via its influence on the hormones of the pituitary gland, and that learning may affect this process; that the brain, as recently discovered, makes its own hormones, which along with other tissue chemicals that act as neutrotransmitters, are contributing to what promises to be a veritable explosion of knowledge concerning the governance of human sexuality and eroticism. This new knowledge will, in all probability, enforce a complete rewrite of the differentiation and development of human sexuality and eroticism early in the twenty-first century.

Cyclicity

Hormones after the maturation of puberty fluctuate the sexuality of most animals in a seasonal or cyclic rhythm of estrus that guarantees the synchrony of impregnation and ovulation. In human beings and other primates, the hormonal fluctuations of the menstrual cycle determine the chronology of ovulation, but without guaranteeing its synchronization with coitus and impregnation. The attempts that have been made to demonstrate a synchrony between phase of the menstrual cycle and frequency of coitus or of imagery of wanting it have been inconclusive for both the woman and her male partner. Hypothetically, it appears that synchrony between ovulation and copulation is weak in those species, especially the human, in which sexual arousal is far more dependent on visual stimulation and imagery than it is on odors (pheromones) and the nose.

Aging

The dominance of vision over smell as a sexual attractant in human beings may account for the fact that human sexuality does not terminate with the female partner's menopause. By contrast, in species in which the male is attracted pheromonally by the cyclic vaginal odor of estrus, when a female's cycling terminates, copulation no longer occurs. In these same species, however, a castrated or an aging male may continue to copulate, provided the partner is a female in estrus. In male primates, including men, there is also a relative, but not complete, independence between androgen secretion, sexual arousal, and copulation.

In the geriatric age group there is great individual variation among couples regarding the timing of the cessation of sexual intercourse. Much of the variation is traditionally attributed to differences in personal and social erotosexual history. Among males, it has been shown that the earlier and more frequent the sex life in youth, the longer and more frequent its continuation with old age. For both sexes, partner availability in old age is a crucial variable, especially for women, since the life expectancy of females exceeds that of males by an average of five or more years.

With advancing years, there is an increased risk of exposure to prescription medications, for example, for hypertension or psychosis, that have an antisexual effect on the central nervous system. There is also an increased risk of diseases, like diabetes mellitus and psychotic depression, one of the symptoms of which is sexual hypofunction. Street drugs, such as heroin, which have a progressive antisexual effect, are presumed to be less used in old age than earlier.

Folklore aside, there is no substance that genuinely qualifies as an aphrodisiac restorer of erotosexual youthfulness. In males with a demonstrated low circulating level of male hormone, a replacement dose of testosterone may be beneficial to sexual performance. In postmenopausal women, replacement estrogen abolishes symptoms of vaginal dryness and fragility. Protection from the feared association of estrogen with endometrial cancer is achieved by combining progestin with estrogen, in imitation of the menstrual cycle. The relationship of these two hormones to erotosexual responsivity is questionable. It is more likely that androgen is the libido hormone, so-called, for women as well as men. In women, androgen derives partly from the ovary and partly from the adrenal cortex.

Hormonal considerations notwithstanding, there are many elderly people who continue their sex lives, albeit at a diminished frequency, into their eighties.[4] Even when the genitalia no longer function well, the sexuality of grooming, that is of cuddling, stroking, massaging, and bodily closeness remains as a source of great joy and contentment.

Recreational and Procreational Sex

In former centuries, the years after the woman's menopause alone was the time when recreational sex and procreational sex were not inevitably tied together. Proverbially, this fact was recognized in the maxim: "Life begins at forty." The modern age of birth control has forever changed that conjunction so that all people, of either sex and any age, are enabled effectively to separate their procreational from their recreational sex-lives. This separation applies as much to the married as the single, and as much to the monogamous as the multi-partnered. Its greatest impact is on the young prior to marriage. Without the fanfare of a moral or political manifesto, youth has been revolutionizing the tradition of its erotic pair-bonding by replacing the ancient Mediterranean tradition of the virgin bride and the double standard with the equally ancient Nordic custom of betrothal and erotosexual equality (Money, 1980).

In ancient times, the betrothal system required people to prove their capability of engendering a pregnancy so that they might get married. In its present-day version, the betrothal system enables young people to live together, proving their potential compatibility as parents, before they embark on parenthood and marriage. The new morality of the betrothal system may rescue the nuclear family from the failure that currently besets it as a social institution. If so, children will be the beneficiaries, for their bondedness with their parents cannot be broken as can the love-bondedness of the parents. Children cannot divorce their parents. Only parents can quarrel, separate, and divorce one another. The children of those who do not are at a great advantage in growing up to establish a healthy sexuality of their own in adolescence, adulthood, and old age.

Reference Notes

1. See Kinsey et al. (1948; 1953). Kinsey's studies were actually preceded early in this century by those of John B. Watson at Johns Hopkins. Watson's data were suppressed, and he lost his professorship because of them (Magoun, 1981).

2. Beach's (1976) concept of proception, meaning the erotic preliminaries of courtship, mating ritual, or foreplay, differs from that of Rosenzweig (1973), meaning the opposite of contraception.

3. See Masters and Johnson (1970), Kaplan (1974); Hartman and Fithian (1974); and Money and Musaph (1977).

4. Today's average life-expectancy in the West is between 70 and 80 years. At the beginning of the twentieth century it was 45 years. In Maryland, at the time of the American revolution at the end of the eighteenth century, 50 percent of infants died before their first birthday; and the survivors had a life expectancy of 35 years. The paucity of survivors beyond the breeding years may in part account for why the antisexualists of the eighteenth and nineteenth centuries, following the example of their ecclesiastical predecessors, did not address themselves to the hazards of recreational sex for and with a postmenopausal partner. The doctrine of sex for procreation without passion ensured, however, the sinfulness of recreational sex in old age. Only recently has sexual emancipation of the elderly begun to be accorded overt respectability.

Bibliography

Acton, W. *The Functions and Disorders of the Reproductive Organs in Childhood, Youth, Adult Age, and Advanced Life, Considered in Their Physiological, Social, and Moral Relations* (6th ed.). Philadelphia: Presley Blakiston, 1875.

American Medical Association Committee on Human Sexuality. *Human Sexuality*. Chicago: American Medical Association, 1972.

Anon. *Onania; or the Heinous Sin of Self-Pollution, and all its Frightful Confequences, in both Sexes, Confidered. With Spiritual and Phyfical Advice to Thofe, who have already injur'd themfelves by this Abominable Practice*. Boston: John Phillips, 1724. Facsimile reprint edition in *The Secret Vice Exposed! Some Arguments Against Masturbation* (C. Rosenberg and C. Smith-Rosenberg, advisory eds.) New York. Arno Press, 1974.

[Aristotle] *The Works of Aristotle, the Famous Philosopher, in Four Parts Containing I. His Complete Masterpiece; II. His Experienced Midwife; III. His Book of Problems; IV. His Last Legacy*. New England: Printed for the Proprietor, 1813. Facsimile reprint edition, New York: Arno Press, 1974.

Beach, F. A. Sexual attractivity, proceptivity, and receptivity in female mammals. *Hormones and Behavior*, 7:105-138, 1976.

Benjamin, H. *The Transsexual Phenomenon*. New York: Julian Press, 1966.

Birkin, A. *J. M. Barrie & the Lost Boys. The Love Story that Gave Birth to Peter Pan*. New York: Clarkson N. Potter, 1979. Distributed by Crown Publishers, New York.

Birnbach, L. (ed.). *The Official Preppy Handbook*. New York: Workman Publishing, 1980.

Boswell, John. *Christianity, Social Tolerance, and Homosexuality: Gay People in Western Europe from the Beginning of the Christian Era to the Fourteenth Century*. Chicago: University of Chicago Press, 1980.

Bremer, J. *Asexualization: A Follow-up Study of 244 Cases*. New York: Macmillan, 1959.

Broun, H., and Leech, M. *Anthony Comstock: Roundsman of the Lord*. New York: Literary Guild of America, 1927.

Bullough, V. L. *Sexual Variance in Society and History*. New York: Wiley, 1976.

Carson, G. *Cornflake Crusade*. New York: Rinehart & Company, 1957.

Cohen, M. N. *Lewis Carroll, Photographer of Children: Four Nude Studies*. Philadelphia: The Rosenbach Foundation; New York: and Clarkson N. Potter, 1979;

distributed by Crown Publishers, New York.

Colp, R., Jr. Profile: Eleanor of Aquitaine. *Medical Aspects of Human Sexuality*, 15:11, 1981.

Commission on Obscenity and Pornography, *Technical Report*, vol. 2. Washington: U.S. Government Printing Office, 1971.

Dixon, D. An erotic attraction to amputees. *Sexuality and Disability*, 6:3-19, 1983.

Friedman, J. Sex and Mr. Buckley: The "good parts" of William Buckley's four spy novels depict a world of preppy perversion. *Forum: The International Journal of Human Relations*. Special Edition: 22-29, 1982.

Gaden, J. R. The church and sexuality—on not getting it together. *St. Mark's Review*, no. 106:13-23, 1981.

Gilbert, A. N. Doctor, patient and the onanist diseases in the nineteenth century. *Journal of History of Medicine and Allied Sciences*, 30:217-234, 1975.

Goldfoot, D. A. Sociosexual behaviors of nonhuman primates during development and maturity: Social and hormonal relationships. In *Behavioral Primatology, Advances in Research and Theory*, vol. 1 (A. M. Schrier, ed.). Hillsdale, N.J.: Lawrence Erlbaum, 1977.

Goldfoot, D. A. On measuring behavioral sex differences in social contexts. In *Neurobiology of Reproduction*, vol. 8. New York: Plenum Press, 1983.

Goldfoot, D. A., and Wallen, K. Development of gender role behaviors in heterosexual and isosexual groups of infant rhesus monkeys. In *Recent Advances in Primatology*, vol. 1 of *Behavior* (D. J. Chivers and J. Herbert, eds.). London: Academic Press, 1978.

Goldfoot, D. A., Wallen, K., Neff, D. A., McBriar, M. D., and Goy, R. W. Social influences upon the display of sexually dimorphic behavior in rhesus monkeys: Isosexual rearing. *Archives of Sexual Behavior*, 13:395-412, 1984.

Graham, S. *A Lecture to Young Men*. Providence: Weeden and Cory, 1834. Facsimile reprint edition, New York: Arno Press, 1974.

Green, R., and Money, J. (eds.). *Transsexualism and Sex Reassignment*. Baltimore: Johns Hopkins University Press, 1969.

Haeberle, E. J. *The Birth of Sexology: A Brief History in Documents*, San Francisco: Privately printed, 1983. Copyright by E. J. Haeberle.

Hartman, W. E., and Fithian, M. A. *Treatment of Sexual Dysfunction*. New York: Jason Aronson, 1974.

Himes, N. E. *Medical History of Contraception*. New York: Gamut Press, 1963.

Hollender, M. H. The medical profession and sex in 1900. *American Journal of Obstetrics and Gynecology*, 108:139-148, 1970.

Huhner, M. *The Diagnosis and Treatment of Sexual Disorders in the Male and Female, Including Sterility and Impotence* (3rd ed.). Philadelphia: F. A. Davis, 1946.

Hunt, M. M. *The Natural History of Love*. New York: Alfred A. Knopf, 1959.

Jackson, J. C. *Hints on the Reproductive Organs: Their Diseases, Causes, and Cure on Hydropathic Principles*. Boston and New York: Fowlers and Wells, 1853.

Jackson, J. C. *The Sexual Organism and Its Healthful Management*. Boston: B. Leverett Emerson, 1865.

Kaplan, H. S. *The New Sex Therapy: Active Treatment of Sexual Dysfunctions*. New

York: Brunner-Mazel, 1974.

Kellogg, J. H. *Man the Masterpiece, or Plain Truths Plainly Told about Boyhood, Youth, and Manhood.* Warburton, Victoria, Australia: Signs of the Times Publishing Association, 1906.

Kellogg, J. H. *Plain Facts for Old and Young, Embracing the Natural History and Hygiene of Organic Life.* Burlington, Iowa: I. F. Segner, 1888. Facsimile reprint edition. New York: Arno Press, 1974.

Kellogg, J. H. *The Ladies' Guide in Health and Disease: Girlhood, Maidenhood, Wifehood, Motherhood.* Warburton, Victoria, Australia: Signs of the Times Publishing Association, 1908.

Kinsey, A. C., Pomeroy, W. B., and Martin, C. E. *Sexual Behavior in the Human Male.* Philadelphia: Saunders, 1948.

Kinsey, A. C., Pomeroy, W. B., Martin, C. E., and Gebhard, P. H. *Sexual Behavior in the Human Female.* Philadelphia: Saunders, 1953.

Ladurie, E. Le Roy. *Montaillou: The Promised Land of Error.* New York: Braziller, 1978.

Levine, M. H. (ed.). *Falaquera's Book of the Seeker (Sefer Ha-Mebaggesh).* New York: Yeshiva University Press, 1976.

Lewis, D. *The Gynecologic Consideration of the Sexual Act.* Chicago: Henry O. Shepard, 1900. Reprinted with Introduction by M. H. Hollender, Weston, Mass.: M & S Press, 1970.

Lewis, D. Gynecologic consideration of the sexual act. *Journal of the American Medical Association*, 250:222-227, 1983.

Locke, F. W. (ed.). *Andreas Capellanus: The Art of Courtly Love.* New York: Frederick Ungar, 1957.

Magoun, H. W. John B. Watson and the study of human sexual behavior. *Journal of Sex Research*, 17:368-378, 1981.

Malinowski, B. *The Sexual Life of Savages in North-Western Melanesia.* New York: Halcyon House, 1929.

Maple, T. Unusual sexual behavior of nonhuman primates. In *Handbook of Sexology* (J. Money and H. Musaph, eds.). Amsterdam-New York: Excerpta Medica, 1977.

Marshall D. S., and Suggs, R. C. (eds.). *Human Sexual Behavior: Variations in the Ethnographic Spectrum.* New York: Basic Books, 1971.

Masters, W. H., and Johnson, V. E. *Human Sexual Inadequacy.* Boston: Little, Brown, 1970.

Masters, W. H., and Johnson, V. E. *Human Sexual Response.* Boston: Little, Brown, 1966.

Moll, A. *The Sexual Life of the Child.* New York: Macmillan, 1912.

Money, J. Discussion on hormonal inhibition of libido in male sex offenders. In *Endocrinology and Human Behavior* (R. P. Michael, ed.). London: Oxford University Press, 1968.

Money, J. Use of an androgen-depleting hormone in the treatment of male sex offenders. *Journal of Sex Research*, 6:165-172, 1970.

Money, J. Paraphilias. In *Handbook of Sexology* (J. Money and H. Musaph, eds.). Amsterdam-New York: Excerpta Medica, 1977.

Money, J. The American heritage of three traditions of pair-bonding: Mediterranean, Nordic, and Slav. In *Handbook of Sexology* (J. Money and H. Musaph, eds.). Amsterdam-New York: Excerpta Medica, 1977.

Money, J. Sexual dictatorship, dissidence, and democracy. *International Journal of Medicine and Law*, 1:11-20, 1979.

Money, J. *Love and Love Sickness: The Science of Sex, Gender Difference, and Pair-Bonding*. Baltimore: Johns Hopkins University Press, 1980.

Money, J. Paraphilia and abuse-martyrdom: Exhibitionism as a paradigm for reciprocal couple counseling combined with antiandrogen. *Journal of Sex and Marital Therapy*, 7:115-123, 1981.

Money, J. Paraphilias: Phyletic origins of erotosexual dysfunction. *International Journal of Mental Health*, 10:75-109, 1981.

Money, J. Sexosophy and sexology, philosophy and science: Two halves, one whole. In *Sexology: Sexual Biology, Behavior, and Therapy* (Z. Hoch and H. Lief, eds.). Amsterdam-Oxford-Princeton: Excerpta Medica, 1982.

Money, J. To quim and to swive: Linguistic and coital parity, male and female. *Journal of Sex Research*, 18:173-176, 1982.

Money, J. Paraphilias: Phenomenology and classification. *American Journal of Psychotherapy*, 38:164-179, 1984.

Money, J. The genealogical descent of sexual psychoneuroendocrinology from sex and health theory: The eighteenth to the twentieth centuries. *Psychoneuroendocrinology*, 8:391-400, 1984.

Money, J., and Athanasiou, R. Pornography: Review and bibliographic annotations. *American Journal of Obstetrics and Gynecology*, 115:130-146, 1973.

Money, J., and Bennett, R. G. Postadolescent paraphilic sex offenders: Antiandrogenic and counseling therapy follow-up. *International Journal of Mental Health*, 10:122-133, 1981.

Money, J., and Ehrhardt, A. A. *Man and Woman, Boy and Girl: The Differentiation and Dimorphism of Gender Identity from Conception to Maturity*. Baltimore: Johns Hopkins University Press, 1972.

Money, J., Jobaris, R., and Furth, G. Apotemnophilia: Two cases of self-demand amputation as a paraphilia. *Journal of Sex Research*, 13:115-125, 1977.

Money, J., and Lamacz, M. Gynemimesis and gynemimetophilia: Individual and cross-cultural manifestations of a gender-coping strategy hitherto unnamed. *Comprehensive Psychiatry*, 25:392-403, 1984.

Money, J., and Musaph, H. *Handbook of Sexology*. Amsterdam-New York: Excerpta Medica, 1977.

Money, J., and Werlwas, J. Paraphilic sexuality and child abuse: The parents. *Journal of Sex and Marital Therapy*, 8:57-64, 1982.

Money, J., Wiedeking, C., Walker, P., Migeon, C., Meyer, W., and Borgaonkar, D. 47,XYY and 46,XY males with antisocial and/or sex offending behavior: Antiandrogen therapy plus counseling. *Psychoneuroendocrinology*, 1:165-178, 1975.

Natress, L. W. *The Amelotatist: A Statistical Profile*. Lawndale, Calif.: Privately printed, 1978. Copyright by Ampix.

Nissenbaum, S. *Sex, Diet, and Debility in Jacksonian America: Sylvester Graham and Health Reform*. Westport, Conn.: Greenwood Press, 1980.

Noyes, J. H. *Male Continence, or Self-Control in Sexual Intercourse*, Oneida: office of Oneida Circular, 1872. Facsimile reprint edition in *Sexual Indulgence and Denial. Variations on Continence* (C. Rosenberg and C. Smith-Rosenberg, advisory eds.). New York: Arno Press, 1974.

Orr, M. T. Sex education and contraceptive education in U.S. public high schools. *Family Planning Perspectives*, 14:304-313, 1982.

Patel, D. A., Flaherty, E. G., and Dunn, J. Factors affecting the practice of circumcision. *American Journal of Diseases of Children*, 136:634-636, 1982.

Richards, F. C., and Richards, E. S. *Ladies' Handbook of Home Treatment*. Melbourne, Victoria, Australia: Signs of the Times Publishing Co., 1905.

Rosenzweig, S. Human sexual autonomy as an evolutionary attainment, anticipating proceptive sex choice and idiodynamic bisexuality. In *Contemporary Sexual Behavior: Critical Issues in the 1970's* (J. Zubin and J. Money, eds.). Baltimore: Johns Hopkins University Press, 1973.

Schwarz, R. W. *John Harvey Kellogg, M.D.* Nashville, Tenn.: Southern Publishing Assoc., 1970.

Shyrock, R. H. Sylvester Graham and the popular health movement, 1830-1870. *The Mississippi Valley Historical Review*, 18:172-183, 1931.

Sprenger, J., and Institoris, H. *Malleus Maleficarum* (trans. by M. Summers). London: J. Rodker, 1928.

Stockham, A. B. *Karezza: Ethics of Marriage*. Chicago: Stockham Publishing Co., 1896. Facsimile reprint edition in *Sexual Indulgence and Denial: Variations on Continence* (C. Rosenberg and C. Smith Rosenberg, advisory eds.). New York: Arno Press, 1974.

Tennov, D. *Love and Limerence: The Experience of Being in Love*. New York: Stein and Day, 1979.

Tissot, S. A. *A Treatise on the Diseases Produced by Onanism*. Translated from a New Edition of the French, with Notes and Appendix by an American Physician. New York: 1832. Facsimile reprint edition in *The Secret Vice Exposed! Some Arguments Against Masturbation* (C. Rosenberg and C. Smith-Rosenberg, advisory eds.). New York: Arno Press, 1974.

Trall, R. T. *Sexual Physiology: A Scientific and Popular Exposition of the Fundamental Problems in Sociology* (28th ed.). New York: M. L. Holbrook, 1881. Facsimile reprint edition, New York: Arno Press, 1974.

Valency, M. *In Praise of Love: An Introduction to the Love-Poetry of the Renaissance*. New York: Macmillan, 1961.

Wallerstein, E. *Circumcision: An American Health Fallacy*. New York: Springer, 1980.

Wesley, J. *Primitive Physic or an Easy and Natural Method of Curing Most Diseases*. Trenton: Quequelle and Wilson, 1788.

Wikman, K. R. V. Die einleitung der ehe. Eine vergleichend ethno-soziologische untersuchung über die vorstufe der ehe in den sitten des schwedischen volkstums. *Acta Academiae Aboensis Humaniora*, vol. 11. Åbo: Åbo Academi, 1937.

Willson, J. R., Beecham, C. T., and Carrington, E. R. *Obstetrics and Gynecology* (4th ed.). St. Louis: C. V. Mosby, 1971.

Wright, J. Sexuality within the Old Testament. *St. Mark's Review*, no. 106:3-12, 1981.

Zabin, L. S., and Clark, S. D., Jr. Why they delay: A study of teenage family planning clinic patients. *Family Planning Perspectives*, 13:205-216, 1981.

Zelnik, M., Kantner, J. F., and Ford, K. *Sex and Pregnancy in Adolescence.* New York: Sage Publications, 1981.

Indexes

Name Index

Subject Index

Psychedelic mushrooms, 33
Psychoanalysis, 103, 122 ff., 158
Puberty, 88, 95, 122-123, 131, 158-159;
lovemap at, 133, 137; love affair during, 180; hormones during, 193, 194,
195
Public executions, and sadomasochism,
141
Putrefaction, 54, 59, 67

Quim, 124

Race betterment, Kellogg's theory of, 84
Rape, 124, 161, 162, 165, 190; as raptophilia, 141; sleeping princess syndrome
mistaken for, 141; vaginal examination
equivalent to, 159
Recreational sex, 196-197
Religion: and lust murderer, 130, 135;
and masochism, 140; and sermon paraphilia, 147; and sexosophy, 169; ideals
of, and the Inquisition, 174
Renunciation, 33, 83, 172-173; in woman's sexuality, 173
Resistance, unconscious, 85
Rubber fetish, 143, 188-189
Russian roulette, 140

Sacrifice, 134, 137, 138-141
Sadism, 138-140, 162, 179; and pairbond-
ing, 190; and murder, 190
Saint and sinner, 126, 132, 135, 137; and
pornography, 151
Salt and spicy food, 23, 60, 95
SAR (sexual attitude restructuring, or
reassessment), 157
Scandal in the media, 150
Schooling: as cause of debility, 65, 122;
and literacy, 87
School(s), 111; integration of, 162
Secret-police methods and pornography,
166
Secret vice, 54, 67, 69 ff., 85 ff., 129;
blamed for syphilis, 54-55. See also
Masturbation; Self-abuse; Self-pollu-
tion; Solitary vice
Self-abuse, 85 ff. See also Masturbation;
Secret vice; Self-pollution; Solitary
vice
Self-pollution, 67, 69 ff.; as cause of insanity,
64
Self-righteousness, 163-164
Semen, 29 ff., 45, 50-54, 63, 73, 171, 172;
blood made into, 50, 52, 62, 171; conservation of, 169, 170; and sports medicine, 170; made from neurine, 171;
drained from brain fluid, 171; analogy
with hysteria in women, 171
Sermons and paraphilia, 147
Seventh-day Adventist religion, 22 ff., 83,
118; Kellogg expelled from, 24, 26
Sex: and the media, 15; without pregnancy, 30; abstention from, on Mondays,
Wednesdays, and Fridays, 31; and
health theory, 59, 74; below the belt,
112, 126, 151; as sin, 135; and eroticism, 178; and aging, 195-196; recreational and procreational, 196-197
Sex difference(s). See Male-female differ-
ence(s)
Sex education, 118, 122, 123, 155, 159, 160;
neglect of, 132; moral depravity of,
165
Sex manuals, 77, 87, 129
Sex offender(s), 129, 154, 158; treatment
program for, 160-161; new generation
of, 163, 164
Sex offense(s), 138
Sex therapy, 127, 157, 158, 160, 164; for
couples, 160-161, 180, 191; for paraphilia, 160, 190-191; squeeze technique
in, 186; ideogogic and somesthetic, 191
Sexology: pediatric, 158-159; science of,
169; no university department of, 177;
animal, 178. See also Sexosophy
Sexosophy, 169, 172, 173, 175
Sexual rehearsal play, 131 ff., 180; in
monkeys, 133, 187-188; of tribal people, 133; and paraphilia, 149; erotosexual hypofunction due to lack of,
187-188
Sexuality: children's, 131 ff., 158-159, 180;
study of, in monkeys, 133, 187-188;
four phases of, 177. See also Sexual
rehearsal play; Women's sexuality
Sexually transmitted disease(s) (STD), 16,
155, 171, 174. See also AIDS, Gonorrhea; Social vice; Syphilis; Venereal
disease
Shredded wheat, 25

Sleeping princess syndrome, 141
Social contagion, 47, 149, 150, 151, 154. *See also* Contagion
Social vice, 54, 87, 129, 142, 171, 172, 174
Society for the Suppression of Vice, 109
Sodomy, 45. *See also* Anal sex
Solitary vice, 67, 85 ff., 171, 172; in girls, 86. *See also* Secret vice; Self-abuse; Masturbation
Somnophilia, 141
Spermatorrhea, 69, 97, 171. *See also* Nocturnal emissions; Wet dreams
Spices and highly seasoned food, 64, 65, 69, 87, 95. *See also* Salt and spicy food
Sports medicine, semen conservation in, 171
Stigmatophilia, 144
Stoic school, 32
Stockholm syndrome, 141
Suffrage, women's 75
Suicide, 131, 134, 166; and lovesickness, 128, 182; autoerotic, 140; masochistic, 140
Supreme Court, 153
Surgery, for self-abuse, 99
Swive, 127
Sympathies, 57, 58. *See also* Nervous system
Symphorophilia, 140
Syndicate, underworld, 112, 163-164
Syphilis, 16, 54-55, 72, 171

Taboo, 32, 132, 143, 145, 158
Tantric Yoga, 29-30
Tattoo, 144
Tea, 19, 23, 60, 65, 70, 87, 103
Teenaged parents, 162
Teenaged pregnancy, 156, 157
Telephone-calling, paraphilic, 147
Temperance: in drinking alcohol, 19; and health theory, 59. *See also* Intemperance
Tobacco, 19, 21, 23, 70, 87, 95, 108
Torrens invisibles, 52
Trancelike state, 150
Transexual(s), 144, 158, 185, 191-192
Transvestite(s), 142-143, 179-180, 191-192
Troubadours, 37 ff., 43, 126
Troy, wooden horse of, 161

Tuberculosis, and masturbation theory, 97

Underworld. *See* Syndicate
Uniforms and paraphilia, 144
Urophilia, 143
Utopia, 79

Vagina, 115, 141, 151; examination of, 158; malfunctioning of, in hypophilia, 184; postmenopausal dryness of, 196. *See also* Lubrication
Vapor(s), 57, 59, 67, 75
Vegetarianism, 17 ff., 23, 75, 83, 87
Venereal disease, 53 ff., 84, 113. *See also* Sexually transmitted disease; Social vice
Victimology, 71, 160, 161
Video technology, 174
Vietnam, 75, 157
Virgin Mary, 40
Vital: spirit(s), 57, 169; fluid(s), 129, 170; energy, 131; function(s), 187
Voyeurism, 146-147, 189

Water cure, 21, 75, 83
Western Health Reform Institute, 23. *See also* Battle Creek Sanitarium
Wet dream(s), 63, 67, 71, 129, 137, 165, 172, 173. *See also* Nocturnal emissions; Spermatorrhea
Will power, paraphilias not controlled by, 149
Wine, 65, 69
Witchcraft, 44 ff., 85, 172
Witches: pagan religion of, 44; intercourse with demons, 44 ff.; burnings of, 45-46
Women's emancipation, 75, 79-80, 112 ff., 121; and sexuality, 113 ff., 122, 161; and ERA, 161; *See also* Women's rights
Women's rights, 162, 193
Women's sexuality, 113 ff., 121 ff., 161, 173

YMCA, 109

Zoophilia, 145, 189